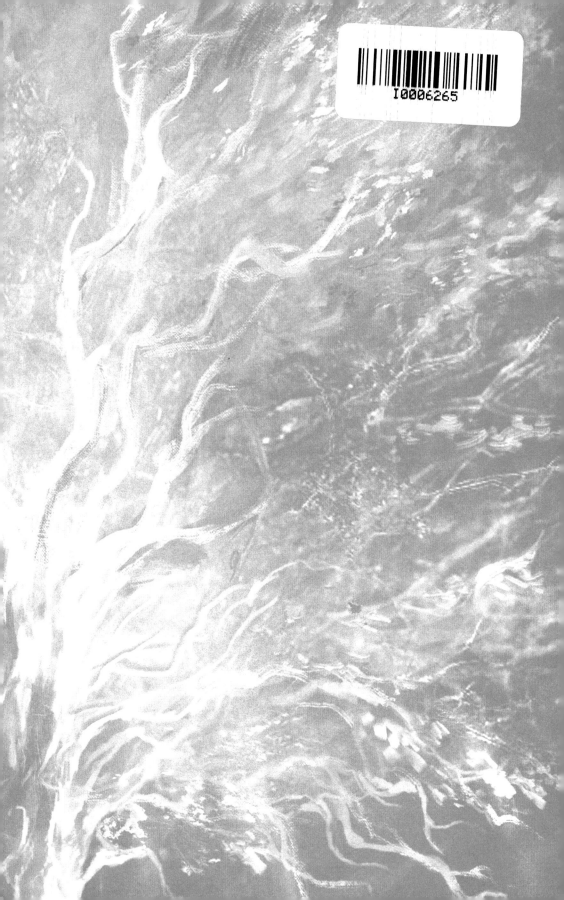

THE MONUMENTAL
ELDEN RING

The Monumental Elden Ring. FromSoftware's Magnum Opus
by Sylvain Romieu
published by Third Éditions
10, rue des Arts, 31000 Toulouse, France
contact@thirdeditions.com
www.thirdeditions.com

Follow us: ✖ @ThirdEditions — ⓕ Facebook.com/ThirdEditions — ⊙ Third Éditions

Publishing Directors: Nicolas Courcier and Mehdi El Kanafi
Edited by: Damien Mecheri
Publishing Assistants: Ken Bruno and Ludovic Castro
Text by: Sylvain Romieu
Proofreading: Pierre Van Hoeserlande (copy preparation) and Charles Vitse (proofing)
Layout: Bruno Provezza
Classic cover: Ali Shimhaq
First Print cover: Gabriel Amalric
Cover creation: Marion Millier
Translated from French by: Michael Ross (main) and Elizabeth Crowell

This educational work is Third Éditions's tribute to the video game *Elden Ring*.
The author traces the history of *Elden Ring* in this unique compendium, which uses original thinking and analysis to explore the inspirations, context, and content of the game.

English edition, copyright 2025, Third Éditions.
All rights reserved.
ISBN 978-2-37784-554-5
Legal submission: November 2025.

SYLVAIN ROMIEU

THE MONUMENTAL
ELDEN RING

FROMSOFTWARE'S MAGNUM OPUS

03rd. THIRD éditions

TABLE OF CONTENTS

PREFACE   07

PART ONE: CREATING ELDEN RING   11
CHAPTER 1: A BRIEF HISTORY OF FROMSOFTWARE   13
CHAPTER 2: THE SEEDS OF ELDEN RING'S DEVELOPMENT   17
CHAPTER 3: CONCEPTS AND DESIGN   27
CHAPTER 4: THE MARKETING STRATEGY   73
CHAPTER 5: COMMUNITIES   79
CHAPTER 6: A HIGHLY ANTICIPATED EXPANSION   89

PART TWO: UNDERSTANDING ELDEN RING   95
CHAPTER 1: AN OVERVIEW   97
CHAPTER 2: THE PAST   107
CHAPTER 3: THE PRESENT   147
CHAPTER 4: ADDITIONAL LORE AND THEORIES   173
CHAPTER 5: THE MANY MEANINGS OF ELDEN RING   235

CONCLUSION: THE NEW MYTH(S)   257
BIBLIOGRAPHY   263
AUTHOR'S ACKNOWLEDGMENTS   271

THE MONUMENTAL

ELDEN RING

FromSoftware's Magnum Opus

PREFACE

ARADOXICALLY, I am writing this introduction last. I've already finished writing the rest of the book. I've actually made a habit of saving the introduction for last. I find that doing so allows me to properly take stock of the work as a whole when writing an analysis or essay such as this one, especially with such a vast subject. Indeed, *Elden Ring* is a game that's larger than life, almost monstrous in many respects.

There's the colossal amount of work that went into the game's production–seven years if you include the *Shadow of the Erdtree* DLC expansion, and around 1,600 people who worked on the project in one way or another.

There's the extensive time needed for players to complete the adventure–150 hours on average when including the DLC, according to the website *HowLongToBeat*.

There's the blockbuster sales–25 million units sold to date for the main game and 5 million for *Shadow of the Erdtree*, making it one of the top 50 best-selling video games of all time.

There's the astonishing number of times players have died in-game–9 billion, an amusing figure announced by the publisher Bandai Namco a year after the game's release.

There's the deluge of awards given to the game by prestigious organizations– over 30 in total.

There's the hundreds of hours spent on research and reflection for me to complete this book, which included countless branches and details on the massive family tree I sketched as part of that research, a solid foundation that helped me wrap my head around the game's mammoth corpus of lore.

Moreover, there's the tremendous and seemingly endless amount of content produced by the title's community, teeming with all sorts of fascinating ideas and reflecting the richness of the game's universe.

For all of these reasons and many others, *Elden Ring* is a monumental work, resulting from the unique ambition and cumulative expertise of FromSoftware.

Elden Ring is the studio's magnum opus.

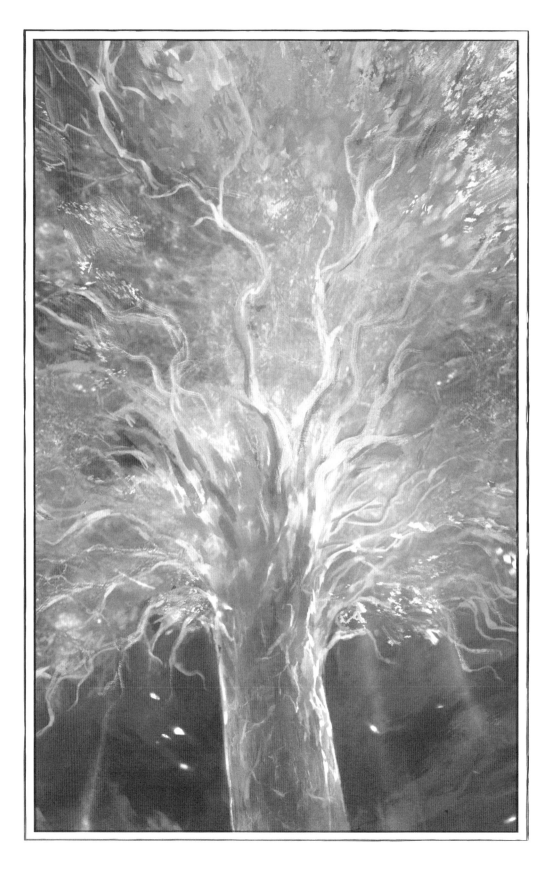

THE MONUMENTAL
ELDEN RING
FromSoftware's Magnum Opus

Part 1
Creating Elden Ring

CHAPTER 1
A BRIEF HISTORY OF FROMSOFTWARE

Before we dive into the making of *Elden Ring*, let's take a few moments to examine the history of FromSoftware and the events that made it into such a beloved studio today[1]. Indeed, FromSoftware's games have not always received such high praise from audiences and critics.

FromSoftware was founded in 1986 as a developer of business software. It wasn't until 1994 that the company developed and self-published its first game. FromSoftware made *King's Field* for the PlayStation, and while the game was never sold outside of Japan, it marked the start of a series of role-playing games that would largely lay the foundations for most of the studio's future productions. Over the years, FromSoftware continued churning out titles at a prolific pace, including both sequels and games set in new universes. The studio's games were almost always self-published in Japan, where the company built its expertise and a decent customer base. FromSoftware also began publishing many of its games internationally and developed a name for itself as a studio producing modest games that weren't always the greatest, but which nonetheless offered variety.

Hidetaka Miyazaki joined the FromSoftware team in 2004, and several years later, he would completely transform the company's reputation. Miyazaki, a former accountant, was enchanted by the ambiance and game design of the game *ICO*, released in Japan for the PlayStation 2 in 2001. After falling in love with the game, he decided to change careers to enter the world of video game development. He joined the FromSoftware team, cutting his teeth as a developer while working on an episode in the *Armored Core* series. From there, he quickly rose through the ranks to become a game director—the person who supervises the development of a game, both in terms of creative aspects and managing production constraints—for two other titles in the same franchise. His work as the

---

1. For a much more detailed analysis of FromSoftware's history, refer to previous books published by Third Éditions on the studio's games: *Dark Souls: Beyond the Grave*, volumes one and two, and *Sekiro: The Second Life of Souls*.

director of *Demon's Souls* (2009) marked a major turning point in his career. The game became the first in a long line of descendants, both direct and indirect.

A cryptic world; confounding difficulty; a dark-fantasy ambiance filled with despair; asynchronous multiplayer mechanics, notably including the ability for players to leave informative messages on the ground for other players; rich and original game design; natural and surprising level design; all of these aspects of *Demon's Souls* were later baked into 2011's *Dark Souls*, FromSoftware's first big commercial success, selling over 2 million copies. *Dark Souls* was more polished and more open, with a more coherent universe and game design. What's more, it benefited from better worldwide, multi-platform distribution, with simultaneous releases for the PlayStation 3 and Xbox 360, then for PC a year later. The game was FromSoftware's first major collaboration with the publisher Namco Bandai Games (now known as Bandai Namco Entertainment), the two companies having previously worked together on less ambitious games.

Hidetaka Miyazaki continued to sit in the director's chair for the offspring of *Demon's Souls* and *Dark Souls*—with the exception of *Dark Souls II* (2014). This included *Bloodborne* (2015), which swapped out the dark-fantasy universe for a Victorian-style setting with a bit of Gothic flavor; *Dark Souls III* (2016), the final entry in the series, widely considered to be a fitting ending; *Sekiro: Shadows Die Twice* (2019), whose sword-based gameplay fit with its setting in feudal Japan; and finally *Elden Ring* (2022), which transposed the *Souls* formula into an open world. Meanwhile, there were some big changes in FromSoftware's structure. In 2014, the studio was acquired by a large company, Kadokawa Corporation. Shortly thereafter, Hidetaka Miyazaki was named president of the studio. It's a role with lots of responsibilities and time-consuming duties, one that would seem to be incompatible with Miyazaki's other role as a game director. However, one of his stipulations when he agreed to become the company's president was that he would remain involved in game development and continue to work closely with the studio's artists and developers.

This was especially important for Miyazaki as he has a very particular way of working with his team when he directs a game. He supervises everything, from the folds in the sleeves of modeled characters to the organic sequencing of shortcuts in level design. But even as he scrutinizes every minute detail, he remains open to suggestions from his team. He's OK with being told that his ideas aren't great, and he has no problem with implementing or exploring good suggestions submitted to him. Still, he drives the overall vision for the games he directs and personally writes the numerous bits of narration, description, and dialogue that cement the unique storytelling of his games. In short, Miyazaki is everywhere all at once and knows himself to be a bit of a micromanager. One has to wonder how he's able to fit so much work into his schedule. The best explanation is that he knows how to dedicate his time to the things that matter, and it shows in the company's results: since Miyazaki became president of FromSoftware, the studio has put out one great game after another, garnering numerous awards and honors, and the company has continued to grow its sales and improve its reputation with both critics and players. Moreover, Hidetaka Miyazaki puts his own ego low on the list of priorities, maintaining a low profile in spite of his success. For example, he grants few interviews, even during media blitzes around game releases. Simon Parkin, a contributing writer for *The New Yorker*, explained in his article published the day of *Elden Ring*'s release that Miyazaki had rescheduled their interview three times. Interviews are simply not a priority for Miyazaki, even with such a prestigious magazine!

To make a long story short, FromSoftware has sold 30 million units in the *Dark Souls* franchise and earned prestigious awards, including one given during the Golden Joystick Awards in 2021 to celebrate 50 years of video game history, the "Ultimate Game of All Time" award. The first *Dark Souls* took home the prize, beating out legendary titles like *Doom*, *Tetris*, and *Super Mario 64*. FromSoftware has created games that have inspired players and developers alike, and although the company is more modest in size than some of its big global competitors like Ubisoft and Electronic Arts, it still knows how to grab media attention and build excitement among its audiences with each new game announcement.

And all that was before the release of *Elden Ring*.

CHAPTER 2
THE SEEDS OF ELDEN RING'S DEVELOPMENT

A new organizational chart

Development of *Elden Ring* began in 2017, just after the release of the second and final DLC for *Dark Souls III: The Ringed City*. At the time, Miyazaki was supervising another game, *Sekiro*, and had to organize his teams in such a way that he could monitor both titles at once. For a time, he focused primarily on game design and art direction (for both visuals and music), and appointed two co-directors—a structure he'd previously experimented with on *Dark Souls III*—so he could delegate all other aspects to them. He selected Kazuhiro Hamatani (lead game designer for *Bloodborne*) and Yui Tanimura (director of *Dark Souls II* and co-director of *III*) for *Sekiro* and *Elden Ring*, respectively.

There were changes to the rest of the team structure, with the addition of a top level of managers that had been absent from FromSoftware's previous productions. Miyazaki added directors of programming, gameplay, level design, environment art and character art, battles, etc. In all, ten directors took the reins of departments that had previously been managed by their respective "leads" (lead programmer, lead level designer, etc.), even while the leads remained part of the team structure. This new level of management allowed the leads to better support their teams, letting them focus on technical ideas and decisions, rather than strategic ones. More broadly, the new organizational chart aimed to respond to the needs of the team's growing headcount and the high ambitions for *Elden Ring*. The website *MobyGames* lists 1,629 people who took part in the game's development, including the staff of contractors and publishers, versus 1,099 for *Sekiro* and 744 for *Dark Souls III*.

In 2017, at the very beginning of the project, before the studio got its full team working on *Elden Ring*, FromSoftware's leaders began imagining what the new game might look like. The general idea was to make a "*Souls*-like" game, following in the footsteps of the studio's storied titles, but with a much bigger, more open world to offer players new sensations and more in-depth exploration. Miyazaki had already announced the previous year that he was personally done with the *Dark Souls* series—comments that were reported by Brian Ashcraft on the website *Kotaku* (September 21, 2016). However, he still wanted to draw from the dark fantasy genre for his next game, just not in connection with the universe and themes of *Dark Souls*; in other words, he wanted to experiment with new ideas that might be incompatible with the studio's flagship series. While the initial concepts for the world of *Elden Ring* trended more towards classic fantasy than dark fantasy, something important happened early in the world-building phase that helped the studio in its goal of breaking away from the constraints of *Dark Souls*: FromSoftware's leaders got the idea to outsource the world-building for their new game to someone not just outside the company, but outside the world of video games entirely, someone with a keen sense of the dark fantasy genre. They turned to one George R. R. Martin.

The writer

George Raymond Richard Martin is a man who needs no introduction. He is the author of several best-selling novels and the producer, and occasional screenwriter, of hit TV series. His *A Song of Ice and Fire* series is, without a doubt, at the heart of his work: it is a series of novels published over the last few decades that have been read by millions of readers and adapted by the American TV channel HBO into the series *Game of Thrones*, which in turn was watched by millions of viewers over the years. Martin was also involved in the production—and even provided the voice for a character made in his likeness!—of the *Game of Thrones* video game released in 2012, a fairly typical RPG developed by the French studio Cyanide. While *A Song of Ice and Fire* was already a highly respected series of novels, with numerous prestigious awards to prove it, the franchise reached the height of its popularity with mainstream audiences during the era of the TV series, from 2011 to 2019. George R. R. Martin, who was heavily involved in the HBO adaptation, became a household name, famous for his dark stories of plotting, betrayal, twisted families, and bold, memorable characters, as well as for his habit of killing off his protagonists, no matter how important, without any warning or moral qualms. He was even named one of the 100 most influential people in the world in 2011 by *Time* magazine. All this to say, whether in writing or in images, Martin has enthralled and traumatized generations of fantasy lovers, or in any case, fans of a darker type of fantasy that's more realistic than other classics of the genre.

Hidetaka Miyazaki counts himself among those fans of George R. R. Martin. And not just for *A Song of Ice and Fire*, which he certainly loves. In various interviews, Miyazaki has cited *Tuf Voyaging*, a collection of science-fiction novellas, and the horror novel *Fevre Dream*, which he considers an absolute masterpiece.

From early in the project that would become *Elden Ring*, the Japanese creator dreamed of collaborating with Martin to create the universe for the new game. However, he hesitated to make the ask, fearing that the writer would categorically refuse. Finally, his executive producer, Eiichi Nakajima, took the plunge and contacted Martin. The author accepted the proposal, and even mentioned his appreciation for the *Dark Souls* games, even though he's not actually a gamer himself, as he has written on his blog[2] (December 18, 2021). Incidentally, in that same blog post, Martin mentioned some of his favorite video games from back in the day, listing management and strategy games from the 1990s, particularly *Railroad Tycoon*, *Romance of the Three Kingdoms*, and *Master of Orion*. So, Miyazaki breathed a sigh of relief and a meeting was scheduled.

In spite of some anxiety, particularly about their 26-year age difference and the language barrier, the first meeting went well. From there, the two creators talked regularly, and Miyazaki laid out for Martin his vision for the game, including its major themes and certain ideas that he wished to put into action in the new universe. On the Xbox official website (article dated June 9, 2019), Miyazaki explains what this period was like: "[We had] many free and creative conversations regarding the game, which Mr. Martin later used as a base to write the overarching mythos for the game world itself. This mythos proved to be full of interesting characters and drama along with a plethora of mystical and mysterious elements as well." Miyazaki then adds: "*Elden Ring*'s world was constructed using this mythos and stimulus as a base."

George R. R. Martin laid the foundations for the new universe and, importantly, described the history of the Lands Between, the fictitious region in which the game takes place, including its peoples, important families, and the connections between them. He established what the game's world was like up until the Shattering, a crucial event that occurred some 5,000 years before the events of the game[3]. Miyazaki explains the approach to *IGN* (June 21, 2019): "Storytelling in video

---

2. George R. R. Martin regularly uses his personal blog, entitled *Not A Blog*, to publish various announcements and musings. While this means of communication is a bit, shall we say, "vintage"—the blog has been around since 2005—it nonetheless lends a certain authenticity to the larger-than-life figure that is G.R.R. Martin.

3. Martin revealed this number in an interview on *The Late Show with Stephen Colbert*, broadcast on October 25, 2022. When asked about the popularity of *Elden Ring*, the writer briefly summarized his collaboration with FromSoftware five years previously. Martin seems to have selected this "5,000" number at random as a way of saying "long before the events of the game." But otherwise, it would be the one and only specific indication of a clear timeline in the entire game!

games—at least the way we do it at FromSoftware—comes with a lot of restrictions for the writer. I didn't think it was a good idea to have Martin write within those restrictions. By having him write about a time the player isn't directly involved in, he is free to unleash his creativity in the way he likes. Furthermore, at FromSoftware, we didn't want to create a more linear and story-driven experience for *Elden Ring*. Both issues could be solved by having Martin write about the world's history instead."

So, the Japanese creator's very peculiar style of fragmented storytelling, as seen in his previous games, was once again used for *Elden Ring*. We will examine this approach in detail in the second part of this book, dedicated to the game's story and universe. For now, I'll just mention that the story is broken up into pieces like a jigsaw puzzle, with each piece cleverly hidden in dialogue and the descriptions of objects, but also in various elements of the backgrounds and in the characters' style of dress and battle habits. As such, it's hard for a player to mentally put that jigsaw puzzle together, especially since many pieces are (purposely) missing, leaving room for each individual to use their imagination to fill in the holes. This type of storytelling is a real trademark of FromSoftware, and especially of Miyazaki, who typically writes all or some of the script for objects and dialogue in his games. For *Elden Ring*, given the volume of content, he did a lot of reviewing of other people's work. However, he notes in an interview with *Famitsu* (June 14, 2021) that he wrote a large portion of the text himself. In this, we can see why Miyazaki insisted on "micromanaging" every aspect of his project, as mentioned previously, always striving to ferret out any inconsistencies and set aside any elements that might reveal more than intended. It was a delicate exercise, particularly when paired with the game's story, which is in many cases more complicated than it initially seems. To understand the story, you need to understand the universe's past, with a hazy timeline that makes interpretation difficult. It all adds up to a sort of mythology, or "lore," composed of the universe's peoples, gods, heroes, and great tragedies.

So, George R. R. Martin developed the history and mythology—the lore—for *Elden Ring*. He wrote a sort of world-building bible, which Miyazaki has compared to the kind of guide used by a game master in a tabletop role-playing game. While developing the game, Miyazaki was able to draw from that "bible," which lays out the key features and laws of the game's universe, along with descriptions and histories of various figures, and even small anecdotes, which, though they may seem trivial, are essential for enriching the story, fleshing it out, and giving it a certain credibility. In his interview with *The New Yorker* (February 25, 2022), Miyazaki notes: "In our games, the story must always serve the player experience. If [Martin] had written the game's story, I would have worried that we might have to drift from that. I wanted him to be able to write freely and not to feel restrained by some obscure mechanic that might have to change in development."

G.R.R. Martin delivered his world-building work well before production of the game began in earnest. After the fact, Martin was amazed at how long the development process took, as he no longer participated in the project after writing his part of it. From time to time, FromSoftware would send him examples of designs for characters or creatures, and even a few visual effects. So, the studio kept him in the loop for a while, but Martin no longer had any direct involvement in working with the lore he'd created.

That said, the game's universe continued to evolve throughout the development process. For example, the Erdtree, the giant, sun-like entity that can be seen from every corner of the Lands Between, was added later, as Miyazaki recounted in an interview with the magazine *Weekly Famitsu* (March 10, 2022). All of the events set in the game's present were built on the foundation laid by Martin. Interestingly, the fantasy author has always employed a similar approach, focusing on the history, major themes, and mythology, rather than on the crafting of dialogue or the fate of his characters. Incidentally, when *IGN* (June 21, 2019) asked Miyazaki about the possibility of the best-selling author writing a book based on *Elden Ring*, he responded: "A novelization would mean that all the secrets and mystery hidden in our game would be revealed. From the point of view of a director, I'm not sure if that would be the right thing to do."

Secrets and mystery have always been at the heart of FromSoftware's games, whether in their respective universes, made to be as cryptic as possible, complex and sometimes unclear rules in game design, and even in their development. As I've said previously, Miyazaki grants very few interviews, and his team grants even fewer. Their responses are always meticulously measured; they make sure to never reveal too much about their work methods or their creative approach. So, all official information on *Elden Ring* has been delivered in dribs and drabs over several years, with tight control by FromSoftware and Bandai Namco, which once again served as the studio's publisher after Activision took on that role for *Sekiro*. All that in spite of audiences and the media being eager for all the information they can get. Unfortunately for the companies, the announcement of their new title did not go quite as planned.

The announcement

In chronological order: George R. R. Martin was the first to mention his involvement in a Japanese video game, doing so in a long blog post in which he bid farewell to the *Game of Thrones* TV series, which had aired its final episode a month earlier in May 2019. No other information was provided, whether about the game in question or even the studio making it. However, rumors began to circulate suggesting a connection with an upcoming title from Miyazaki. Still, the gaming world would have to wait several months before learning any more about the mysterious collaboration mentioned by the author.

Even as audiences awaited the announcement of a DLC for *Sekiro*, the game having been released earlier in the year, FromSoftware suddenly and unexpectedly found itself making headlines in the video-game world. Due to a security flaw on the Bandai Namco website, Daniel Ahmad (alias ZhugeEX), an analyst specializing in the Asian video game market who is very active in the gaming community, revealed confidential data on FromSoftware's upcoming game on June 7, 2019. He was able to share the name *Elden Ring*, the logo with interlocking golden circles, the platforms that would receive the game, and the fact that it was the much-talked-about collaboration with George R. R. Martin.

The official announcement was made a few days later at the 2019 edition of E3, the video-game industry trade show, with a trailer packed with mysteries. Eagle-eyed viewers will note that the trailer actually revealed one of the game's biggest secrets, concerning the link between Marika and Radagon, which we will discuss in detail in the second part of this book. The unveiling of a new game by FromSoftware is always a big event, but the tagline "A new world created by Hidetaka Miyazaki and George R. R. Martin" pushed the excitement to the next level. After the announcement, the team granted a handful of interviews, in which they shared a basic overview of the new game. However, over the next two years, no additional information was shared with the public. Even still, at the Game Awards, *Elden Ring* was named the "most anticipated game" in both 2020 and 2021. So, well before its release, the game had a real aura around it.

Development under constraints

Little information about the actual development of *Elden Ring* has been shared in FromSoftware's official communications. However, we know of two things that created real challenges for the game's team.

When the project was first launched, a portion of the studio's employees were still busy with *Sekiro*. Miyazaki managed both projects at the same time, but he has noted several times that the two games did not really influence each other. On the PlayStation blog (January 28, 2022), Miyazaki discusses the overlapping development period: "I'd have to say that, [even though] *Sekiro*'s development overlapped with *Elden Ring*'s to an extent, there's nothing that directly came through from that [*Sekiro*] project. But there were several indirect examples there. For instance, the enemy stance break mechanic in *Elden Ring* is similar to *Sekiro*'s successful posture system. We even referenced *Sekiro*'s player traversal for the horse mounting system and how you traverse the map in *Elden Ring*." Indeed, players enjoy very fluid movement as they explore the Lands Between on horseback, especially with the double jump, which allows you to reach great heights, much as you can with the grappling hook in *Sekiro*. Players also have the ability to break an adversary's stance, although *Elden Ring* differs from its predecessor by hiding this stat. In contrast, *Sekiro*'s more intimate approach to storytelling, with a true protagonist instead of the "empty shell" avatars found in the studio's previous games, did not return in *Elden Ring*. On the other hand, the game's designers focused more on character development, an approach likely introduced by George R. R. Martin and his descriptions of the major families of the Lands Between.

Working on two projects at once, especially with a title as ambitious as *Elden Ring*, requires considerable resources. As we've already seen, FromSoftware seriously beefed up its teams, both internally and by outsourcing to partners, but hiring more help isn't the only solution for the problem of development lead times. For example, the studio saved time by having 80% of the open world's vegetation be procedurally generated, with staff making manual touch-ups afterward. For comparison, almost everything was done by hand in *Dark Souls*, in which the environments were much more limited in size. What's more, as *Elden Ring* was produced by Bandai Namco, the publisher of *Dark Souls III*, FromSoftware was able to reuse numerous assets, including both graphic and audio resources, and also probably part of the older game's engine. Of course, a lot of work was required to adapt the game engine to handle an open world, not to mention the work required for the thousands of new assets that had to be created, but without that foundation, the game's development would have taken a few years more, or it might never have gotten off the ground as the level of risk would have deterred all sources of funding. Miyazaki suggested as much in an interview with *4Gamer.net* (June 24, 2022). All in all, the game took five years to create. At the same time, that length was influenced by an external factor that no one saw coming and which affected literally the entire world: the COVID-19 pandemic.

In 2020 and 2021, Miyazaki had to deal with all sorts of complications: staff out sick, everyone working remotely full time, and eventually shortages of certain pieces of computer equipment. That was true for the *Elden Ring* project, but also for the rest of FromSoftware, as Miyazaki is the company's president. He talked about these difficulties to *Edge* magazine (issue 367, February 2022): "It would be false to say it didn't affect *Elden Ring*'s development in any way—we had to change how we approached a lot of the aspects of game development, including communication, which was obviously a big part of it. It was a big challenge to adapt at first, but we succeeded thanks to the team." Before the pandemic, FromSoftware had already started allowing its employees to work remotely more often, but the new constraints, which came on fast and strong, really interrupted the company's routine.

The homestretch

In June 2021, during the annual Summer Game Fest, FromSoftware showed a new trailer for *Elden Ring*. Unlike the video revealed two years earlier, the new trailer was made up entirely of sequences from the final game. The audience got its first look at the Lands Between, along with a steed, dragons, and a slew of bosses. The trailer was a big hit and ended with the announcement of a release date: January 21, 2022. It was also revealed that the game would be available for the latest generation of consoles, the PlayStation 5 and Xbox Series X and S.

The release date was eventually pushed back to February 25, 2022. "The level of freedom that we wanted to ultimately achieve in *Elden Ring* exceeded what we were initially planning for. This [complexity] gradually built up, and the time needed to debug and QA in particular took a lot more effort," Miyazaki explains in the *Edge* interview. Was this delay caused by pandemic complications or did Miyazaki want to avoid wearing out his team with a brutally long crunch time? Again, it's hard to know exactly what was happening inside FromSoftware. While Miyazaki has tried to ensure optimal working conditions for his team, telling *4Gamer.net* that the work environment has greatly improved in recent years, he also talks about a "peak time of development" in his interview with *Edge*.

Anyone who has worked in the realm of software is sure to be familiar with these "peak times of development." As a delivery or "code freeze" (when you can no longer touch the source code before it's sent into the final testing phase) date draws near, any number of situations can imperil the late stages of development, including last-minute critical bugs and outages of crucial infrastructure. And then there's the unfortunate fact that developers can almost always count on Murphy's Law: "anything that can go wrong, will go wrong." There are all sorts of tools to help prevent these kinds of situations, along with proper upstream risk management, with choices made accordingly. But in spite of all that, studios are rarely able to avoid a peak in activity in the critical final stages of development. With a bit of lucidity and the right decisions, it's manageable. But otherwise—and this is unfortunately often the case for projects under strong financial pressure or with high anticipation, as in the video game world—that peak in activity can extend over a longer period and become a true "crunch time." It's a vicious circle in which exhaustion and distraction, or even circumvention of procedures to save time, can lead to new problems and drag everyone into development hell.

In any case, Miyazaki has described a "peak time of development" for *Elden Ring*, but he still tried to ensure proper working conditions for his employees. And that's all we'll ever know, at least from official channels. A few months after the game's release, a number of articles described appalling reviews of FromSoftware from its employees on the Japanese community website *Career Connection*. Indeed, the studio received some less-than-admirable scores and comments on the site, shining a light on problems with gender parity and equality, as well as a lot of regular overtime work. If we take a closer look at the reviews, the worst ones are several years old, with some from 2016 and 2015, but most from 2012. In November 2022, a new article on the subject was published on the website *Games Industry*. This one relied on more recent testimonials, though the individuals remained anonymous as FromSoftware does not allow its employees, whether current or former, to give interviews. Depending on the department, some of those interviewed described two to three months of crunch time, along with fairly low pay given the amount of work they did. On FromSoftware's official website, all of the company's job postings list a generic monthly salary starting at 260,000 yen (as of November 2022), or about $1,857, with actual amounts varying according to the candidate's skills and experience. Staff also get two bonuses per year. For comparison, that's slightly above the lower end of the normal pay range for a video game developer in Japan, which is about $1,648, according to the reference values on the website *SalaryExplorer*. We don't have much more concrete information than that, especially since the *Games Industry* article is vague on a number of points, such as the actual number of people they talked to or the departments in which those people work. It's a touchy subject and FromSoftware has refused to comment on it, which doesn't help us get a firm and objective understanding of the situation. Moreover, the article in question says that not everyone the journalist talked to was unhappy. It ends with a short paragraph mentioning "multiple sources"–once again, a vague description–who had a positive experience. Whatever the case may be, we hope that FromSoftware's management is taking working conditions and respect for employees seriously, and more importantly, that management is constantly working to improve them.

Returning to the delay in *Elden Ring*'s release, one month is not actually that much of a delay. That extra month was barely enough time to fine-tune a day-one patch that corrected a few critical bugs after release. That said, one month can also be the time a team needs to catch its breath and gain some clarity, depending on the state of the project they've been working on. Although the game was very highly anticipated, the announcement of the delay was received quite positively. Over the years, audiences have come to realize the complexity of developing a video game and they generally prefer to wait a little longer in order to get a better level of polish and a better experience. In any case, the video-game market is so diverse and intense that players are never bored.

In spite of the extra month for testing the game and fixing bugs, several critical issues remained when the title was released, including failures to save on the PlayStation 5 and unstable performance for the PC version. As some players experienced an inexplicable drop in the frame rate and jerky performance, things started to get heated. On the day of the game's release, Bandai Namco published on its website a list of known problems, with a few work-arounds, particularly for saving issues—after all, what could be worse for a player than losing their progress?

Thankfully, most people had no problem while playing the game. And so, on February 25, 2022, millions of people—over 760,000 on Steam alone—finally discovered *Elden Ring*, diving into an unknown and hostile world, for an experience much more intense and extensive than most players probably expected. For weeks, which flew by for players exploring the Lands Between around the clock, the media devoted all its attention to FromSoftware's latest production, leaving all other announcements and releases by the wayside. But before we talk about the game's critical and commercial success, a record-shattering period for FromSoftware, let's examine in more detail what the game itself has to offer.

CHAPTER 3
CONCEPTS AND DESIGN

Open world

◈ Let's define it

The open world is not a genre, but rather a way of designing a game's environment. It offers a response to linear games that unfold through a series of levels and narrative sequences, with a certain control over the pacing (X passage is estimated to take Y time to complete), but also over the difficulty (the first level is easier than the fifth), the progression of the story (information given at the end of a level will lead to revelations in the next), and even rules in the game design, since it's easier, for example, to add or experiment with a more complex gameplay idea within a clearly defined level.

This classic and effective structure is obliterated when you design your game as an open world, in which the goal is generally to offer a more immersive experience, giving the player much more flexibility in discovering the game's universe and story. The freedom of movement given to the player, and thus the ability to really explore, makes it impossible to "organize" the player's experience into levels, i.e., units in a sequence, or at least organized into a carefully thought-out order. It's true that the designers can always orient the player's progression with a main storyline, or even block off certain zones, whether physically with sealed passages or cliffs, for example, or artificially by ramping up the difficulty to an insurmountable level, a sign that the location in question is outside the natural sequence of the adventure. But the designers must be careful, as imposing too many restrictions detracts from the open-world experience. Thus, the openness of the world will depend on how much the designers wish to control the experience they offer to players. As a result, some games offer semi-open worlds, others are much more closed and linear while giving a false impression of openness (which is not at all meant to be a criticism), and others still offer so much freedom that it's almost like playing in sandbox mode. All sorts of different games offer open worlds, and that's what makes this approach so difficult to date and define. Still, we can retrace the evolution of open-world philosophies to better understand the approach used in *Elden Ring*.

✦ Emergence and evolution

The Legend of Zelda (1986) was one of the first mainstream games to offer an open world. Up to that point, only a niche group of PC gamers had been familiar with the concept, for example, people who played the RPG series *Ultima*, of which the first installment was released in 1981. In fact, *The Legend of Zelda* adopted certain ideas from *Ultima*, like the top-down perspective. This was revolutionary at a time when most games were side-scrollers, in which the avatar is seen in profile and moves from left to right to advance. Changing perspective opened up new directional possibilities. With the newfound ability to explore to the north, south, east, and west, players' relationship to the world and gameplay therein changed radically, and *The Legend of Zelda* became an instant classic. Years later, *Ocarina of Time* (1998), which successfully brought the series into a 3D universe, introduced its own bundle of innovations while at the same time taking a step backwards in terms of the player's freedom to explore. Indeed, the only truly open area in *Ocarina of Time* is Hyrule Field, which serves as a hub between other, more closed areas; however, the game offered the novelty of allowing players to cross Hyrule Field on horseback. The cycling between day and night in the game also had an impact on the changing standards for open worlds. The idea of a very open central hub that links together more limited and detailed areas, like villages and dungeons, became quite common in a segment of games aiming to offer more openness without giving the player total freedom. It became a good compromise for a semi-open world, while illustrating the difficulty of developing such an approach in a fully 3D environment.

For that very reason, 2001's *Grand Theft Auto III* was viewed as revolutionary. The title from Rockstar Games impressed the industry with its sandbox-style world. The first few installments in the series had already allowed players to freely explore the streets of an entire city, whether on foot or by car, and to live the life of a gangster while completing various missions for the local organized crime syndicate. But with one (huge) difference: they were in 2D. *GTA III* brilliantly brought the series into a 3D world, managing all of the implications of a revamped game design (shooting, driving, freedom of action, etc.) and changed perspective, thus setting a new standard for open worlds and the immersiveness that's so important for game designers.

The Elder Scrolls is another hit series of games that has always preferred to offer an open-world experience. Among the most notable in the series, the third installment, *Morrowind* (2002), delivered an enchanting, "handmade" open world, in which every element was placed manually, from the vegetation to the houses in the various villages. This was in response to the game's immediate predecessor, *Daggerfall*, with its 80,000 square miles (200,000 km²), 15,000 towns, and 750,000 characters, all procedurally generated using algorithms. That approach allowed the developers to automatically create a large volume of content using some basic rules; however, it naturally results in a lot of redundancy or, as in the case of *Daggerfall*, a lot of emptiness. *Morrowind* went in the opposite direction, with absolutely everything being carefully crafted in a much smaller world, but one which was still quite vast. Additionally, the 3D graphics added a vertical dimension to the universe, and the developers also put special care into creating various side quests. While playing the game, it's not uncommon to get side-tracked far from the main plot as you solve the problems of different villagers or complete guild missions to climb through the ranks. It's fascinating stuff. With *Morrowind*, the open-world concept opened up further, moving in the direction of a captivating universe in which the player's interest is constantly renewed by the game's storytelling. *Skyrim*, the fifth volume in the *Elder Scrolls* saga, was also extraordinarily successful, outperforming *Morrowind* by far: as of 2023, the game had sold over 60 million copies. That's an astronomical figure that reflects the larger-than-life nature of the epic adventure, which has inspired numerous developers over the years. While *Morrowind* already contained the heart of the *Elder Scrolls* open-world philosophy, *Skyrim* brought the concept to a much wider audience. In *Skyrim*, even more than in its predecessors, the player follows the on-screen compass, but also intriguing sights. What secret might be hiding on the snow-capped peak? What treasure might this cave have in store for me? Via the approach to its level design, *Skyrim* became a real free-roaming game, in which the player explores all the different natural structures in the game's snowy environment.

At the same time, the open-world concept received some major updates from Ubisoft, which became one of the most prolific publishers of games using the approach. The amazing *Assassin's Creed* (2007) established a number of elements that were perfected two years later in its sequel, notably an approach based on the placement of numerous point-of-interest icons on the map. While at first refreshing, this strategy was then deployed *ad nauseam* in most of the studio's productions. It has gotten to the point that many players now lament this systematic approach: scaling dozens of towers to find pieces of a map, collecting tons of resources and other objects, completing numerous side quests that are often generic and rarely interesting, whether in terms of gameplay or in terms of storytelling. All of these ideas—which, while acceptable, get truly repetitive over dozens of hours of gameplay and over dozens of games—were infused into the specifications for many other projects after the commercial success of *Assassin's Creed*. As such, for many years, a whole host of studios tried to apply the Ubisoft formula, often with lackluster results. The problem was only made worse by long development lead times and the resulting inertia. Meanwhile, many gamers found themselves getting increasingly frustrated with this standardization.

That said, as open-world games became more common, they also became more diverse. While there were more and more RPGs and action-adventure games, other genres tried their hand at the open world: racing games like *Burnout Paradise* (2008) and *Midnight Club: Los Angeles* (2008), pirate games like *Assassin's Creed IV: Black Flag* (2013), puzzle games like *The Witness* (2016), and the astounding *Mortal Kombat: Deception* (2004), setting a "versus-fighting" game in a semi-open world. And then came *The Witcher 3: Wild Hunt* (2015), which brought its own innovations to the open-world concept, this time in terms of storytelling. The two previous series installments had also put an emphasis on storytelling aspects, with fascinating quests and characters; however, they were set in semi-open levels. The ambition for the third installment was to bring that same quality of writing into a fully open world. The thing is, those two things are often incompatible. Indeed, most often, an open world means dull "filler" quests with very little connection or interaction between them. As the player can explore every part of the open world in any direction and complete quests in any order, storytelling is often a weak spot for these games. *Fallout: New Vegas* (2010), in its time, succeeded in pairing good writing with real choices affecting the fate of the player's avatar. However, with its modest budget, the game was unable to go toe-to-toe with AAA titles, whether in terms of the target audience or production values, and that's where *The Witcher 3* shined upon its release. It's an incredible world, a long and dense game, and above all, it has outstanding writing. While the game's main quest is, overall, pretty conventional, the creators put a lot of effort into developing the secondary characters and side quests. The side quests, in particular, are truly captivating, at least for the most important of the lot. It's not unusual for them to intersect with one another, with references to certain situations and characters. This gives the whole a real sense of coherence, making for a natural, organic progression. Unsurprisingly, given its complexity, this storytelling system is not free from bugs. But sincerely, we can salute the game's boldness and ambition, which it accomplished, as it set a new standard for storytelling in an open world. It meant that, going forward, competitors would have to get out of the comfort zone of humdrum, independent side quests. To do so, studios would have to reach farther into their already deep pockets to develop convincing storylines.

Over the years, the standardization of AAA games—the big blockbusters of the video-game industry, with colossal budgets to match their colossal sales ambitions—

gradually trended toward the use of open or semi-open worlds. The RPG series *Final Fantasy* offers some interesting examples. The series' twelfth episode (2006) largely opened up its areas for exploration, while the thirteenth episode (2009) imposed a very linear and closed first part before offering a much more open environment once the characters arrived on Gran Pulse. *Final Fantasy XV* (2016) implemented a true open world, through the lens of a strange road trip with a gang of friends, on the tragic backdrop of a war between kingdoms. The increasing power of gaming consoles from generation to generation has made it possible to open up game environments, but as we've seen, developing such games remains a long and expensive process, making them risky undertakings. Indeed, the development of *Final Fantasy XV* was absolute hell and lasted for at least a decade, first being announced in 2006 as a spin-off from the thirteenth installment in the series.

Another game-changer arrived in 2017. Inspired by *Skyrim*, *Breath of the Wild* (2017) marked the return of the *Zelda* franchise to a completely open world, as first popularized by the game's ancient ancestor. *Breath of the Wild* actually transcended that legacy by offering a multitude of ideas which, while not necessarily new, had never before been integrated so cleanly. The game is a giant sandbox, with logical and natural laws of physics. Wood burns, metal conducts lightning, you can die of cold or collapse from exhaustion, etc. The result is what's called "emergent gameplay," meaning that each player comes up with their own way of progressing through the adventure, solving puzzles, and fighting the most formidable foes. Moreover, everything is explorable and anything can be climbed. It was a real crowning achievement for the open-world concept after three decades of experimentation. Added to that were a few truly intriguing elements, like the map. A true blank map, nothing like the standards seen in the 2010s with maps covered in dozens or even hundreds of annotations, some relevant but many not. In *Breath of the Wild*, the player adds their own notes. They have a vague notion of which direction they need to go, guided by a series of quests from the beginning of the game, but they don't know exactly what path to follow. The player is forced to observe their environment to get their bearings. This choice in game design went against the grain, but offered a breath of fresh air for aspiring explorers.

Death Stranding (2019) is another open-world game that stands out from the crowd. Developed by Kojima Productions, and thus by creator Hideo Kojima, best known for the *Metal Gear* series, *Death Stranding* is a game centered on delivering packages in a post-apocalyptic world. The title really threw down the gauntlet, challenging the many open-world games filled with many such tasks, referred to as "FedEx quests," often criticized and viewed as uninteresting. *Death Stranding* went ahead and centered itself entirely on these quests! Of course, the game has much more to offer—great writing and a fascinating journey, among other things—but on its face, it was a perplexing choice. A game with walking at the heart of its gameplay: that wouldn't be an easy title to market if it wasn't for the name of the creator. In any case, the game was reasonably successful.

So, the open-world mode of game design has continued to gain traction and has been the subject of a wide range of experiments. And that's true not just for AAA productions, but also for independent studios with more modest budgets, who have tried to approach the "genre" differently, particularly in terms of storytelling, offering, for example, a more minimalistic story, free of NPCs and explicit side quests. There's *Subnautica* (2018), which followed a popular trend at the time of survival-oriented open worlds, popularized by *Minecraft* (2011), adapting the concept to a hostile underwater world. The game involves fascinating discoveries in different stages, each offering different crafting possibilities and deeper knowledge of the environment. Then, there's the equally fascinating *Outer Wilds* (2019), set in space, which offers a new approach to an open world, reaching the scale of an entire solar system that only exists and evolves for a fixed period of time before resetting. The entire game is a puzzle, an enigma, in which freedom of exploration is crossed with segmented storytelling and the need to decode the universe's mysteries. It's a mystifying experience. At the beginning, everything seems foreign, but the player learns the ins and outs as the game progresses. Indeed, there's no need to be a gaming veteran to play *Outer Wilds*, as experienced players will find themselves just as lost as novices. The player must observe and learn—some basic instructions that also happen to characterize the games of FromSoftware. Could it be, then, that the open-world approach has been a natural evolution for the studio's games?

◈ FromSoftware productions

Indeed, what about the *Souls* games, *Bloodborne*, and *Sekiro*? Are they open worlds? Well, no, not really, although they have borrowed some interesting ideas and sensations from some of the games previously cited.

Demon's Souls offers open levels, but they are not directly connected to one another. The player can use five "Archstones" to travel to the different levels, which are each divided into several segments. Each level offers a certain degree of freedom, particularly thanks to ingenious level design, and is dotted with shortcuts to facilitate exploration and help the player build a mental map of the spaces. There's no on-screen map; the player must follow their own sense of direction and learn organically how to get around. *Demon's Souls* also introduced an element that would become a mainstay for its successors: the game's segmented, puzzle-like storytelling. While the title's storytelling isn't necessarily typical of open-world games, it does encourage the player to explore every nook and cranny in hopes of finding an object or a clue that might reveal a little more of the lore of a particular area. And indeed, players are rewarded for their efforts.

The *Dark Souls* games and *Bloodborne* offered more openness, transposing the *Demon's Souls* formula, including its storytelling, into a series of coherent and connected environments. The already-successful level design was adapted to the rest of the game environment, with shortcuts connecting different areas in all sorts of improbable ways. *Dark Souls* added a significant vertical dimension to its semi-open world, making the game environment feel both enormous and labyrinthine. While this perception is absent from the first few hours of gameplay, as indications remain brief, you feel it more and more as the adventure progresses. Not every area is accessible at the beginning of the game—far from it—but the player can follow several different paths, creating a certain sense of freedom. *Dark Souls II* and *III* maintained the major aspects of the first installment, but with a more linear construction, while still offering choices for exploration—first this zone, then that zone—without really imposing a specific order or logic. The third installment, while not actually offering an open world, visually creates the impression of one, as Drangleic Castle is the central point of the game, both geographically and narratively. It can be seen from most areas of the game, which allows you to easily get your bearings. It serves as a real spatial marker, even if it can't be accessed in a straight line from any given location, as there is only one path to get there.

Finally, *Sekiro* kept the same spirit, even while being a bit more restrictive, or even more linear. On the other hand, it added gameplay elements that reinvigorate the sensation of freedom. Jumping—it's impossible to do a good and useful jump in the *Souls* games!—and the grappling hook add a bunch of vertical movements, and it's not unusual in the game to visit different areas by crossing over rooftops, adding new perspectives, both visually and in terms of gameplay.

◈ Great expectations

Again, none of FromSoftware's previous titles could claim to offer true open worlds. They borrowed some ideas from the open-world concept and experimented with various sensations, but just as they did with many other concepts and genres. They did, however, revolutionize—or at least significantly update—the action-RPG genre with certain game design rules now used here, there, and everywhere in recent productions, and a style of level design that many studios have tried to reinterpret in their own games. The *Souls* games, especially *Demon's Souls* and *Dark Souls*, truly left their mark on the entire video game industry.

For that very reason, when a new game from Hidetaka Miyazaki was announced, it got the attention of the entire gaming world. Especially given that the game would take on the new challenge of offering an open world. As we've already seen, the open-world approach is a costly one, and while trendy, an open-world game can end up being disappointing or even redundant once in the hands of players. Excellent open-world games are rare, and even rarer still are those that update the recipe with zesty new ingredients. Still, there are success stories, like *Horizon*, *Ghost of Tsushima*, and the *Marvel's Spider-Man* games, which stand out from the crowd thanks to their universes and gameplay sensations.

Although games like *Breath of the Wild* and *Death Stranding* have proved that it's possible to make a hit while infusing an open world with a different philosophy, the "Ubisoft way" remains very popular and relevant as it meets the primary expectations for an open-world game: immersion and a feeling of freedom, reinforced, moreover, by increasingly stunning graphics.

Indeed, a few years before *Elden Ring*, a AAA game with an open world made its mark on the video-game industry thanks to its bold, extraordinary vision: *Red Dead Redemption II* (2018). Developed by Rockstar, the studio behind the emblematic *GTA* series, *Red Dead Redemption II* took just about everyone by surprise when it was released. Both for better and for worse, mind you. In terms of structure, it's a classic Rockstar game, with its quests, long rides accompanied by dialogue, chase sequences, shoot-outs, etc. On the surface, the game's open world seems to follow the typical philosophy. In terms of application, however, the title aims to be extremely realistic. For example, the approach to "fun" of the studio's previous games was replaced by a whole host of controller manipulations allowing the player to carry out various actions and moves. It's a bold artistic decision that immerses the player in a Wild West world that feels credible in every way, from the gameplay to the graphics—not to mention the incredible weather-management system!

Much like *Death Stranding*, *Red Dead Redemption II* exposed audiences' curiosity, with players always ready to experience new sensations; it also proved that a game with a big budget and high expectations can still deliver an artist's vision, no matter how daring it may seem, and even when the game appears to rely on tried and true approaches.

As such, expectations were very high for Miyazaki's next game. Would *Elden Ring* prove to be as revolutionary as *Dark Souls* in its time? Would the title set new standards for open-world games?

⊕ FromSoftware's approach

"There are many definitions to the term 'open world,' and I might not be phrasing it correctly, but we have simply tried our own approach to a game with a large, open field to play in," Miyazaki states in an interview on the Xbox official website.

More or less ignoring what their competition was doing—although they would have certainly done a deep and thorough analysis—FromSoftware's teams chose to transpose their expertise and game style, which they had been developing for over a decade, into a much larger environment.

The studio maintained the same approach it had used for its previous titles. While the team wasn't sure that an open world would be the best approach, they laid out their initial vision for the project, including its major features and components. They prioritized gameplay aspects above all else—a sort of philosophy for the studio that has proven to be successful in the past, and which guided the team at many different stages of the *Elden Ring* project. The game's developers played around with different ideas to find the right size for the world and the right variables to adjust in order to deliver the ideal experience, as Miyazaki explains to *Edge*: "There are a lot of areas in which we've had to use trial and error since creating the *Dark Souls* series, iterating on those mechanics and formulas, expanding on them in this new sense of scale."

One of the greatest challenges that the developers encountered was the issue of pacing. Would this be another game in which players would traverse large, empty spaces and complete numerous unimaginative and redundant quests? That was out of the question. The team wanted to do everything possible to avoid boring their players. They made it a priority to deliver fun and a sense of freedom. They adjusted the number of NPCs and events that would appear during exploration, but they also simply shrunk down the different areas to prevent them from feeling too big or too time-consuming to explore. In a video entitled "Pre-release Production Staff Interview," published on February 24, 2022, on Bandai Namco's YouTube channel, the FromSoftware community manager Yasuhiro Kitao describes this adjustment process as a long and highly complex stage of development. He also talks about concerns the developers had, like the speed of the horse or how far it would jump, as the steed is key to exploration in the Lands Between.

There was nothing revolutionary about having players travel the world on horseback. Many other games had done so in the past, and by studying some of those games, the *Elden Ring* team was able to make certain decisions—sometimes to avoid copying others' work! Ultimately, their goal was to provide players with a horse, a means of transportation, that would be easy to maneuver. They had no interest in making a horse that would refuse to listen to the player, or get lost in the environment and become impossible to find again. They also didn't want one that would be hard to handle or offer challenges during mounting and dismounting. As a result, Torrent, *Elden Ring*'s spectral steed, listens without question, can be summoned or sent away using a quick command—even while running!—and is easy to control, including in terms of speed and double jumping. During the Japan Media Arts Festival (September 22, 2020), Miyazaki explained that he received advice from certain members of the team behind the *Game of Thrones* TV series—a connection most likely made by George R. R. Martin—regarding how to manage large spaces and what their exploration on horseback should look like.

Once the horse had been fine-tuned and the size of the environments more or less set, the developers had to figure out how they would captivate players throughout their adventure, especially given its considerable length. "*Elden Ring* has a vast world with an open overworld, so we were faced with the ordeal of how we maintain our gameplay style while offering a renewed sense of openness," says Miyazaki on the PlayStation blog. The title's gameplay borrows from the studio's previous games, but with more bosses, weapons, spells, and, overall, more possibilities. The battles while riding Torrent through wide-open spaces add an epic sensation, but even still, the game's battles generally feel similar to *Dark Souls*. A few welcome innovations, like the Spirit Ashes, were added to make the adventure more accessible for players and win over new audiences who may have been turned off by the difficulty of FromSoftware's previous titles. The open world alone goes a long way toward breaking down difficulty barriers—a game-design choice brought over from previous titles—by allowing players to simply go to another spot to acquire equipment and experience. We'll come back to these notions of difficulty and accessibility later on.

In terms of storytelling as well, adjustments had to be made to accommodate the open-world environment. For example, without more guidance than in the *Souls* games, players could quickly find themselves disoriented in the Lands Between. Miyazaki tells *Famitsu*: "The basic policy of telling a story in this work is the same as in the *Dark Souls* series. The textual information is presented in pieces and is intended to be connected in the user's mind or to be imagined by the user. The reason for this is that we want the gameplay itself to be the story of the user. However, I think that NPC conversations are more straightforward than in past works." Indeed, in quests for NPCs, these side characters tend to indicate where they're heading and thus more or less where the next step in their journey lies. Still, it's not unusual for a player to miss a few steps or rendez-vous points, as there are so many to keep in mind. A month after the game's release, patch 1.03 added to the world map the location of most NPCs from whom the player has accepted a quest. This makes progression through the game less chaotic for the player, who will inevitably forget some of the many irons they have in the fire, especially since there's no journal that automatically records quest instructions. This map update is a rare example of an in-game aid provided by FromSoftware, and it proves to be useful.

So, the game's storytelling is more direct, at least as concerns the story's development. The player is also guided by Grace, rays of light that discreetly indicate Sites of Grace, safe places where the player can rest. Following the golden glows helps the player avoid getting lost and it gives them an objective. This is convenient at the start of the game, even though the rays of Grace insidiously lead the player to Stormveil Castle—where the difficulty level really ratchets up for the first time! In terms of visual markers, the central Erdtree plays its part perfectly. It can be seen from just about anywhere in the Lands Between, helping the player easily get their bearings. The adventure begins south of the Erdtree and the game's overall objective is to reach it. It's as simple as that. There are many other visual elements in the landscape that give perspective. Buildings and natural land formations can also be seen on the map, offering guidance for the player across the vast expanses of territory.

The map is a key component of *Elden Ring*'s world. Every point of interest appears on it, not in the form of invasive icons, as seen in most of the game's open-world competitors, but added naturally by the imaginary cartographer who crafted the map once upon a time; that same unknown figure is also responsible for the map's very refined aesthetic, as if it were drawn by hand. However, at first glance, the map appears complex, detailed, and sometimes difficult to understand. As the game progresses, the player learns organically how to decipher it and use it, quite simply, like a real map. The various markings, in addition to adding an aesthetically pleasing touch, often indicate a region's key sites, as well as different types of points of interest and practical details about topography. As with the horse, Miyazaki wanted the map to be simple and fun to use, and he wanted its pieces to be easy to find.

In addition, a number of villages appear on the map. Now there's a real mainstay of open-world games! Villages are typically safe havens where the player can stock up on supplies, pick up some new quests, or learn new things that can help them understand the game's universe. You can forget about that in *Elden Ring*: most of the time, the villages are every bit as hostile as the rest of the world, either abandoned or inhabited by bloodthirsty creatures. "Creating a more open game is a big challenge for us. If we were to add towns on top of that, it would become a bit too much, so we decided to create an open world-style game focused on what we are best at," Miyazaki told *IGN* (June 21, 2019). Indeed, such safe zones—which also, in a way, serve a utilitarian purpose—were always absent from the *Souls* games, or were extremely rare and limited. While this design choice may be attributed to a real lack of expertise and resources, it nonetheless distinguishes the game from its competitors while staying true to the studio's legacy.

◈ Can we really call it revolutionary?

To say that players were eager for a FromSoftware style of open world is an understatement. Many were hoping for a sort of revolution, like the *Souls* games brought in their time to the action-RPG genre, or at least an avalanche of good ideas and possible disruptions to the standards. So, did FromSoftware deliver on that? As we've seen, Miyazaki and his team focused more on their areas of expertise rather than totally reinventing the wheel. They took on an ambitious project using existing resources—a task that would have been impossible otherwise given the team's modest size at the start of development. Given audiences' high expectations, it was hard for the studio to shoot for a daring, revolutionary vision—a phantasm of fans nostalgic for the revolution brought about by *Demon's Souls*. The team also had to think about expectations for commercial success. Still, the fact of transposing the studio's expertise, that *Dark Souls* ambiance, into a new game environment was interesting in its own right.

Much as, five years before *Elden Ring*, the developers of *Breath of the Wild* had sensed that they needed to introduce a slew of innovations to the open-world concept, innovations that have now become mainstays, the FromSoftware team knew that it would become harder and harder for future open-world games to rely on the same formula of "a map chock full of markers and icons + redundant quests and situations + nonexistent or uninspired level design." While that model had worked for many years, it was beginning to run out of steam. Especially since certain successful games—again, *Breath of the Wild* for mainstream audiences, but also *Death Stranding* and *Outer Wilds*, and even *The Witness* (2016), with its organic blend of an open world and puzzles—had already made a real paradigm shift by placing trust in the player and their ability to adapt to a world with new rules, without spoon-feeding them with explicit instructions. The discovery of a unique universe brings with it novel sensations, all tied to exploration of the unknown. *Elden Ring* fully embraces that philosophy.

That's not to say that the game's open-world formula is perfect. In particular, it's worth critiquing the title's borrowing of certain features long exploited by the studio. For example, the crafting system proves to be quite a disappointment. Classic in both its form and its function, *Elden Ring*'s crafting system largely serves to get the player out of a tight spot when certain objects are in short supply. When that happens, the player can create, on the spot, all sorts of consumables, from arrows to antidotes. The thing is, players don't tend to run out of supplies very often in the game, and meanwhile, their attention is constantly drawn to crafting resources sitting on the ground, shining brightly, distracting them from explo-ration. The player goes around picking up resources over and over again, hundreds of times throughout the game, detracting from the fluidity of discovering the Lands Between, and thus detracting from the overall rhythm of gameplay.

The same is true for certain ancillary spaces—catacombs, caves, ruins, mines, and tombs—that are numerous and often redundant. Many have criticized these mini-dungeons as being almost indistinguishable from one another, in spite of the surprises they spring on players, occasionally offering some interesting situations. For example, among those welcome surprises, the player gets to ride on the blade of a giant guillotine to reach an upper-level corridor in the Black Knife Catacombs. In the Giant-Conquering Hero's Grave, the enemies only become vulnerable upon being exposed to a special light. And a final example of an original idea: who among us can say they weren't tripped up by the clever level design of the Leyndell Catacombs, believing (incorrectly) that they were going around in circles? There are just over 50 of these mini-dungeons scattered across the Lands Between—for comparison, that's far less than *Breath of the Wild*'s 120 shrines. Still, their regular presence throughout the game's world makes them feel a bit like filler, much like *Bloodborne*'s supplementary Chalice Dungeons, which were procedurally generated according to certain rules, making them seem both clumsy and repetitive. Thankfully, in *Elden Ring*, the mini-dungeons prove to be more successful; however, it's still worth questioning their utility given the already prodigious length of the adventure.

Is *Elden Ring* too long? It's a fair impression that some have, and thus a fair question to ask. While, after studying the game's lore, there's an amusing theory that might explain the choice to make a never-ending game (and we'll get into that in the section of this book on the game's universe), the issue of a game's lifespan can be a double-edged sword when it comes to sales. While a lengthy game was once an important criterion for players, especially in the RPG market, they now see things quite differently. Few players still demand a long lifespan from their games, focusing instead on pacing over length. As such, a tighter experience without lulls in the rhythm will be much more popular than long series of redundant situations. It's about intensity over routine. For that very reason, a bit of marketing for *Dying Light 2: Stay Human*, a game set in an open world filled with zombies, completely backfired. A month before the game's release in early 2022, its creators touted 500 hours of content. This led to a massive outcry from the community that had been eagerly anticipating the title up to that point. While the first volume in the series, in spite of its strengths, was no model of originality in terms of its story-telling, the idea of an even more extensive sequel—likely to be even more generic given the amount of content—caused even the most enthusiastic fans to lower their expectations. Put in a tricky position by its ham-handed marketing, the publisher then struggled to explain itself and justify the outrageous number.

Elden Ring took a somewhat different approach: to offer an intense and varied experience over a long duration. According to the website *HowLongToBeat*, the game's average play length sits at over 100 hours, and apart from the critiques of the number and redundancy of certain side dungeons, as discussed previously, players do not seem to characterize their experience as one of boredom. Still, it must be said that some zones near the end of the game get a little monotonous—the snow-capped mountains, for example, are not the best of the game's locations. As for the rest, *Elden Ring* maintains the intensity of the *Souls* games, with the player exploring every nook and cranny while always on the lookout for danger, given the world's hostility. And yet, *Elden Ring* is twice the length of *Dark Souls III*, which was already considered an extensive challenge! The gameplay sensations remain similar and the rhythm doesn't slow down too much in the open spaces. The feeling of solitude–at least when playing in single-player mode–adds even more weight to the experience. *Elden Ring* is a challenging, taxing game, particularly because it imposes a fast pace over a long period. No time to get bored, not a lot of routine gameplay; instead, varying degrees of exhaustion begin to set in over time–a fact that can also be considered a flaw. Balancing these different variables is in fact astonishingly complex.

Beyond the player's overall experience, the design and discovery of *Elden Ring*'s open world offer some interesting innovations. For example, there are strange portals scattered hither and thither across the Lands Between. Entering one of these portals will teleport the player to an unknown location, which might be nearby or might be on the other side of the map! Sometimes the location and destination of a portal will shed light on some of the game's lore, but above all, the portals give the player a glimpse of still-inaccessible locations, like Farum Azula or the Eternal Cities. A little taste of places to be discovered at some point in the future, effectively piquing the player's interest. Once again, it's a matter of rhythm—doing everything possible to prevent the player from getting bored. Still, the developers had to be careful to not ruin all the surprises of future locations and to not send the player down rabbit holes with new zones to be explored. In general, the teleporters tend to take the player to isolated areas that are fairly limited in size, revealing just enough to intrigue the player and stimulate their curiosity. In terms of game design, a portal can only be used in one direction, which gives the player a shiver of excitement, both before entering (Where will it send me?) and after crossing it (Where am I? How do I get out of here?). Using a teleporter is basically like choosing to abandon your current phase of exploration, get out of your comfort zone, and head into the great unknown. It's not such an easy choice to make, and it's one that can be quite destabilizing depending on where you end up. There are also a few traps–teleporters activated automatically, for example, when you open a chest, unexpectedly transporting the player to some unknown location. Some of the destinations can be so far from known territory that the map of the new region will be completely blank and show nothing but fog.

Elden Ring's map is one of the most interesting features of this open world *à la* FromSoftware. The principle of opening and consulting a map in this kind of game is commonplace–it's even baked into the open world's DNA. Once upon a time, the maps were distributed in paper format in the game boxes–the fabric map for

Ultima IX (1999) was both original and magnificent. Then, over time, as technology improved, maps were integrated into the games themselves. *Grand Theft Auto: San Andreas* (2004) came with a paper map and, finally, a detailed interactive map that could be accessed via an in-game menu. While it was far from being the first to include such a feature, the game's influence was such that many titles followed its lead after its release. For the next generation of consoles, the PlayStation 3 and Xbox 360, the interactive map became a standard. Over the years, multiple layers of information were added to game maps. Place names, portal locations, quests, and various points of interest. It got to the point that, in *The Witcher III* for example, the initial map became absolutely covered in all sorts of different icons, transforming an indispensable tool into an avalanche of information that began to irritate some players. *Breath of the Wild* "innovated" by making a much-needed turn in the opposite direction, providing a blank map, or at least one with just a minimum level of information. The player is then able to place certain markers, whenever they want and in the form of their choosing. The player becomes a cartographer–to an extent, as the basic map is already drawn. They chart their own course, their own path of discovery through a previously unknown world.

This crucial idea is perfectly in line with the approach adopted by the FromSoftware team for *Elden Ring*. "[The designers] want the gameplay itself to be the players' stories," Miyazaki states in an interview with *Famitsu*, translated in an article on the website *Frontline Gaming Japan* (March 5, 2022). The gameplay, the constant lack of direction throughout the game, the hazy storytelling: everything is designed so that the player can write their own story and have a unique experience. It's an idea that the studio had used since *Demon's Souls*; however, in *Elden Ring*, the sensation is magnified by the possibilities of the open world, as well as by the crucially important map.

Aside from the Sites of Grace–functioning like handy teleporters, quickly transporting the player to any Site of Grace previously visited–and the locations of quests, added with patch 1.03 (a practical feature, even if it contradicts the designers' original vision for the game), nothing else is highlighted on the map. The player can, however, zoom in and out and comb over every inch of the map to occasionally uncover hidden and important locations. Indeed, every point of interest appears right on the map: minor Erdtrees, ruins, certain cave entrances, churches, ponds, etc. The level of detail is impressive, and yet not everything is included on the map. Each location holds numerous hiding places and other points of interest, something you can't tell from just looking at the map as, of course, it shows a two-dimensional view of each area that doesn't account for the vertical dimension of structures.

Like many other open-world games, from *Assassin's Creed* (2007) to–yet again– *Breath of the Wild*, the player must carry out an action to reveal map details. In the aforementioned games, that means climbing and "activating" towers; in *Elden Ring*, it means collecting map fragments from map stelae. And in fact, the player can actually see the stelae marked on the map in the fog that appears before regions are revealed. As such, it's not particularly difficult to acquire a map fragment; it's sort of an implicit homage to the routines of older open-world games.

On the other hand, where *Elden Ring*'s map innovates–perhaps we can even call it a small revolution?–and offers a sensation still uncommon in the world of video games is that it grows as the player explores the Lands Between. Really, it's all a matter of scale. At the start of the game, when the map covers only the Limgrave region, it appears to be quite big. Exploring this first region takes time and there are many cliffs marking its borders. Still, the player can make out other lands in the distance, though there's nothing to indicate that the player will eventually travel there, or even how they might do so. However, the player is able to discern paths and bridges that seem to continue past the edges of the map. The unknown in the great unknown–absolutely fascinating. The borders of the map eventually expand outward, and the view zooms out a bit at a time to establish new contours for the world. As the game progresses, Limgrave becomes smaller and smaller on the map, giving a real indication of scale, not just in terms of how the player perceives distances, but also what the player actually experiences.

So, the map expands many times throughout the game, sometimes giving the player a sort of virtual vertigo. And let's not forget the incredible moment when you take the elevator down to the underground region known as the Siofra River, revealing a new map superimposed on the first. It's a striking moment in every way. How big is this map really? How much will it keep expanding? In the end, the game's environment is truly massive, especially with the large underground areas to be explored. While other open worlds are markedly bigger–for example, those of *Just Cause 3* (2015) and *Assassin's Creed Odyssey* (2018), which wow players from the very beginning with the magnitude and ambition of the adventure in store for them–*Elden Ring*'s approach is particularly interesting in that the player's sense of wonder is renewed with each expansion of the map. Once again, it's a matter of pacing.

Finally, with regard to level design: it often proves to be quite basic in open-world games because it's much more difficult and time-consuming to structure–both naturally and with originality–movement through expansive zones. Depending on the means of transportation offered and the nature and diversity of the places to be visited, level design can create real headaches for the teams in charge of it. Given FromSoftware's reputation and the studio's expertise in level design, expectations were particularly high for this aspect of *Elden Ring*. As we've seen, the important vertical dimension of their previous games was translated into the open world, along with numerous nooks and crannies hiding various treasures, some rarer than others. Most of the time, the player just goes around exploring and collecting crafting resources. Then all of a sudden, a winding path, previously hidden from other viewpoints, appears and leads the player down to a grotto, a treasure chest, or a formidable creature. The player is guided by their own observations, constantly leading them astray from their original path. A fallen tree, a boulder, or a building in ruins can take the player to previously inaccessible places. Travel is facilitated by Torrent—the player's steed with the crucial double jump ability—and exploration of the Lands Between unfolds organically.

When the player isn't coming across well-concealed hiding spots, they're discovering absolutely breathtaking landscapes. After the battle with Godrick the Grafted at Stormveil Castle, a passageway takes the player outside to a spot overlooking Liurnia of the Lakes. The panorama extends infinitely—or so it seems, even though it only covers part of the region—offering a sensational view. It's a moment that has stayed with many players—at least those who didn't arrive at nighttime in pouring rain with reduced visibility! Like *Dark Souls III* before it, *Elden Ring* is a game of impressive panoramas. These vistas are placed and designed to give the player geographic indications: there's the ever-visible Erdtree, but also important landmarks like Stormveil Castle at the beginning of the game and the Academy of Raya Lucaria overlooking Liurnia of the Lakes, as mentioned previously. The buildings stand tall in the landscapes, clearly visible. They also appear on the world map, although their complexity is not evident at first glance. Indeed, once you finally enter one of these locations, the sensations of exploration change to offer a more confined experience, more like that of the *Souls* games. The player cannot call on Torrent in these places, the bosses are formidable, and the level design becomes extremely dense and precise. Welcome to the "legacy" dungeons!

Good old-fashioned dungeons

Numbering six in total, excluding the DLC expansion, and spread across the game's various regions, the "legacy" dungeons—a term used by Miyazaki himself in interviews—are real highlights of the adventure that is *Elden Ring*. They are reminiscent of the best aspects of the game's predecessors, allowing the player to escape for a time from the open world and its vast spaces to focus on an enclosed space with multiple layers and branching paths.

"Perhaps especially players who have played a lot of the *Dark Souls* series will find this refreshing," Miyazaki tells *Famitsu* (June 14, 2021), according to a translation by Reddit user theangryfurlong. Miyazaki adds: "Imagine the areas in the *Dark Souls* series. Only this time, the scale is larger and there may be new places you can reach by jumping, which should make exploration even more enjoyable."

The addition of jumping, or at least a form of jumping that's more precise and more effectively implemented than in the *Souls* games, offers a useful tool for building levels with an engaging level design. The studio developed considerable expertise in this respect while working on *Sekiro*, while nonetheless taking a somewhat different approach with *Elden Ring*. Indeed, the jumping and grappling hook features of *Sekiro* were implemented more in service to action, allowing the player to improvise when faced with a band of enemies, for example; in *Elden Ring*, jumping allows the player to explore every inch of the environments, which are filled with numerous shortcuts and secret passageways.

The first of the legacy dungeons, Stormveil Castle, is a real work of art, perhaps even the game's most effective dungeon in terms of level design. There's only one way in and it's guarded by the terrible Margit the Fell Omen. The battle is grueling, marking an initial spike in difficulty as part of the player's natural progression. Once the path into the castle is cleared, a new obstacle presents itself: the portcullis is down, blocking the main entrance. Gostoc, the castle's gatekeeper, is found not far away. He advises you to take a secret path via an opening that leads along the castle's ramparts. He can also order that the portcullis be raised. From there, a set of stairs offers a faster path to Godrick the Grafted, the castle's demigod owner and the main objective of this first part of the adventure.

So, there are two paths offered for two totally different approaches: one is more direct and difficult, with a well-armed welcoming committee that even has a ballista; the other path, the most logical one at this stage in the game, offers a more accessible detour. If you look closely at the moat, you'll notice passages below you. It's risky to go down into the moat, as you might not be able to get back up, but in any case, it offers more opportunities for exploration. Some of the passageways will lead to objects, others to new places to be explored. The number of paths and nooks is impressive. Farther on, the player can travel across the rooftops or they can instead explore the basement, which holds shadowy mysteries.

The impression of inspecting a giant medieval castle is particularly striking. You get lost, you poke around, and then you eventually get back to a place you recognize. You try various approaches, you fail, and then you start over with new ideas. Stormveil Castle is an example that should be studied by every student of video game design! The level design and game design–for example, with the insidious Gostoc constantly spying on the player and stealing a percentage of their runes each time they die–are flawless; visually, the entire place is grandiose and coherent, from the architectural inspirations to the lighting and ambiances, which change from one part of the castle to the next. This first legacy dungeon is stunning in many respects, and each time you come back to it, you might find a new secret passageway. A hidden door, an elevator that has remained inactive, or a nearly-invisible ladder: exploration of the castle takes hours, and you're never 100% sure that you've gotten to everything.

There are other castles—secondary dungeons—scattered here and there across the Lands Between, though they are not as extensive as Stormveil. Passing under the portcullis or discovering a hole in an outer wall, allowing you to begin your exploration, or even simply spotting a fortress in the distance through the fog: these are always powerful moments in the adventure. It's a sort of childhood dream that many works using various media have tried to capture, with varying levels of success; it's worth noting that *Elden Ring* does quite a good job of it and with a certain elegance and captivating aesthetic.

The game's climax, the moment when the excitement of discovery reaches its apex, comes when the player arrives at the royal capital, Leyndell—another legacy dungeon. The Erdtree is finally close; in fact, it stands quite literally at the heart of the city, and we've heard about this extraordinary place since the start of the game. And what a sight! Instead of entering through the main gate, which has been blocked since the Shattering, you take a secondary path with an elevator that takes you to the top of the ramparts. From there, you look out across the entire city. It's a breathtaking view and time seems to stand still. It's a moment reminiscent of the discovery of Anor Londo in the first *Dark Souls*. It would be hard to make a more elegant and aesthetically pleasing sight: the golden tones of the rooftops, the view of the various neighborhoods and the main street below, the giant petrified dragon standing in the center of the city, and the impressive buildings standing around the trunk of the Erdtree, like a sort of dream version of Mont Saint Michel, enhanced by the environment art department. Of course, you can explore every nook and cranny of this extraordinary location—you can even get lost in the city's sewer system and discover a secret underground area that just keeps going down into the depths of the earth. It's an absolutely dizzying experience.

Beyond this incredibly impressive visual aspect of the legacy dungeons, the pieces of lore that they reveal form the heart of the game's story. For example, Leyndell holds the shameful secret of Marika and Radagon, as well as the vestiges of several wars, from the war against the Ancient Dragons to the Shattering wars. Beneath the city, the sewers and dungeons conceal their own batch of surprises, leading the player deeper and deeper until they finally encounter the mysterious Three Fingers.

The other legacy dungeons are equally fascinating to explore in search of clues about the universe's past. There's the Academy of Raya Lucaria with its different strains of magic, sullied by the decline of Rennala, who remains there forever clutching her strange amber egg. There's Volcano Manor, the site of the unspeakable blasphemy of the demigod Rykard. There's the Haligtree of Miquella and Malenia, the cursed Twin Prodigies. And finally, there's Farum Azula, the lost floating city that holds a power stolen long ago by Maliketh, the Black Blade. The six main legacy dungeons—and other, smaller dungeons, like Mohgwyn Palace and Caria

Manor—are the sources of most of the stories that form the glue that holds together the lore of *Elden Ring*.

Don't you worry, we'll cover all of this in greater detail in the chapter dedicated to the game's universe. For now, the important thing to note is this dichotomy between, on the one hand, the macroscopic approach of the open spaces you can travel through on horseback, offering a true feeling of freedom and exploration at various levels, and on the other hand, the microscopic approach of the legacy dungeons that you explore in minute detail, conveying a certain ambiance and plenty of lore.

And while it's easy to flee from a tricky situation with help from Torrent, surviving the traps and bosses of the legacy dungeons requires more patience and tenacity. *Elden Ring* is a challenging game and, like its predecessors, the subject of its difficulty is worth taking some time to discuss.

Difficulty and accessibility

◆ The state of play

Thanks to word of mouth, *Demon's Souls* managed to capture a niche audience willing to tackle a dark, twisted, and challenging game. Still, a little guide was included in the game box, offering a number of helpful tips and tricks, including effective approaches for taking on different bosses and the locations of certain key objects. FromSoftware's subsequent productions were less obscure and gained increasingly large audiences. The fact that marketing focused heavily on difficulty and the fact that players would die over and over again—the PC version of *Dark Souls* was even subtitled *Prepare to Die*—did not help the reputation of the studio's games. However—and this cannot be overstated—dying is not a fatal end in the *Souls* games; it's a way of learning.

FromSoftware's games are not really that difficult per se, when compared to manic shooters, for example, or the legendary *Teenage Mutant Ninja Turtles* for the NES. They do, however, have a high learning curve due to how they break existing video game codes and differ from the standards of their competitors. Tutorials are minimal or nonexistent, there are no immediate objectives or explicit instructions, their storytelling is cryptic, their bosses are strong and outrageously difficult, their health meters are limited, etc. These are game-design choices that force the player to learn new ways of doing things. And depending on the player, that learning phase can be long and difficult. It also depends on players' willingness to invest time and effort, to immerse themselves in a sinister and hostile universe. Those who manage to adapt experience the great sense of accomplishment that Miyazaki has described in many interviews. The creator has made difficulty a key part of his game-design philosophy because it's when players overcome certain obstacles, especially after feeling frustration or exasperation, that they get that feeling of accomplishment that Miyazaki strives to provoke. These emotions, both good and bad, are part of the game, of the experience as imagined by Miyazaki and his team. And it's precisely that vision of the creator, in the artistic sense of the word, that you must respect, or at least understand, when you enter into their world and discover their works. With all that said, it raises the question of what a video game should offer players. Entertainment, via success and positive emotions alone? A moment of fun, with no room for frustration? Or should players accept that they might have to deal with negative emotions so that, if things work out, they can trigger positive emotions with much greater impact? Everyone has their own opinion on this subject, and thus some will be more receptive than others to what games like *Dark Souls* or *Bloodborne* have to offer.

Beyond questions of difficulty and the developers' intentions, FromSoftware's games have never been very generous when it comes to accessibility. Difficulty and accessibility are related concepts, but they are two distinct considerations for game designers. Difficulty is about the level of expertise the player must reach to get past various stages in the game, for example, finishing the first level, beating the final boss, or tackling additional content post-game. Accessibility is about helping the vast majority of players reach that expected level of expertise. A simple example: if a rule of game design requires the player to manage different colors in one of the game's systems, that is going to immediately create a barrier for people with color blindness. Thinking about issues of accessibility means taking into account this sort of situation: allow players to customize the colors used to make them distinguishable, use symbols or sounds in addition to colors, or quite simply, avoid the problem altogether by eliminating color-coding from your game design. There are numerous accessibility considerations and it can be very costly to account for those considerations depending on the stage of development. At the end of a project, it is very hard to implement anything new; the priority is to fix bugs and, basically, to just make sure the game works. Still, the notion of accessibility has gradually been incorporated into the habits of game designers. In the world of board games, for example, many accessibility rules have been standard for years now. Most game designers take them into account and develop game systems and materials accordingly. In the world of video games, accessibility rules are also becoming increasingly standardized. AAA games like *Uncharted 4* (2016) and *The Last of Us Part II* (2020) have incorporated many options to include as many players as possible in the experience offered. Some independent games, notably *Celeste* (2018), have made accessibility a point of pride.

And where does FromSoftware stand on all of this? Well, when it comes to accessibility, the studio falls short. For many years, FromSoftware was spared a lot of criticism on this subject because its games were considered to be for a niche audience, in spite of their millions of units sold. However, largely because of that success, the studio found itself in the hot seat after the release of *Sekiro* in 2019. At the time, the big debate over "easy mode" was covered more than the game itself! Should we focus on respecting the exact original vision of the creator (the artistic dimension) or focus on facilitating access for the greatest number of people (the popular dimension)? It's an impossible question to answer, with irrefutable arguments on both sides, and so we won't be able to resolve the matter here. In any case, the consensus was that *Sekiro* is not an accessible game. Could a mode offering less difficulty have solved the problem? Yes and no. It certainly would have enabled a segment of players to access the game, but in a version with characteristics different from those imagined by Miyazaki, resulting in a different experience and emotions. And with that said, preserving the emotions intended by the creator while making some atypical adjustments is a tricky thing to pull off.

Developing another difficulty mode is extremely complex work. What parameters do you play around with? Some will still find that the game is too hard, or on the contrary, they'll say it's too easy, completely suppressing the emotions that the game designer intended to transmit to players. The notion of difficulty is subjective. Creating different difficulty levels allows you to bring in certain audience segments, but the game will never be 100% inclusive. *Hellblade: Senua's Sacrifice* (2017) offered adaptive difficulty, a particularly interesting concept in the context of this debate. The player has no idea what parameters are being adjusted behind the scenes. The force of hits? Enemies' health meters? The speed of their reactions? We have no idea, and it all depends on how the player reacts and exerts themself when faced with obstacles. The system is a black box that leaves us to assume that it's working, and only the developers would be able to tell us what's going on inside and if a given player's experience is easier or harder than normal. *Hellblade* does not rely on a particularly complicated game design; instead, its emphasis is on the atmosphere and story, but the idea of adaptive difficulty is still quite remarkable. Such a system is far from unprecedented. *Left 4 Dead* (2008) implemented adaptive difficulty, with hordes of zombies being repeatedly directed at the most skilled teams of players. *Deathloop* (2021) uses a similar system, and Electronic Arts, again in 2021, filed for a patent on an adaptive-difficulty system. The patent filing indicates an interesting market positioning for the American video game giant: in addition to being able to optimize the duration of engagement for its own players with a meticulously controlled experience, the company could also sell certain tools and collected data to other studios and publishers, saving them valuable time on research and development. That said, adaptive difficulty also has its faults. What happens to the player's learning curve? Can it just be flattened or ignored? If so, how do you remedy that?

In the end, lowering or adapting the level of difficulty is not really the same as accounting for issues of accessibility. Because of these complex, and thus costly, problems, *Sekiro* decided to ignore the issue altogether. That earned the game its fair share of criticism, and probably cost it some sales as well. As soon as *Elden Ring* was announced, the debate resurfaced, this time with–understandably–high expectations from audiences.

◈ Controversy at the time of Elden Ring's announcement

A few months after the release of *Sekiro*, as the storm surrounding easy mode was beginning to clear, *Elden Ring* was announced at E3 2019. From there, it became inevitable that the subjects of difficulty and accessibility would resurface with every new piece of information revealed about the game. But in spite of all the noise before the game's release, in the end, once *Elden Ring* was installed on consoles all over the world, the clamoring gradually subsided. And yet, easy mode is nowhere to be found among the game's features. So, what happened? We have this statement from Miyazaki on the PlayStation blog: "In *Elden Ring*, we have not intentionally tried to lower the game's difficulty." Well then, if the difficulty didn't budge but the audience isn't raging about it like they did with *Sekiro*, then something must have changed in terms of accessibility!

Indeed, *Elden Ring* is more accessible than its predecessors. This is notably thanks to its open-world design, which logically allows a player to go explore another area if they get stuck on a boss or a particularly tricky passage. When you put it like that, it sounds like an obvious solution. It makes me think of the first boss of *Dark Souls III*, Iudex Gundyr, who discouraged a certain number of players from the very first hour of the game, leaving them without any hope of getting around him or finding a way out. In the case of *Elden Ring*, if you follow the glow of Grace at the beginning of the game and end up losing repeatedly to Margit the Fell Omen (the first truly difficult enemy to beat), you can–and it's even recommended, to avoid pointlessly tearing your hair out–go explore other parts of the Lands Between. Doing so allows you to pick up some equipment that might be more powerful, but it also allows you to hone your skills and improve your weapons using Smithing Stones. After that, beating Margit will be nothing more than a formality as both you and your avatar will be stronger. You, thanks to the natural learning curve that has always been part of FromSoftware's games; your avatar, thanks to all of the typical leveling-up rules you find in any RPG.

A few additional features come with the open world. In particular, there are new ways of guiding the player: as we've seen, the player is able to follow the light of Grace; they can also navigate based on recognizable landmarks seen in different panoramas; and there's also the fact that storytelling is more to the point for quest stages. There are also statues of Rosus standing above the landscape at various points in the Lands Between, pointing in the direction of the nearest catacombs. While the catacombs may just be additional content, the presence of the statues helps the player understand their environment, with the idea again being to make exploration of the open world more accessible. A critique often leveled at the *Souls* games concerns the fact that players always have to redo the path from their respawn point to the boss that keeps killing them. That path can sometimes be quite long and be scattered with enemies that are strong or difficult to avoid, making the passage that much more arduous and annoying. In *Elden Ring*, Stakes of Marika stand right near boss areas, allowing the player to respawn at the closest one, thus allowing them to immediately take on the boss again.

"Boss fights are a special experience, one of the high points of the game. At the same time, we hope to minimize instances of being unable to advance in the game because the boss is too hard," Miyazaki tells *Famitsu*, again according to a translation by Reddit user theangryfurlong. So, the development team wanted to make sure that players didn't get stuck. Of the game's more than 150 bosses—an impressive number when you think about the fact that the first *Dark Souls* had 26 bosses when including the DLC—only a dozen are required to progress all the way to the end. Incidentally, it's amusing to note that *Elden Ring* includes probably the hardest boss of any FromSoftware game: Malenia, who has certain characteristics that just seem totally unfair, like her ability to steal your health, but also her two forms that you must battle and special moves that are practically unblockable and unavoidable. Thankfully, it's an optional battle, but it's one that has stirred a lot of discussion and pushed many to tears in the community of players. Another example, this one an enemy belonging to the main quest: Radahn is a particularly difficult boss. He also happens to be Miyazaki's favorite boss, and we can understand why, given how good the dramatization of the battle is. On a gigantic battlefield, where you can summon a whole group of allies, adding an intriguing, epic dimension to the battle, you charge at Radahn while riding Torrent, ready to rip into a boss described as "the most powerful of the demigods." The battle can be long and taxing. But that said, it's not actually required, as not all the demigods need to be slain. You need to defeat at least two to enter Leyndell, but that doesn't necessarily mean you have to take on Radahn. And besides, if you dig just a little bit into the game's lore, you'll quickly learn that Radahn is vulnerable to the scarlet rot. Certain objects and weapons inflict this illness, and while they may not be easy to find or craft initially, they are so effective that Radahn will hardly put up a fight.

Finally, depending on the character build chosen by the player, certain bosses will be more difficult than others. The Fire Giant, toward the end of the game, is a required boss who has left an impression on many a player thanks to his toughness. Others will point to Maliketh, also toward the end of the adventure, as being particularly difficult to beat.

The occurrence of inevitable surges in difficulty at the end of the game feels more acceptable as the player, by that point, has grown a lot and knows the game well. What's more, the player can easily change their build to overcome those surges in difficulty. Indeed, Rennala has the power to reset all stat points allocated when leveling up. As such, in a matter of minutes, you can go from being a warrior to a mage. However, you have to then use the smithy to improve the weapons for your new specialty, but again, that's not all that difficult to do given the availability of the necessary materials at that point in the game.

Other points of gameplay were also added to make battles more accessible. Most capabilities are explained in the game's tutorial, which became obligatory after the release of patch 1.04 in April 2022. Indeed, the tutorial is found deep in a cave at the beginning of the game and many players walked right past it without even realizing it! It is now a required stage, making the game a little more accessible thanks to explanations of the different features of gameplay. Certain situations can be approached with a touch of stealth, with the player hiding in tall grass to pick off their enemies one by one using the element of surprise. This simplistic system can help the player gradually chip away at areas with a lot of opponents. Fighting on horseback also offers some significant advantages, with Torrent's speed and double jump helping you quickly get to safety when a dangerous situation arises. Unlike in previous games, the player can make jump attacks when on foot. This new move adds to the element of improvisation in battles or ambush situations. A strong jumping blow also has a chance of momentarily immobilizing the enemy, offering an opportunity for you to get in a few more hits. The Ashes of War offer special abilities that can be applied to or removed from weapons at will. In its time, *Dark Souls III* offered this idea of special attacks, but without the modularity. There are around a hundred Ashes of War that can be found across the Lands Between, and their usefulness will depend on the battle strategy the player wishes to pursue. All of this brings diversity to battles—a bit less rigidity for greater accessibility. Crafting also allows the player to create various consumables on the fly when stocks get low, which in practice most often means arrows and crossbow bolts.

Spirit Ashes round out the list of the new "aids" added to *Elden Ring*. Spirit Ashes allow the player to summon various creatures that can lend a hand to the player during boss battles. There are many different types of Spirit Ashes, each with very distinct characteristics. Archers, strong monsters, kamikazes, sorcerers, etc. The player can level them up using certain resources, just like they can do with weapons by visiting the blacksmith. Certain Spirit Ashes contain the souls of unique and particularly strong characters. That said, there's a higher cost (in the form of magic or health points) of summoning one of these more powerful beings. As such, you have to carefully choose the creature you want to summon based on the boss in question and your own chosen build. An example of an effective combination would be to summon a knight who will enter into hand-to-hand combat with a boss while the player character shoots arrows or casts spells from a distance.

In practice, and with Ashes at a solid level–at the start of the game, the spirits don't last long–the spirits are most useful for temporarily distracting a boss, allowing the player to catch their breath, heal, or relentlessly attack during that time. This sometimes results in fairly "mechanical" battles in which the boss, if on their own, just constantly switches between targets. For a moment, the boss focuses on the player and allows the spirit to attack without any real danger, then the boss changes targets, giving the player a chance to execute their own tasks. Of course, there are all sorts of subtle factors that enter into the battle depending on the boss. Some bosses cast spells affecting an entire area, others act with incredible speed, and others still will call in an ally to help–there's never an end to the surprises. Still, it has to be said that the pattern of "you make a hit, I make a hit" recurs regularly, and sometime after the game's release, that pattern was severely criticized by certain players who would have preferred a more strategic approach to battles.

At the far end of the spectrum, some players pointed to Spirit Ashes as the real problem, claiming that they simplify battles too much, creating a quasi easy mode. So, does that mean that Spirit Ashes are forbidden and rebuked by purists?

◈ Is there a "right way" to play Elden Ring?

There is a very simple and obvious initial answer to this question, which is: "No, each player gets to play *Elden Ring* however they want." No one can force anyone to do anything, especially when it comes to entertainment. The important thing is for everyone to have a good time. Some will discover the game with others using the multiplayer mode, others will play on their own or share their experience with a community via streaming. "Speedrunners" aim to exploit every possible loophole to finish the game as fast as possible, while the most motivated players will defeat each and every boss without getting so much as a scratch. And they can do all that while systematically using Spirit Ashes, or not! Furthermore, each of these players will experience different emotions from playing the same game. Incredible, no?

Still, it's interesting to ask ourselves, what is the best way to play if you want to stick as closely as possible to the developers' original intentions? In other words, what is the best way to play if you want to feel the emotions that the developers intended for you to feel while playing the game? It's a valid question for *Elden Ring*, but also more broadly for any video game. Truth be told, it's a valid question for any work created with an intention behind it, a characteristic that differentiates it from pure entertainment, no matter the medium. Now, not everyone will necessarily be interested in using such a lens to view a work; it all depends on one's approach to different art forms.

Having one's emotions stirred by a work of art doesn't require specific cultural baggage, and again, those emotions can vary greatly from one person to the next. But for those who wish to dig deeper, that emotion constitutes a first step in a larger journey in which the person will learn more about the work, for example, its origin, then about its creator or the historical and technical background of its creation. There are so many things one can learn, and with more detailed knowledge of the work, one can understand it better and perhaps feel new things more in line with the artist's original intention, or even other emotions beyond that. That knowledge, that growing cultural and artistic understanding, can then help a person more easily approach other works, ones they might not have known about before or that might have been inaccessible without the right keys to understand them.

Where might that personal journey take you? Now there's a real existential and philosophical question. Do you need to speak fluent Korean to appreciate the full artistic value of the film *Oldboy*, a cinematic masterpiece by Park Chan-wook? Do you need to see it specifically in a movie theater? Watch it at the time it was created, while living in a neighborhood of Seoul? Do you also need to have read the manga on which the film was based? Of course not. Those are extreme requirements, and each person can experiment with where to place the limits according to their own preferences and means; the extremes shouldn't set the standards for the appreciation of an artistic work. One's own feelings about a work of art shouldn't be subject to social judgment.

To address this issue of how the audience can discover and (try to) understand an artistic work using their own mental toolkit, their own cultural and societal perspective, the notion of accessibility comes into play. Translating a book, grouping together certain paintings and sculptures in a public museum, making available online resources about various works, their creators, and their context, all of these things help make the art in question more accessible.

For video games, the principle remains the same; however, you have to add to that the interactive aspect, which is fundamental to the medium. Someone who has played *Dark Souls* will not have the same approach to *Elden Ring* as someone who has never played a FromSoftware title before. Nor will they experience the same emotions, to tie back to the previous discussion. The same is true for a veteran gamer, even one not familiar with the *Souls* games, versus a novice: each will have a very different experience while playing the game. For this very reason, there is no "right way" to play *Elden Ring*–or any other game. Each individual will discover a work of art in the way that suits them personally.

However, a word of advice: it's better to avoid any spoilers when playing a game for the first time as you want to preserve the feeling of surprise that comes with discovering a game. The emotions are that much stronger when, in the course of your adventure, you find yourself astonished by a situation or design choice specifically inserted by the creators at a particular point, rather than reading about it beforehand on a wiki or seeing it in a video or during a stream. In fact, Miyazaki recommends that very mindset in his interview for the PlayStation blog: "If possible, we want players to try and steer clear of spoilers or guides and go in with a completely fresh, open mind and enjoy that initial sense of adventure. That's how we'd want to experience the game if we were going into it for the first time. And that's how we hope our players can experience the game comfortably at their own pace with this new sense of wonder." It's an approach the creator had previously talked about in an interview with *IGN*: "What we want to do is retain that sense of players discovering things for themselves and enjoying uncovering the world both in terms of action and narrative for themselves. We don't want to force anything on the player."

Avoid spoilers and take advantage of your freedom while playing: those are clear instructions from the game's creator. So, can we consider that the best way to discover *Elden Ring*? Whether you want to take on every boss while remaining at level one or summon spirits at every opportunity, have at it! Use every aid offered by the game to make the experience as fun as possible, or in any case, to make it as close as possible to what you want to make of it. Some people enjoy difficulty, others do not. I would say that *Elden Ring*, while it may be difficult and presents an incredibly hostile world, also offers features that make it more accessible to a much broader population of players than its ancestors the *Souls*. "In general, I'd like new players to feel unpressured and that they can approach the game at their own pace. I don't want to enforce any play style or particular route because I'd like them to experience that sense of freedom. And I realize that while we offer games with a high level of challenge, we design them in a way that feels fulfilling to overcome. [...] As for a starting class, it's entirely up to the player. It's an RPG, and they can approach it however they like and choose whichever looks the coolest to them. But I would recommend against choosing the naked one (known as the Wretch). As before, it's probably the most difficult starting class!," Miyazaki explains, again on the PlayStation blog.

In any case, the improvements made by the developers have paid off. *Elden Ring* is more accessible without necessarily being easier. Many newcomers to FromSoftware's games have tried their hand at it, sometimes with great apprehension about the difficulty. Among them, some have made it all the way to the end of the adventure, discovering along the way a style of gameplay that ended up winning them over. In spite of the moments of doubt and the steep learning curve, it seems that the balance of the game's design has proven to be persuasive. As an example, if we compare the Steam success rates for the challenging mid-adventure bosses between *Elden Ring*, *Dark Souls III*, and *Sekiro*, we find some revealing figures. We can see that 55.6% beat Radahn, versus 52.6% for the Abyss Watchers in *Dark Souls III* and 46.5% for Genichiro Ashina in *Sekiro*. Given that the success rate for *Elden Ring* covers many more players than its predecessors, if the accessibility efforts had not panned out, the figures for successful completion, as well as reviews from critics and audiences more broadly, would have been quite different!

Coherence of design

In addition to striking the right balance between difficulty and accessibility, what also—and particularly—holds players' attention is the game's design. Since the beginning of this chapter, I've talked a lot about "game design" and "level design," crucial factors for the video game medium. There's also character design, which deals with the visual aspect of characters and creatures, and narrative design, meaning the way that the creators tell the story through all of the different elements that make up a game, from text to interactions, from music to backgrounds. These design concepts can be identified and applied very mechanically or academically. We know what works well with players and what doesn't work so well. Meeting certain specifications will ensure that a game is at least enjoyable to make your way through, without any surprises, whether good or bad. However, a dose of creativity and daring can make a game remarkable. In this respect, *Elden Ring* cultivates a sort of elegance in its design, both in terms of form and function, which results in a sense of coherence that's absolutely fascinating.

Let's look at a few examples to really understand what coherence looks like in a video game. As mentioned previously, Radahn is vulnerable to the scarlet rot. When you know about this weakness, beating the boss becomes nothing more than a formality. The reason for this weakness can be found in the character's past, when he long ago fought Malenia during the Shattering wars. Their duel lasted for what seemed like an eternity and appeared to reach a stalemate. Malenia, who is also known as the Goddess of Rot, put an end to the clash by unleashing her poison on the entire Caelid region, where her troops had been battling Radahn's, forever turning the territory into a wasteland. Radahn was driven to madness by the rot. Ever since, he has continued to wander around the battlefield. In spite of his immense size, he continues to ride around on his tiny horse, using the gravitational magic that he studied in his youth to avoid crushing the poor creature. In short, everything about his character design is consistent. It matches both his personal history and his personality. Visually, Radahn is gigantic—he's supposed to be the most powerful of the demigods, and often in the *Souls* games, a character's size is directly proportional to their strength—and we can barely see his horse under the tons of armor that he wears. The battle takes place on a large battlefield—the same one where he long ago lost his mind, a place that has been synonymous with him since time immemorial. When battling, he uses gravitational magic and he remains weak against the scarlet rot. In this example, character design, level design, game design, and narrative design all converge to deliver a remarkable duel.

Let's look at two other examples that dig down into a level of detail that becomes meaningful when you know the game well. The first is the infamous battle with Malenia. It turns out that Malenia is vulnerable to attacks with heavy weaponry. Indeed, according to her lore, she appears to have no weaknesses—they say that she has never lost a battle—and when you yourself confront her, she is probably the most formidable boss ever created by FromSoftware. And yet, she is made up of nothing more than a bunch of prostheses and a half-rotted body, and she has a perfectly ordinary build, one that seems almost frail in comparison to other bosses. As such, a good, well-placed hit from a mace will easily knock her off balance, affecting an unseen stat, stance, that was already present in the *Souls* games but was used more effectively thanks to updates made for *Sekiro*. The second example concerns Rennala, with a particularly juicy detail. Have you noticed how there's no Stake of Marika near the location where you battle Rennala? No chance of respawning right next to the battle site; instead, you have to redo the whole passage each time. The same is true for the other boss in the Academy of Raya Lucaria, the Red Wolf of Radagon: no Stake of Marika to be found. There's a reason for the absence of these statues: Rennala hates Marika with every fiber of her being. Rennala's ex-husband, Radagon, left her long ago for Marika in order to become the new Elden Lord, abandoning poor Rennala with nothing but her grief. So, there was no way she would allow any statues of that loathsome Marika to be put up in her academy!

Details like this can be found all over the place in *Elden Ring*. The gameplay and storytelling are constantly interweaving with one another to form what we might call "ludonarrative consistency." FromSoftware's previous games were also infused with this approach, this interaction and resonance between the various aspects of design, *Bloodborne* being a particularly good example of this. Transposing that desire for consistency into an open—and enormous!—world like that of *Elden Ring* was a real feat for the development team to pull off.

The ludonarrative consistency is accompanied by art direction, for both visuals and sound, that is always on point. We'll come back to the music specifically in a bit, but let's spend a few moments looking at the game's visual style. In *Edge* magazine, Miyazaki makes a few confessions: "Graphical fidelity is not something we put as the top priority. What we ask for on the graphics side depends on the systems and requirements of the game itself, and it takes less priority compared to the other elements of development." He will also, of course, admit that his team did good work on the technical side of things, but it's interesting to note this avowed decision to not place the quality of graphics above all else in his games. That said, it's undeniable that *Elden Ring* is absolutely magnificent. It has some purely technical bugs in the graphics, but visually, the game will constantly wow you.

The presentation of different areas, in the creators' artistic quest to create the perfect panorama, is captivating. Miyazaki often talks about the desire to give his games a painting-like appearance. The website *Frontline Gaming Japan* offers a translation of such comments made by the creator: "Miyazaki says that the Erdtree's first purpose is to represent the visuals of the game, showing that it is a mythological world, and to make it easy for anyone to identify the game as *Elden Ring* with a quick glance at the screen. [...] Moving on to the field design of the game, Miyazaki says that the aim was to give the world a mythological, fantastical, painting-like look, with a feeling of Romanticism in solitude."

Indeed, with just a glance at some *Elden Ring* artwork, or even a screenshot, you know immediately what game it comes from. The colors, the lighting, and the ambiance of the images are unique. They also very clearly evoke the 19th-century Romantic movement, in which, in direct opposition to the existing Classicist and Rationalist movements, artists took the liberty of replacing reason and imitation with an explosion of feeling. Passion and pure exaltation, whether personal, political, or spiritual, came to characterize their works, with the goal of making them sublime. That sublime state—with dreamlike colors and lighting, for example, or conversely, the torments and fantasy of Dark Romanticism—is what interests us here in connection with the visuals of *Elden Ring*. And *Elden Ring* is hardly the first game to make this stylistic association, as the *Souls* games borrowed numerous elements from masterpiece Romantic paintings. What's more, Miyazaki is constantly talking about his love of Romantic art and the many books on the subject he has lying around his office, offering him a deep well of inspiration. In *Elden Ring*, real-life paintings seem to come to life before the player's eyes. Depending on the lighting, weather, and viewpoint, you might catch sight of the *Chalk Cliffs on Rügen* by Caspar David Friedrich (1818) or *Medieval City on a River* by Karl Friedrich Schinkel (1815), or even the rugged promontory of *Storm off the Coast of Belle-Ile* by Théodore Gudin (1851).

Elden Ring also shows different sides of Romanticism, taking players on a journey from the lighter conventional Romanticism to the shadowy Dark Romanticism. While the game is certainly brighter and more colorful than its predecessors, sometimes giving it a high-fantasy atmosphere, it still remains a bit gloomy, faded, tarnished... And it never forgets where it came from, regularly offering chillingly dark environments. "Light looks more beautiful in darkness. When there is something beautiful in the middle of a wasteland, we are able to appreciate it more. One jewel doesn't look like much when you have a pile of them, but if you find one jewel in the midst of mud, it is worth so much more," Miyazaki astutely observes in an interview with *IGN*. He adds: "Personally, a world that is happy and bright is something that just doesn't feel realistic to me. It may sound like I have a trauma or something."

Incidentally, the creator apparently has trouble showing this dark side of himself to his loved ones. When the journalist Simon Parkin asked him if his children play his games, Miyazaki responded: "I don't want to let my family play my games, because I feel like they'd see a bad part of me, something that's almost unsavory. I don't know. I'd feel embarrassed. So I say: no *Dark Souls* in the house." That's understandable. In spite of the fantasy world and all the abstraction of universal themes and fictional characters, you have to wonder sometimes where he gets his ideas. He must have a very dark unconscious mind, but isn't that the hallmark of the greatest creators of horror and strange fiction?

Finally, to close out our discussion of the game's visuals, and before we move on to analyzing the game's music, let's briefly talk about the remake of *Demon's Souls* by the American studio Bluepoint Games, released on November 12, 2020, between *Sekiro* and *Elden Ring*. While it maintained the same gameplay as the original, the artistic aspects were completely revamped. Updating the game exclusively for the PlayStation 5, and thus the newest generation of consoles, Bluepoint Games used every bit of expertise it had to revisit FromSoftware's first critically-acclaimed hit and produce a fantastic remake. Out of nowhere, it set a new standard by which *Elden Ring* would be judged: in the eyes of audiences, the open-world game would have to offer graphics at least as beautiful as those of the updated *Demon's Souls*. Speaking to *Edge* magazine, Miyazaki complimented the graphics of the Bluepoint Games remake. He also noted that he had not yet played it, which is understandable given that, at the time, he was busy promoting his new game, *Elden Ring*, which he had to make his priority to talk about and sell. But he also added this: "I just don't enjoy playing the games that I've made in the past." And in fact, it seems that many creators find themselves unable to enjoy their own works after they're finished. Truth be told, Miyazaki and the members of his team have probably "played" the game for thousands of hours across every stage of development, in hundreds of different versions with varying levels of polish and stability.

As such, it's no wonder that they want to move on to something else once production is complete!

The music

Exploration of the Lands Between and the epic battles that punctuate the adventure would not have the same feel without a fitting soundtrack. Heading up the composition and sound-design team was Tsukasa Saitoh, a FromSoftware veteran: he has worked on the *Armored Core* saga, as well as titles like *Eternal Ring* (unrelated!), *Bloodborne*, and *Déraciné*. Saitoh was the one responsible for setting the tone for *Elden Ring*'s musical aesthetic, and he was also responsible for coordinating the work of his colleagues. Alongside him was Shoi Miyazawa, a sound designer (*Bloodborne*, *Dark Souls III*) who gradually started taking on composition duties starting with *Déraciné*, and Tai Tomisawa, a newcomer to FromSoftware who had previously produced a few additional tracks for *Final Fantasy XV*. Also on the in-house team was, of course, Yuka Kitamura, the lead composer for *Dark Souls III* and *Sekiro*, and whose feverish music also accompanied certain memorable battles in *Bloodborne* and *Dark Souls II*. Kitamura left FromSoftware in 2023, but she nonetheless composed several ambiance tracks for *Shadow of the Erdtree*, working as a freelancer. Finally, coming straight from the studio Basiscape, where he notably worked on the soundtracks for *Odin Sphere Leifthrasir* and *13 Sentinels: Aegis Rim*, Yoshimi Kudo also wrote several tracks for *Elden Ring*. However, he was not part of the *Shadow of the Erdtree* project, being replaced by Soma Tanizaki, who wrote his first compositions for the studio after working on arrangements for *Armored Core VI*.

◈ The Lands Between orchestra

Following in the footsteps of the *Souls* games, the soundtrack for *Elden Ring* was developed with a decidedly orchestral flair. To really enhance that approach, who better to perform the music than... an orchestra? That said, turning to an orchestra has not always been a given for the studio. Oddly, FromSoftware's games have had quite uneven results when it comes to musical production since *Demon's Souls*. While *Demon's Souls* and the first *Dark Souls* used recordings of real instruments, the second *Dark Souls* made do with digital instruments and various samples. The third volume, meanwhile, upped the quality slightly by using a choir, but it was one made up of only five singers. As such, the job of mixing in post-production was essential to create the illusion of a much bigger choir, with the voice recordings stacked on top of each other multiple times. The result, strictly from the perspective of music production, was only made more disappointing when compared with *Bloodborne*, released the year before *Dark Souls III* and for which Sony pulled out all the stops by hiring a massive orchestra and choir, as well as dedicating an entire team to music supervision (producers, orchestrators, mixers, etc.), not to mention the fact that they had the music recorded at the prestigious AIR and Abbey Road studios in London. So, a lot of resources went into *Bloodborne*'s music–something Sony often does for its exclusive titles–but the same has not always been true for the *Souls* games. From there, the *Sekiro* team opted for a hybrid approach: the digital instruments and samples were intermingled with recordings of actual instruments, particularly for the strings and *shinobue* flute.

    Elden Ring, in spite of its extraordinary proportions by FromSoftware standards, did not receive the same level of resources for its music as seen for *Bloodborne* or for the remake of *Demon's Souls*, also under the aegis of Sony. Still, the upgrade was significant compared to *Dark Souls III*: while FromSoftware still used a hybrid approach, with many digital instruments and samples structuring a segment of the soundtrack's pieces, the studio also hired a real-life orchestra made up of over a hundred musicians, the Budapest Film Orchestra, as well as the VoiceStation Choir, comprising 45 choristers and seven soloists. The real instruments offered key advantages for ensuring that the boss-battle music would deliver the right power to fit the situation. It's interesting to note that both musical groups are based in Hungary: recording music in Eastern Europe is a common practice thanks to the lower costs. *Shadow of the Erdtree*, on the other hand, benefited from the talents of the Tokyo City Philharmonic Orchestra and of the Philharmonic Chorus of Tokyo. Notably, the recording of the DLC's music was coordinated by singer Sumika Inoue, who lent her own voice to three tracks.

    Overall supervision was provided by Harmonics International, which served as an intermediary. Harmonics had previously worked on various video-game projects, notably managing the soundtracks for *Resident Evil 6* and *Sekiro*. For *Elden Ring*, recording the music was more complicated than it normally would have been, as Koji Suga, the recording coordinator for Harmonics, told me when I asked him to comment for this book: "FromSoftware first contacted us in fall 2019 [for the *Elden Ring* project]. We are honored to have been able to work with the studio and produce such beautiful music in spite of the complicated social situation created by the COVID pandemic." For the pieces written for *Elden Ring* to be performed by the Budapest Film Orchestra and VoiceStation Choir, they needed to be prepared by orchestrators, i.e., the people responsible for adapting the initial compositions by choosing the most appropriate instruments (and number of each) from each section of the orchestra and ensuring that they work well together, refining certain parts to make them better match the specific timbre of each instrument or the stylistic effects used. This work was carried out by Paul D. Taylor and Zac Zinger, with support from Kentaro Sato of Wiseman Project, and in direct collaboration with the composers. As Koji Suga explains: "The composers would give us specific instructions and directions for most of the tracks, but they would also listen to suggestions from Paul, Zac, and the rest of the team. We feel that Paul and Zac used their experience and talents well to create beautiful orchestrations while respecting the composers' visions." Finally, as is often done, the choir and orchestra were recorded separately to allow for greater flexibility with mixing—managed by Satoshi Mark Noguchi of Mirai Sevens—to ensure that the final tracks would be cohesive and clear. For *Shadow of the Erdtree*, recording was again supervised by Harmonics, and the studio Wiseman Project oversaw the orchestrations, which were handled by Kentaro Sato, Tomomichi Takeoka, and Shunsuke Abe.

❖ A new dynamic for accompaniment

For the *Souls* games and *Bloodborne*, there were clear lines to divide how sound was paired with gameplay: with few exceptions, exploration was only ever accompanied by background sound effects, while musical explosions were reserved for boss battles, thus amplifying the impact of those clashes. Due to the fact of being structured as an open world, *Elden Ring* called for a different philosophy. In the end, the game followed in the footsteps of *Sekiro*: not only is exploration colored by music, but the music actually employs a "dynamic" approach. The accompanying sound changes in real time, with fluid transitions, according to what's happening on screen. So, if you find yourself in an enemy camp, the music will become more menacing as you stealthily make your way inside, then more martial when you eventually cross swords with an adversary. As the phases of traveling and wandering around the world of *Elden Ring* make up a large portion of the experience, the dynamic music aims to maintain the player's interest, to stimulate their senses, without detracting from the feeling of solitude that pervades the desolate lands of the game's world.

Moreover, the accompanying music proves to be quite understated and discreet: it whispers a certain atmosphere, certain emotions, rather than imposing them. The first notable ambiance-setting track is, of course, "Limgrave," written by head composer Saitoh. It includes the essential characteristics of such tracks: a subtle melody and instrumentation mainly focusing on strings (violins, violas, cellos, etc.), with the instruments being used for various stylistic choices aimed at conveying a feeling of tension: long, sustained notes, tremolos, etc. In "Limgrave," as in many of the game's tracks, a feeling of discomfort dominates, but the tone is not yet at the point of despair. A sort of luminosity emanates from the track's piercing orchestration.

In spite of the surface-level similarities between the various environmental tracks, certain unique features in each allow us to unconsciously associate them with their locations, and thus shape the identity of those places. Yuka Kitamura, in particular, wrote several of these place-based tracks (in addition to playing the violin for some of them), giving them various notable distinguishing characteristics: effects like echoing, rustling, and whispering for the mines; a bell, voices, and sighs for the intoxicating Eternal Cities; chimes whose crystalline timbre underscores the magical and mysterious dimension of the Academy of Raya Lucaria, etc. And let's not forget, of course, the dissonant notes that accompany exploration of the Caelid region: the humming of strings, organic sounds bordering on the super-natural, a masculine voice delivering a deep "ohm" like a Tibetan chant—these lands consumed by the scarlet rot give off a palpable feeling of unease. The Realm of Shadow, meanwhile, is characterized by the presence of voices, as if to under-score the ambivalent nature of the region, where death and massacres have been covered up by a veil. This is particularly noticeable with the choir of deep, masculine voices heard in Belurat and Scadu Altus, but in any case, the majority of the DLC's ambiance-setting tracks include singing.

Never invasive, these place-based songs introduce subtle factors that enrich the palette of sensations provoked by the game's fascinating artistic choices. However, there's a cost that comes with the constant accompanying music: monotony and repetitiveness can more easily set in, especially given the fact that the tracks always start from the beginning, from the same point over and over; it might have been interesting to implement a system that would have started tracks randomly at other measures to avoid the feeling of redundancy whenever you return to a place you've already explored for several hours.

However, the game keeps some surprises in store, using "diegetic" or "source" music, meaning music that belongs to the game's universe, and therefore that the characters themselves can hear. In addition to songs performed by merchants on their strummed string instruments, a feature that notably indicates to the player that a merchant is somewhere nearby, the *a cappella* singing by the warriors before the battle against Radahn is among the most memorable moments in the adventure [4], along with the first encounter with the Chanting Winged Dames. In the case of these harpy-like creatures, while out exploring, even before you see the enemies in question, you are hailed by the sound of an elegy (entitled "Song of Lament" on the

---

4. In order to lend consistency and credibility to the situation, since the warriors would probably not be a bunch of master vocalists, the singing was not performed by professionals, but rather by musicians in the brass section of the Budapest Film Orchestra!

soundtrack): a woman's voice expresses great pain in a very beautiful song with lyrics in Latin. The contrast with the harpy's repulsive appearance is all the more striking and reflects the ambiguity of the emotions conveyed by *Elden Ring*. Moreover, the Chanting Winged Dame's song offers the only intelligible lyrics in the whole game. As confirmed by Reddit user Magister Organi, a student of Latin who decided to dig deeper into this issue by talking directly with the relevant people on the production team, the singing that we hear, particularly in the boss-battle music, is pure gibberish, just syllables strung together for no other reason than to give the *impression* of listening to ancient Latin, the idea being for the meaning of the lyrics to be opaque. So, there's no hope of learning more about *Elden Ring*'s universe by analyzing the lyrics to the battle music!

And as for that battle music, as the boss clashes follow the same structure as in *Bloodborne* and the subsequent titles, generally divided into two distinct phases, the same is true for the music. The divide is stark: there's no dynamic transition, although certain timbres and motifs are translated from the first part to the second to ensure aesthetic continuity.

◈ A (too?) consistent aesthetic

Generally speaking, the music of *Elden Ring* offers few surprises for anyone who has played the *Souls* games or *Bloodborne*. Massive, grandiose orchestrations, largely driven by blaring choir singers, brass instruments (horns, trombones, trumpets, etc.), and strings[5], imposing percussion (notably the sound of timpani), dissonance, a very dense composition style to convey a sense of horror or chaos, violin and cello solos: there's no doubt about it, this is all familiar territory. So familiar, in fact, that the game's main theme, simply entitled "*Elden Ring*," strangely borrows the melody that opened *Demon's Souls*. This is not the first time that the studio has made this kind of self-reference: the *Dark Souls* theme, for example, was also derived from the *Demon's Souls* theme. However, composer Tsukasa Saitoh made no mention of this reference when he talked about the track on the PlayStation blog in 2022; even worse, he explained that, for the composition, they "wanted the music to reflect the fact that this was something different from the *Dark Souls* series or *Bloodborne*." So, are we expected to believe that the recycling of this motif was pure coincidence? It seems unlikely. What's more, the way in which Hidetaka Miyazaki's creations play off of one another makes his total body of work seem like

---

5. The woodwinds section (flute, oboe, clarinet, bassoon, etc.) often fades into the background or simply goes unused. These instruments generally help give an airy quality to music, even adding lightness, which is not the goal in this case.

a sort of palimpsest, with ideas being constantly rewritten while all being layered on top of the same base, the material being continuously refined and reinvented. Coincidence or not, the return of the motif from *Demon's Souls* is perfectly consistent with this broader approach. And to bring everything full circle, the *Elden Ring* theme that we hear on the game's title screen also serves as the base for the music during the battle with Radagon at the end of the game. It's an eternal cycle: the concepts found in the lore of Miyazaki's games can also be found in a more meta reading of the construction and design of the games themselves, with that interpretation underscored here by the music.

It would be an understatement to say that *Elden Ring* is dense. Indeed, given the incredible vastness of the game's world, if offers a huge number of bosses, both major and minor—in fact, a much greater number than in the studio's previous games. However, the increase in the number of musical tracks to accompany the boss battles is more modest: there are around 30 of these tracks for the main game, with another dozen for *Shadow of the Erdtree*, versus 20-ish tracks for the studio's previous titles. The reason is simple: *Elden Ring* recycles a lot of major enemies, particularly to fill the catacombs and mines, and the real number of unique bosses is actually much smaller, even though the DLC rebalanced the equation a bit. In any case, the composers and orchestrators did everything they could to underscore the epic dimension of these battles.

How can you not tremble with fright when facing Godrick the Grafted, whose monstrous, unnatural appearance is echoed by the dissonant and humming sounds of the orchestra? How can you not be racked with terror of the unspeakable when facing the God-Devouring Serpent, as the tremolos of the strings and the soprano soloist convey the nightmarish majesty of the creature? The second part of that battle then delivers a big reveal: Rykard becomes one with the serpent. A choir of bass voices replaces the soloist, and the glissandos of the violins accelerate to accompany the apocalyptic chaos that has become the battle arena. While Godrick's music is the work of Shoi Miyazawa, the serpent's was composed by Yoshimi Kudo. That said, the musical identities of the composers become somewhat indistinguishable when considering the soundtrack as a whole. The primary objective, with the help of the orchestrators, was to offer a cohesive whole for the game's sound, to conform to the mold initially fashioned by Saitoh and clearly derived from the musical aesthetic of the *Souls* games and *Bloodborne*.

However, each composer found moments to shine. The most melodic tracks quickly won the hearts of players, including "Those United in Common Cause" by Soma Tanizaki, which lends a feeling of melancholy to the fateful battle against Leda at the end of *Shadow of the Erdtree*, or the track written by Tomisawa for the Godskin Apostles, notable for its particularly prominent choir. Tomisawa again relied on the sound of the choir for the battle against Godfrey, for example, with the music conveying both the nobility and ruggedness of the character using masculine voices and a meticulous orchestration, even using the all-too-rare woodwinds.

On that note, it's the tracks that dare to use different sounds that, unsurprisingly, prove to be more memorable. This is the case for the music during the spectacular duel with the dragon Fortissax: the epic and dramatic dimension of the battle is generated in no small part by its music written by Kudo. The track in question is divided between the sounds of a thundering orchestra, flights of staccato strings, a cello solo with a violin playing a counter-melody, and, above all, the imposing presence of an organ. Like many songs on the soundtrack, Fortissax's track makes no attempt to be delicate, but it's hard not to tremble while listening to the music's fury being unleashed—which is indeed the soundtrack's primary objective! The same is true for "Mohg, Lord of Blood," for example, in which the dialogue between the low, masculine voices and higher, feminine voices singing in counterpoint offers interesting color, evoking both the duality of Miquella and the pact made between Mohg and the Formless Mother. This track is also distinguished by its various changes in rhythm—a stylistic effect that Miyazawa seems to be particularly fond of—as well as the notable presence of a harpsichord. Miyazawa also wrote the tempestuous "Divine Beast Dancing Lion," remarkable for prominently featuring woodwinds—finally!—whose spirited glissandos contrast with the gravity of the choir and the rhythm of the strings. This aesthetically pleasing dynamic is perfectly adapted to accompany a creature with the power to control lightning, wind, and ice.

As Saitoh explains on the PlayStation blog, as they wrote their pieces, *Elden Ring*'s composers drew inspiration from various sources: the instructions from Hidetaka Miyazaki, concept art depicting the bosses or battle arenas, the actual renderings of the bosses and arenas in the game, etc. And while an epic feel, chaos, and excess characterize most of the musical aesthetic, the battles called for more unique tones and timbres. We can hear this, in particular, in the music for Astel, written by Tomisawa. The track is slower and aims to be more troubling and mysterious than warlike: it's made up of the distant sound of a choir, trembling strings, and stifling management of the volume, creating a nagging feeling. The song's progression is increasingly stressful, leading up to the arrival of the brass section, which introduces an additional dramatic dimension to one of the most beautiful battles in all of *Elden Ring* from the standpoint of the atmosphere and overall design. In contrast, the battle with Midra, Lord of Frenzied Flame, set to music by Miyazawa, aims to be terrifying. The distorted sounds of certain instruments, the dissonance, the squealing sound of the waterphone, the harrowing sound of the choir, and the melodic line of the cello: the track's plunge into unfathomable horror is reminiscent of some of the greatest moments of *Bloodborne*.

Meanwhile, Yuka Kitamura played her own cards just right, as she so often does. In addition to writing the music for the traumatizing battle against Malenia, with all the elegance and variety of stylistic tools Kitamura is known for when it comes to using sound to create a harmonious blend of violence, sadness, and tragedy—by the by, we find in Malenia's battle music one of Kitamura's signatures: swift arpeggios from the strings section—she also wrote two of the soundtrack's most unusual pieces, which accompany two equally memorable battles. The first is Rennala's track. Piano, chimes, a choir of ethereal feminine voices, woodwinds, and languorous strings create a magical, intoxicating atmosphere for this battle tinged with a dreamlike quality; incidentally, composer Tai Tomisawa echoed the track in certain passages of the music for Rennala's sister, Rellana. That dreamlike quality is also found in the second memorable track by Kitamura, "Regal Ancestor Spirit." The majestic stag is represented by a gentle and mysterious song in which we can hear, in particular, a rainstick, a feminine voice, a harp, a violin solo, layers of synth, and a flute played in an Asian style that adds a woody note, further enhancing the sublime impression of this singular composition. It's a real moment of grace.

Interestingly, Saitoh uses a similar poetic touch to conclude the adventure in the final battle against the Elden Beast: a harp gently reprises the introductory *Elden Ring* theme, while a soloist delivers a magnificent lament to accompany the appearance of the tremendous being. It's an otherworldly and timeless moment. The soloist is then joined by a choir of ethereal feminine voices, echoing the visual design of the Beast and of the stellar backgrounds. The unrelenting rhythm of the strings evokes the forward march of destiny and the influence of the Golden Order, but it's truly the voices that give substance to the strange beauty of this final battle. You end up regretting that the music for the end credits doesn't follow the same trajectory—as was the case for the superb, melancholy final tracks of the *Souls* games—instead settling for a bellicose medley that strings together, in chronological order of their occurrence in the adventure, the themes for Godrick, Morgott, Maliketh, and the Elden Beast.

While the *Elden Ring* soundtrack often remains in familiar territory, even to the point of sounding *too* uniform when listening to it on its own, it perfectly executes its primary function: to fiddle with players' emotions, to make them feel the titanic strength and chaotic horror of the bosses, to elevate the adventure into more mystical and unfathomable realms.

The job of the publisher

People talk a lot about the game development studio, FromSoftware, but rarely about the publisher, Bandai Namco Entertainment. And yet, Bandai Namco played an important role in delivering the final product. While FromSoftware handled the publishing of *Elden Ring*—and other titles before it—in Japan, Bandai Namco handled the job of publishing the game everywhere else. However, the game's Japanese version, like the *Souls* games before it, uses the English voices. It's quite an interesting approach, given that the English text is translated from the original Japanese, then the English dubbing becomes the reference audio; however, the Japanese subtitles are then added using the lines of dialogue as originally written!

◈ The English localization

The English translation was provided by an outside company called Frognation. It's an important name in the industry, having collaborated with FromSoftware as far back as *Demon's Souls*, which was published by Sony Computer Entertainment. Since then, Frognation has participated in each of FromSoftware's games, whether under the aegis of Sony or Bandai Namco, another of the company's clients. Only *Sekiro*, published by Activision, was localized by a different firm. Incidentally, many criticisms have been leveled against the various translations of *Sekiro*. It must be said that Frognation has always worked very closely with FromSoftware on its localization projects. More specifically, translator Ryan Morris has developed a close working relationship with Miyazaki over the years, becoming his main point of contact at Frognation and collaborating with him to produce an English script that's as faithful as possible to the original Japanese.

It's funny to note that Morris discovered and learned Japanese through works of pop culture, particularly in the genres of fantasy and science fiction, including manga series like *Akira* and *Ghost in the Shell*. Miyazaki had a similar journey to learn English, working his way through books like *The Lord of the Rings*, struggling to understand and then letting his imagination fill in the holes. Their paths finally crossed, thanks to Frognation, while working on *Demon's Souls*.

With each new project, Frognation and FromSoftware collaborate closely. The original text is loaded with so much meaning that direct, precise communication is essential. "The text was very dense and very unusual. It uses a lot of very unusual *kanji*, which sort of reminds me of the density of some English fantasy translated into Japanese. Translators who were very good, who were able to capture the meaning, but also to adjust it to Japanese so that it has this kind of authentic, archaic feel. It wasn't just a bunch of transliteration of English terms, it was a good localization," Morris recalls about *Demon's Souls* in an interview with *PC Gamer* (March 11, 2022). Correspondingly, Morris also used dated terms from older dialects of English, adding that very peculiar touch that has become a mainstay of FromSoftware's games.

On Frognation's side, at regular intervals, they receive the Japanese text, ranging from lines of dialogue to descriptions of objects to be translated. While generally the text is delivered by character or at least by theme, the translators don't get a lot of information about the context. Where are these characters or objects located? Is this character speaking to a man? A woman? A creature? It's hard to decipher the meaning without that kind of crucial data. The translators sometimes get access to a debugging version of the game so they can explore and discover the characters and objects in their environment. Still, it's not always easy for them to find the information they're looking for. As such, their questions are frequently resolved during wide-ranging question-and-answer sessions with Miyazaki and his team.

"We ask hundreds of questions, but some of the more subtle things, like levels of absurdism, are a little bit too abstract to really discuss. We usually ask a lot of factual stuff, like 'what's going on? And why? What's the relation here? And what's the background here?,' so we know what language can be used and what can be left out while still mapping to the facts," Morris explains, again to *PC Gamer*. He adds: "There's not a big augmenting handbook that will give us a bunch of context that he takes the time to write. [Miyazaki is] really too busy for that. So we do the text, the scripture that we run off first, and then we have to consult him to find out what the context is so that we don't make errors. Errors are inevitable, if you don't have context, and text alone is not enough to translate correctly."

⬧ Dubbing

In the same interview, Ryan Morris says that Miyazaki loves his characters and feels that each one must be treated with the utmost care. As such, once the translation of the dialogue is complete and approved, Morris and Miyazaki both attend the voice-recording sessions at the Liquid Violet recording studio in London. For *Elden Ring*, due to the COVID-19 pandemic, they didn't go each time—according to Morris, they attended about half the sessions. But still, they tried to maintain the necessary communication with the voice actors.

Liquid Violet and Frognation have a long history together going back to the earliest *Souls*. And in fact, Liquid Violet specializes in video game dubbing, delivering the voices for games like *Borderlands 3*, *Overwatch*, and *Xenoblade Chronicles 3*. The people involved all have the processes down pat, with various unusual actors always at the ready to play the studio's enigmatic characters. "*Elden Ring* presents complex family relationships, and we came up with Welsh and Cornish regional dialects, since both are derived from the Brythonic language spoken in Britain before and during the Roman occupation and fit the premise," Lynn Robson, the founder of Frognation, tells *PC Gamer*.

Elden Ring's cast includes dozens of British actors who most often work in the TV industry, using their range of vocal talents to immerse players in a different, older universe. Among the actors, there's Joe McGann (Sir Gideon Ofnir and various traveling merchants), with his strong North-English accent; Cara Theobold (Nepheli Loux), who you may have seen in *Downton Abbey*; Aimee-Ffion Edwards (Ranni) of *Peaky Blinders* fame; and Gemma Whelan (Tanith), who played Yara Greyjoy in *Game of Thrones*. Some of the smallest parts offer a few surprises: Hannah McCarthy, Liquid Violet's casting director, lent her voice to certain Ancestral Followers, and Ryan Morris is listed as the voice actor for Goldmask... a character who has zero lines of dialogue! It's a "joke" that the translator has repeated a few times now, as he was responsible for the grunts of Horace the Hushed in *Dark Souls III*, Nico of Thorolund in the first *Dark Souls*, and the discreet messengers in *Bloodborne*. It seems that going with Miyazaki to meet the actors and actively participating in the supervision of the dubbing sessions inspired him to take on these great roles!

❖ The other languages

In addition to Japanese and English, *Elden Ring* is available in twelve other languages. As the other localizations were done off of the English version, the English had to be impeccable. For that reason, FromSoftware always has the final say on the translations proposed by Frognation, and the studio only confirms the translated text once it has verified that all of the meaning of the original text is accounted for. As such, the English version becomes a solid foundation allowing the other translators to execute their work, with English generally being more accessible than Japanese—in practical terms, and thus in terms of price.

Each language of translation requires the involvement of a dedicated team at Bandai Namco and its contractors; consequently, each language comes with its own process. Marina Ilari and Guido Bindi, working under Bandai Namco with other colleagues, handled the Latin-American Spanish localization. The two of them answered many questions about their work on *Elden Ring* on the website for Terra Localizations (April 6, 2022). "There were many translators, so it was a challenge to keep consistency throughout. [...] We used a dynamic sheet to create an internal glossary and a style guide, and that helped a lot. We could exchange comments there and work towards using the same terminology and style in-game," explains Bindi. He and the other translators use what are called "computer-assisted translation" tools that automate certain tasks to allow the user to focus on their core responsibility: the game's localization.

In their software, the translators mainly just see text—no images and not a lot of context. "Context is everything because the meaning and intention of a text can change dramatically depending on context. Thankfully, we had good lines of communication within the linguistic team and the project manager, and we were provided a space to ask questions when needed so as not to provide a faulty translation. An additional challenge we had was that the source text was being adjusted rapidly and we would receive new updated strings throughout the course of the project," adds Marina Ilari.

One key tool the translation teams had at their disposal was a glossary, to which they could refer whenever needed. On that topic, Guido Bindi has this to say: "The glossary in English was particularly helpful since it contained most terms used in the game, their explanations, other background information about characters, abilities, etc. We also checked terminology from previous FromSoftware games, mainly the *Dark Souls* saga. We considered it important to keep a resemblance in terms and lore with those previous games." Indeed, certain elements were borrowed from previous FromSoftware games, like the Moonlight Greatsword or the NPC Patches, which have appeared in various titles. The translation teams must remain vigilant at every stage of the process.

There are numerous subtleties that must be accounted for in each localization. For example, when it comes to replicating the archaic-English style: how do you, the translator, create that archaic feel using elements of your own language? Well, you can do it through grammatical constructions, word choice, or just ways of speaking—there are numerous ways to lend an authentic feel to the universe and characters.

✦ What is a video-game publisher?

As we've seen, distributing a Japanese video game outside of Japan, with dubbing and translation into various languages, involves a gargantuan amount of work. Wires can easily get crossed between departments or when moving from one stage to the next, which can deform the creators' original intentions and thus undercut the impact of the game, depending on the resulting quality. Although the localization teams collaborate with the development studio, this rigorous work actually falls under the responsibility of the publisher.

The role and tasks of the publisher go far beyond just localization. The publisher handles everything that the studio can't, like the logistics of distribution to stores or the work that goes into making the game available on download platforms. The publisher also does some quality-control work, handles all of the game's marketing and press relations, and manages player communities in various countries. So, the studio is responsible for creating the product, while the publisher is responsible for making it available to the public.

For *Elden Ring*, that also includes, for example, setting up and maintaining servers for the multiplayer mode. Hosting millions of online game sessions requires solid infrastructure, and it's the publisher that provides that expertise, while also providing long-term maintenance. If on the day of the game's launch the servers go down because there aren't enough of them or they aren't powerful enough to handle the large influx of eager players, that's often considered a failed release. Additionally, online functions represent a major cost center, and it's up to the publisher to decide when to take them down because activity becomes insufficient. In 2018, for example, *Demon's Souls* made headlines once again because of the joint decision between Sony, Altus, and Bandai Namco, the game's three publishers covering different regions of the world, to shut down the game's servers. The announcement sparked nostalgia, with players going online for one last session, playing among the last few ghosts and messages left by other players.

In November 2021, four months before the release of *Elden Ring*, Bandai Namco organized a "closed-network test" spread across five sessions of three hours each. The sessions were a way to introduce the beginning of the game to thousands of ecstatic players over a short period in order to test the infrastructure's ability to handle the load. They also served as an opportunity to collect a lot of data—in particular, on how players explored zones or summoned friends—for the decision-makers at FromSoftware, helping them adjust or improve their game, or at least make plans for their future day-one patch. Collecting feedback on the user experience—UX for short—is now a key part of the process for the video-game industry, given concerns about the usability of its products. Designers and developers get so close to their creations that they sometimes lose sight of the question of an average user's ability to pick up the product and play it. On the PlayStation blog, Miyazaki talks about the benefits of closed-network testing: "Overall, we saw some relatively good reactions from the network test, which was nice. I don't tend to look at the raw user reactions; that can be a little scary. I typically get filtered feedback that comes down through various sources on the team, both on our side and the publisher side, so I get to look from a more holistic view."

The publisher's purview also includes supporting players in their discovery of a new title. The idea is to make sure not to immediately lose the player because of the immensity of the game's world or because of the difficulty, which is, of course, a key concern for FromSoftware's games. The publisher wants to make sure that players don't get scared off. The company does so by working to familiarize players with the gameplay, exploration, and story. For example, they use tutorial videos or simple and direct communications via social media, or even assistance tools within the game itself. The assistance tools may be planned from the beginning by the development studio or they may be suggested by the publisher. When it comes down to it, the publisher aims to offer solid advice to the developer in order to make the game accessible to as many people as possible, to ultimately maximize sales.

Indeed, the main job of the publisher—which, after all, is a business like any other—is to sell as many copies of a game as possible. Generally speaking, the publisher is often the one who funds a game's development, at least in large part. Beyond all of the tasks briefly discussed in this section of the chapter, which are often contracted out to third parties, the publisher is mainly concerned with the business aspects of making a game. The publisher provides the funding and does everything it can to get an adequate return on its investment. That means the publisher develops a marketing strategy to fit the game it wants to sell.

And there's no denying it: the marketing strategy for *Elden Ring* paid off big time.

CHAPTER 4
THE MARKETING STRATEGY

A new approach

FromSoftware's games had always been marketed for their difficulty, for the challenge they represented. That angle was attractive for a niche group of gamers, but it turned off many others. Not everyone is drawn to a high level of difficulty, and many players never picked up a *Souls* game because of their reputation for being "tough games," a reputation largely promoted by the games' own marketing over many years.

In 2019, after the successful release of *Sekiro* and before the announcement of *Elden Ring*, the names FromSoftware and Hidetaka Miyazaki were well-known in the world of video games. *Dark Souls* enjoyed a good reputation, even though mainstream audiences didn't necessarily know it all that well. For the announcement of their new game at E3 2019, FromSoftware and Bandai Namco decided to take a whole new approach. A new franchise—even though the game is clearly a spiritual successor to *Dark Souls*—required new ideas to promote it. The famous phrase "A new world created by Hidetaka Miyazaki and George R. R. Martin" that opened the announcement trailer proved to be clever and evocative in many respects. First, it immediately put the emphasis on the game's universe, and not on its gameplay or difficulty. Second, it paired Miyazaki's name with Martin's. The game creator and the novelist. While Miyazaki already had his fans, he wasn't really famous; Martin, on the other hand, was a household name. It really didn't matter what came after that in the trailer—which was actually quite good; audiences got the message. The announcement worked; the marketing machine was up and running.

However, for the next two years, the game's team shared absolutely zero news about *Elden Ring*. The title was named a few times as the "most anticipated game," but no relevant information was revealed. Some even began to speculate that the project had been canceled. Then, in late 2020, a bit out of nowhere, Phil Spencer, the head of Xbox, made mention of the game, saying how impressed he was with its quality. It seems unlikely that his enthusiastic declaration was part of Bandai Namco's plan to stoke players' expectations. Indeed, all of the communications about the title remained quite humble. While the publisher could have capitalized on Martin's participation, even though he only took part in the very beginning of the project, or on the reputation of *Dark Souls*, which during this same period won the prestigious title of "The Ultimate Game of All Time," Bandai Namco rolled out its marketing plan without highlighting any particular aspect. Conversely, *Cyberpunk 2077*, developed and published by CD Projekt, constantly monopolized media attention, notably touting Keanu Reeves's involvement in the game as part of its marketing campaign. The Polish studio went as far as to say that the actor had played the game and loved it, which Reeves denied. In short, CD Projekt pursued a much more aggressive marketing strategy, one that was also likely more costly, but in any case, it worked very well, with many players champing at the bit to play the game. The disappointment when *Cyberpunk 2077* was finally released was considerable—perhaps proportional to the hype the studio had generated. In the end, it seems that the philosophy of not trying to do too much, or at any rate, of not overselling a game, no matter how good it may be, may sometimes be the best solution.

Two years after the initial announcement at E3 2021, a new trailer for *Elden Ring* became the talk of the town. This time, the video included images directly from the title and showing its gameplay, along with a release date, set to arrive within a few months. With that, Bandai Namco kicked off the second phase of its marketing plan, a phase that was much more eventful than the first. Two major trailers were released: one dedicated to the story, with certain visuals that have remained exclusive to that video (the death of Godwyn, the War of Leyndell, Malenia's floral eruption, etc.), the other giving an overview of the game. The latter was shared a few days before the closed-network test and showed the game's possibilities, limited to the (admittedly extensive) area of Limgrave. The title is constructed in such a way that it's easy to reveal a lot of different elements without really spoiling the actual adventure. The thousands of players selected for the closed-network test explored that same zone and—another subtle cog in the marketing machine—shared their experiences with those who weren't able to participate. "Free" publicity, from player to player, reminiscent, in a way, of the word-of-mouth that had propelled *Demon's Souls* to success 12 years prior. It's a daring strategy, but it's one that works when the game is good.

Audiences were ready for *Elden Ring*, but they also accepted the one-month delay in its release. Bandai Namco took that extra time to adapt its marketing for the release, taking into account some of the feedback received from the closed-network testing. In an interview with *Games Industry* (October 3, 2022), Arnaud Muller, the CEO of Bandai Namco Europe, recalls: "*Dark Souls* has always been perceived as a difficult [series] and *Elden Ring* is a difficult game, but I think with the work we've done to explain properly to our fans the way they could discover this adventure, this new game has touched a larger audience and has made it more accessible. It's a combination of the type of game it is and the positioning of it. And I think it worked very well."

In a meeting with investors, Bandai Namco revealed that it projected to sell around 4 million copies of *Elden Ring* by the end of the Japanese fiscal year on March 31, 2022. The game was released on February 25, 2022, and 20 days later, a joint press release from Bandai Namco and FromSoftware announced they had sold 12 million units.

Smashing success

Dark Souls III, which was a huge hit for FromSoftware and Bandai Namco, sold 10 million copies in four years. *Elden Ring* exceeded that number within three weeks. The game's 12 million units sold in such as short time was a colossal figure, absolutely destroying all of the forecasts that had been made and immediately shifting the balance of power among the heavyweight studios in the video game industry. For comparison, *Breath of the Wild* sold just under 4 million copies in the first month after its release, and *Skyrim* sold 10 million. FromSoftware didn't quite reach the level of *Cyberpunk 2077*–13 million units sold in ten days–and landed far behind the mammoth that was *GTA V*, with its 20 million units sold in the first month, but *Elden Ring* nonetheless had one of the most impressive releases in recent history.

Beyond its stellar sales, one of the most fascinating things to see was how FromSoftware absolutely dominated video-game news. For weeks, all other titles were crowded out in video game coverage, no matter how good they might have been–special shout-out for Andrew Shouldice's incredible *Tunic*, released two weeks after *Elden Ring*. Everything else got drowned out by the flood of news and reviews relating to the new phenomenon. Video game media shared every small detail about the game: tips, interesting finds, players' impressions, the slightest signal from Bandai Namco or FromSoftware. Meanwhile, social media platforms were inundated with players' reviews and screenshots–in spite of the absence in the game of the very fashionable photo mode, a strange choice given that the game is seemingly designed to make you want to immortalize each and every panorama. While Twitter Gaming was reporting (April 5, 2022) that *Elden Ring* ranked as the seventh most-tweeted video game in the world for the first quarter of 2022, including mobile games and online social games in the mix, YouTube Gaming announced that videos pertaining to the game had received 3.4 billion views in the first 60 days after release, making it the best launch ever, beating out *GTA V* (1.9 billion) and *Red Dead Redemption 2* (1.4 billion).

This frenzied attention for the game lasted quite a while—a pretty rare phenomenon in the contemporary video game world. Normally, a new game quickly eclipses an older one, no matter how popular the older one might be. Perhaps *Elden Ring* was able to consume people's attention for so long because of its long lifespan and the fact that it is so intense and incredibly addictive once you've immersed yourself in the Lands Between. Millions of players were enthralled for dozens, or even hundreds, of hours, forgetting about the rest of the video game industry for that time, while other games might have bored players faster, leaving room for the next best thing.

At FromSoftware, Miyazaki was left pondering the game's success. In an interview with *4Gamer.net* (June 24, 2022), he says that he created *Elden Ring* with the same passion he put into his previous works. He started analyzing and trying to understand why this game was a hit with a much wider audience than was the case for *Dark Souls III* or *Sekiro*. Perhaps it was the open world or perhaps it was George R. R. Martin, he thought. Or perhaps, quite simply, it was the fact that the game is excellent, just like its forebears, but the emphasis in marketing was put not on its repellent difficulty, but instead on more engaging elements with greater appeal for mainstream audiences.

After *Elden Ring*'s release, the publisher continued to pursue the same marketing strategy. It had a healthy budget to do so, but still wasn't particularly aggressive in its approach. Truth be told, players and the media, as they talked incessantly about the game, voluntarily participated in generating widespread hype. Moreover, that had been the positioning of Bandai Namco from the beginning of the marketing campaign: the publisher let players' expectations speak for themselves and only chimed in on rare occasions, for example, to deliver a new trailer or interview. In the end, Bandai Namco implemented a fairly traditional approach, but paced it in such a way that it worked effectively. The publisher's restrained approach to marketing was even covered in an article on the website of the business magazine *Forbes* (December 13, 2020), entitled "FromSoftware's '*Elden Ring*' Marketing Is Pure Genius."

The merchandising component of the campaign was also rolled out quite slowly and over a long period of time. For example, Bandai Namco collaborated with Future Press to create fantastic official game guides, published in three volumes with releases staggered from late 2022 to late 2024. Fans were also offered an art book in two volumes, a special set of the game's soundtrack on vinyl records, and, most surprising of all, a jazz concert featuring music from the game, with online and in-person viewing options. All of this special merchandise is expensive, but of high quality. And we can't forget the fact that rights were again sold to Steamforged

Games to create a monumental board game set in the game's universe. The board game's Kickstarter campaign took in over €3.8 million (the campaign for *Dark Souls* hit over €4.3 million). In short, *Elden Ring* is big business, and so we can understand why Bandai Namco and FromSoftware chose to exercise extreme control over all communications concerning the title. They chose to turn each bit of information shared, each window into the future, into a big event. No doubt about it, Bandai Namco has found a new golden goose to add to its collection of high-potential franchises (*Dragon Ball*, *One Piece*, *Tekken*, etc.).

CHAPTER 5
COMMUNITIES

Given *Elden Ring*'s resounding success, with millions of players immersing themselves in the Lands Between within days of the game's release, the community dimension, which was very important for FromSoftware's previous titles, returned in a big way for the new game. In addition to the fact that the game's multiplayer mode, with both cooperative and competitive components, has been very popular with players, the active community that has come together around the title has been particularly impressive.

Information sharing

The most valuable aspect of the game's community has to be the sharing of information and collection of data that happens within it. Wikis—collaborative spaces where anyone can create and edit a web page on a particular topic—are part of the essence of the *Souls* games, and that is now true for *Elden Ring* as well, along with numerous other video games and media more broadly. These wikis provide dedicated pages to every aspect of an artistic work, in this case *Elden Ring*, with each and every user being able to contribute. The tone is always as factual and objective as possible; any writer who strays from that editorial line is swiftly corrected by one of the site's moderators, who are always ready to enforce the wiki's rules.

For *Elden Ring*, you'll find, for example, pages on the different bosses, with their stats, techniques, rewards for beating them, etc.; pages on the different places to be visited, with the location of each object, trap, etc.; pages on every object in the game, including their descriptions, which are particularly useful for lore hunters, who also are able to comb through every bit of dialogue that has been transcribed by the community.

The amount of work that goes into these wikis is impressive, and it is shared between thousands of users, who develop the databases to be as comprehensive as possible. Wikis are publicly accessible and almost always free of charge. However, because these fan wikis are administered and hosted by private third parties (individuals or companies), there is no guarantee that all of the collected data will be available in the long term. Given the growing flow of web traffic for each new game, along with the significant costs of data hosting and bandwidth usage, no one can guarantee that these wikis will still be accessible in another five, ten, or 20 years. Most often, wikis are funded through donations, an approach that is far from being sustainable, but Fextralife, the best-known of the wikis on the *Souls* games and *Elden Ring*, recently created a subscription-based VIP section. Among other things, the subscription masks the Fextralife Twitch stream that appears on each page of the wiki. A questionable–and frequently questioned!–"advertisement" given its invasiveness and heavy bandwidth consumption. For example, if you open ten tabs at the same time to get information on various talismans, you end up with ten Twitch streams running all at once. In short, we all have to bear in mind that as comprehensive and indispensable as these wikis are for the whole community, they are still managed by third parties and their situations might change quite rapidly, for better or for worse.

The other information-related aspect of gaming communities is something called "data mining." It involves searching through a game's files to dig up all kinds of information. Data miners sometimes find nearly complete game elements that ended up not being implemented, like the quest from the merchant Kalé leading to the encounter with the Three Fingers, which was left out of the final game, even though the game's files include all of the dubbing for the quest's dialogue. People have also dug up many lines of dialogue excluded from the final game. There's no clear reason for these deletions. They can likely be explained by creative choices, a lack of time, or the presence of bugs. Data mining sometimes even produces hints about the game's future. For example, a file entitled "DLC1" was quickly found in patch 1.08, the "Colosseum Update," getting fans dreaming of more DLCs to come.

In response to the incredibly tight lid that Bandai Namco and FromSoftware have kept on information, ever since the closed-network test and with each patch release, data miners have shared their discoveries on Reddit, another very important discussion forum for *Elden Ring*'s community. Each piece of information mined is then analyzed by hundreds of people, generating all sorts of fascinating theories.

Data mining is no easy task. You have to have strong computer skills and even knowledge of software architecture. You also have to understand how games are structured and developed. Obtaining and analyzing segments of code, extracting resources or lists of assets–anything can turn up development secrets. One particularly talented data miner is Lance McDonald, who has been at it for years, analyzing all sorts of media. He has especially focused on video games and immediately got to work after *Elden Ring*'s release. He and other fans, including one Sekiro

Dubi, have dug up numerous items left out of the game's final version, or even hidden for future versions. For example, in patch 1.07, they turned up new maps, along with ersatz versions of the colosseums and haircuts made available in the following patch.

Artistic inspirations

In a totally different segment of the community, numerous artists have been inspired by *Elden Ring* to produce new content, often that's quite good. Their inspiration comes from all sorts of things—characters, bosses, emblematic locations—and they use that inspiration in all sorts of different ways.

Two such creators graciously agreed to talk with me about their personal journeys, their artistic sensibilities, and their connection with *Elden Ring*, as well as with the *Souls* games more broadly.

The first is John Devlin, a prolific illustrator whose drawings feature precise, undulating lines. He has made a habit of dedicating his Inktober (an ink-drawing challenge held annually in October, in which each participant produces a drawing a day) creations to a FromSoftware game. Devlin recounts to me how, years ago now, he got sucked into the shadowy universe of *Dark Souls*: "I remember that some friends kept telling me about a game called *Dark Souls* that had just come out. They were always talking about its extreme difficulty. 'You lose all your experience if you die,' or, 'It took me five days to kill that boss.' I told myself that there was no way I'd like that, so I didn't play it. Why would I do that to myself? It didn't seem even the least bit fun to me. I also didn't care for the visual style, and that's a crucial aspect for an illustrator like myself. I wanted the games that I played to influence me artistically, and I was much more interested in the rich and bright aesthetic of fantasy worlds, like those of *Final Fantasy IX* and *Legend of Mana*. I never saw the appeal of the Gothic aesthetic of dark fantasy, and I thought I'd never change my mind about that."

From there, John Devlin admits that a year and a half later, he bought a copy of *Dark Souls* he found on sale, for no other reason than the fact that it came with an art book. "I love art books. I actually have a problem—I buy them all the time!," he jokes. Still, he started playing the game that very night. Even though he wasn't immediately sold on it: "Two weeks later, I had beat *Dark Souls* multiple times and I was pushing my girlfriend to finish it. [...] Even though I initially felt like the game's world was just dull, monochromatic dark fantasy, I eventually learned to appreciate the aesthetic and the game's appeal. I came to realize just how real the universe felt. Locations like Anor Londo, the Kiln of the First Flame, the unending torture that is Blighttown, the Painted World of Ariamis that sucks you in... I felt drawn to all of these places. I fell in love with the *Souls* games, both for the games themselves and for their artistic style. And they have influenced me ever since."

It was in 2014, for Inktober, that Devlin began drawing characters from *Dark Souls*. "The first day, I drew a Channeler from *Dark Souls*. I always loved the design and movements of the Channelers, and I was excited to draw the armor. I remember commenting on the image something like: 'Maybe I'll do a *Dark Souls* character every day?' And that's exactly what I ended up doing that month." While he admired the great wealth and diversity of the weapons and armor of the characters created by FromSoftware, the artist brought his own touch—his own artistic style and sensibility—to the drawings.

Bloodborne further deepened Devlin's fascination with the studio's creations. He found himself enamored with the game's design and its horror and Lovecraftian themes. More generally, each new game released by FromSoftware inspired him with new visuals to explore, offering fertile ground for his imagination: "Those games got me out of my comfort zone and made me the artist that I am today. That never would have happened if I hadn't bought that copy of *Dark Souls* on sale and if it hadn't come with that incredible art book."

The artist adds that for *Elden Ring*, he had a similar approach, with a keen interest in the lore and the backstories of certain characters, especially Ranni. He was so inspired that he produced around a thousand original drawings based on the game!

The other artist I talked to for this book goes by the name Plumy. She is an illustrator and author of comics. As she started the *Elden Ring* adventure, she decided to keep an illustrated journal of her progress, initially posting each page on the social media site X. She then published the charming journal as a booklet entitled *My Elden Ring Journey*. She tells me about her experience: "*My Elden Ring Journey* was sort of a happy accident. I hadn't planned to do anything. When I bought the game, I read comments from several people on Twitter [X] recommending that I keep a journal because there was no quest log in the game itself. I immediately thought of keeping an illustrated log, a sort of travel journal. It's a format that I really like and that comes naturally to me. It's something I do when I go on vacation. I almost started my log using a leather-bound journal for a very RPG feel, but I ended up using my usual sketchpad to not put pressure on myself."

Truth be told, Plumy didn't really think that the venture would last more than a few pages. But in fact, she found herself totally enthralled, sketching situations that aren't even possible in the game, "like the possibility of sitting [her] character in one of the chairs at the round table for a quick nap." In general, Plumy likes FromSoftware's games, especially for their unique manner of storytelling: "Its games leave so many gray areas that I can let my imagination run wild and create my own version of the adventure that I experience while playing." For those unknowns in the plot, Plumy sometimes fills the holes with her own illustrations!

In the case of *Elden Ring*, she particularly focused on the different characters, who she found to be more appealing than those of the studio's other games. As an example, she mentions Boc, an especially minor character. The conclusion to Boc's storyline left her so upset that she dedicated two pages to him, using a comic-strip format, in *My Elden Ring Journey*. Other characters, like Millicent, are absent from the journal because of the feeling of weariness that set in for Plumy by the end of the game.

"The journal's format evolved as I advanced through the game. I began to make humorous drawings of the characters, comic strips based directly on my own reactions while playing, full pages of much more serious comics, as well as illustrations delving into the lore... It really became a log of my personal experience with the game. [...] I shared it bit by bit on my Twitter, where it got a positive reception that really surprised me." While many players in the community worked to create the best-possible character build and bragged about their triumphs over the various bosses, Plumy simply recounted her adventure, including her exploration of the Lands Between and her discoveries pertaining to the game's rich lore. As she pondered the face of Godwyn seen in the basement of Stormveil Castle, "an image that stuck with me," she began to study up on the game's universe and all its details via videos by YouTube creator Zullie the Witch: "As I'm very attuned to details, I would do my own research when something caught my attention, like the first encounter I had with the statues of Malenia and Miquella hidden in a spot near Leyndell. When I first saw the twin statues, I recognized Malenia, but not Miquella. It wasn't until later that I put all the different pieces together in my mind."

"It was the first time that I'd done something like this. I think I might one day do something similar with my favorite FromSoftware game, *Bloodborne*, which I have been obsessed with ever since I first discovered it in 2016. But it's a very time-consuming and preoccupying undertaking: I spent four months working on this journal, encompassing 200 hours of gameplay, and that's time I couldn't spend on my other personal projects." After *Elden Ring*, Plumy tried to repeat the journal experience with *Dark Souls III*, but unfortunately found that it didn't have the same appeal. It was a question of sensibilities: "*Elden Ring* is probably FromSoftware's most accessible game thanks to its gameplay, but also thanks to its universe and characters, who, even while they are often hard to fully understand, are much more human and real, in my opinion, than the characters from the studio's other games. The game's universe, too, with its open-world aspect and the impression I got of endlessly discovering new places and new atmospheres, totally contributed to the game's appeal for me, that sensation of adventure and exploration that I got throughout the game. Whenever I'd read the description of an object or discover a new place, the puzzle pieces that make up the world would come together in my head, maintaining my interest in the game's universe."

Video creators have also produced a massive amount of content related to *Elden Ring*, with some videos being more original or creative than others. I'd like to give a shout-out here to the YouTube videos of VaatiVidya, the most famous lore hunter, who's been at it since *Dark Souls*. For *Elden Ring*, he decided to adopt more of a "short film" format for his videos. Assisted by other creators, notably to capture battle scenes, each video really has a cinematic quality to it. That said, he strays away from deep analysis of the lore to offer strong narration of the major quests from the game's characters. So, the videos are different from his past work, but are still just as interesting. Finally, another shout-out to SunhiLegend and their short battle videos. With the game interface hidden, great presentation, with slow-motion sequences and careful management of the camera to make sure to capture every attack and dodge, the scenes captured are truly incredible!

Role-play

Within the game's community, role-playing—the idea of embodying a character in terms of their style of dress and their battle habits—happens not just in the game itself, but also in the real world. Indeed, there are many fans of cosplay in the community, as has always been the case for the *Souls* games. *Elden Ring* has lent itself well to cosplay with its particularly distinctive characters: Ranni and Malenia leading the pack, but also Melina and even Margit the Fell Omen, with his much more imposing style! The costumes take many hours to create and are worn by people of different profiles, from passionate actors to players who simply want to adopt the role and appearance of a beloved fictional character for a short time. There are also costumes sold on specialized websites. It's a niche business, but one that is absolutely available for those who might not have the time or skills necessary to create their own cosplay outfits.

Within the game itself, a good number of players take the RPG's role-playing a step further. This is particularly the case among fans of player-versus-player (PvP) battles. The virtual knights and magicians engage in fights to the death, with all sorts of rituals like special greetings before the battle and limiting their use of healing objects. With the addition of the battle arenas in patch 1.08, this aspect of the community took on a new dimension, with specific rules applying to each colosseum.

However, the in-game role-playing also sometimes happens outside the context of PvP battles, with players adopting the appearance of characters from other franchises, like Shrek or the Teenage Mutant Ninja Turtles. And then there's the story of a mysterious player named "Let me solo her." Wearing nothing but skimpy underwear and a jar on his head, and armed with two samurai swords, the avatar has become iconic for the entire *Elden Ring* community. Players could summon him before the battle against Malenia–who, I'll remind you, is the game's hardest and most unfair boss–and Let me solo her would finish her off in no time. His unambiguous name, essentially telling other players, "Don't you worry, I'll handle her myself," his absurd style, and his regular presence made him into a real celebrity. In early July 2022, he announced on Reddit that he had beat Malenia over 2,000 times! Tales of his exploits even reached Bandai Namco, which sent him a few goodies, including a gorgeous sword. "I can still remember my first experience with the *Souls-Borne* series and almost quitting because of Iudex Gundyr[6] in *Dark Souls III*. I'm glad I persisted and went on to enjoy the game, because this community is one of the most passionate and dedicated people I've ever seen in a game, and I'm proud to be a part of it," Klein Tsuboi, the person behind the extraordinary character, writes on the social media platform X. Like many players, he had so much trouble beating Malenia that afterward, he took on the personal challenge of building up his skills to the point where he'd be able to easily defeat her, with the goal of helping others get over this spike in difficulty. Along the way, he adopted his strange getup and username. Role-play in its purest form!

Great feats

Let me solo her fits somewhere in the space between role-playing and the performance of great feats, having trained himself to the point where he knows every single one of Malenia's moves and she's no longer able to touch him. A few streamers have also specialized in this kind of impossible challenge. MissMikkaa managed to finish the game while remaining at level one and playing with only one hand. And by the way, it took her 12 hours just to beat Malenia! MissMikkaa pulled off another feat, using a dance pad and a controller to play two sessions of *Elden Ring* at the same time. Very impressive. As you can see, it's not unusual for certain streamers to try to spice up their sessions by imposing various off-the-wall rules. They'll try to beat the game while not taking a single hit, or they'll use a very specific, even improbable, character build, or they'll only use torches or kicks as

---

6. This boss was mentioned in a previous chapter when discussing the great difficulty of the beginning of *Dark Souls III*.

weapons. These eccentric approaches become everyday life for players who have already completed every aspect of the adventure. With 200 million hours of streams dedicated to *Elden Ring* (figure as of April 2022), the streamers have to offer their viewers a bit of variety.

Speedrunning is another category that has been undeniably popular, especially because of *Elden Ring*'s open world. Indeed, the bigger the playing field, the greater the desire to race to the end of the adventure in record time. As of the end of 2022, the record was held by a player who goes by FirstTwoWeeks, who finished the game in 19 minutes and 49 seconds, excluding loading times. To achieve this incredible completion time, the speedrunner exploited certain glitches in the game to go faster and avoid entire sections of the adventure. However, there are several categories for speedrunning competition, including one that prohibits the use of such glitches. In that category, the player Forsa is the reigning champion, with a time of 58 minutes and 42 seconds. There are other, equally fascinating categories with more stringent completion criteria, like having to take on all the major bosses (record: 1 hr. 1 min. 14 sec.) or earning all the achievements and trophies (record: 2 hr. 49 min.). No matter the category, these players achieve superhuman levels of performance.

And yet, there's nothing superhuman about speedrunners–OK, maybe just a little. Above all, they go through a very long and sometimes complex learning process, but in the end, it's "just" about executing an extremely precise game plan, calibrated down to every millimeter, health point, endurance point, and magic point. The game plan in question is developed through crowd-sourcing, in which different community members provide their own tips and some even report glitches, test them, and report back on their effectiveness. All of this evolves over time as players make new discoveries and as patches intervene to fix certain glitches, while occasionally creating new ones. So, in a way, the speedrunners do some very important QA work for the developers, often with the support of automation and collaborative-research tools. Once the game plan has been prepared and mastered, the speedrunner takes a bit more time to perfect their racecourse, adding in a jump here, an acceleration there–I'm just giving the most basic examples here as the speedrunner juggles numerous parameters–in order to shave off fractions of a second throughout the game.

They measure their performance with precise tools that allow them to accurately calculate the time elapsed, overall and at each stage, like during boss battles, for example. It's very much like an official sporting event. Speedrunning is really a very particular approach to gameplay. Some speedrunners have never followed the story or the normal course of the adventure. They are solely focused on the technical aspects, completely breaking down the game to the point where all they can see is the fastest shortcuts between essential points. *Elden Ring* is far from the only popular title among speedrunners, but FromSoftware's creations, in general, are well-loved among this segment of players—I'm reminded of the feat pulled off by player Mitchriz while playing *Sekiro*: he finished the game while blindfolded in just two hours at GDQ 2022, a charity event dedicated to speedrunning. Perhaps the appeal for them is the games' reputations for difficulty, making their feats all the more impressive for their audiences, especially people who aren't familiar with the ins and outs of speedrunning. And yet, a speedrun in *Elden Ring* is similar to one in *Far Cry 6*. The approach is the same—it may even be easier to set new records with *Elden Ring* thanks to the bigger community—and once the speedrunner has mastered the game plan, they "just" need to execute it while maintaining their concentration for the time needed.

So, there you have it: there are many fascinating facets to *Elden Ring*'s generous community. I could mention here that the community also includes certain toxic and aggressive players, but I don't want to give them too much of my energy. Statistically, there will always be a group of such lunatics in a community, unfortunately often making a lot of noise. But that said, they are a minority of players and are easily eclipsed by the rest of the community, which constantly comes up with great things to contribute. I also didn't spend a lot of time talking about the lore hunters, who have become increasingly numerous since *Demon's Souls*. They offer an inexhaustible store of food for thought about a universe that is at once opaque and profound, as we will discuss very soon. But before that, I'd like to give the final word of this chapter to our dear Miyazaki, who talked about the community in his interview with *The New Yorker*: "That power of imagination is important to me. Offering room for user interpretation creates a sense of communication with the audience—and, of course, communication between users in the community. This is something that I enjoy seeing unfold with our games, and that has continued to influence my work."

CHAPTER 6
A HIGHLY ANTICIPATED EXPANSION

Announcements

The fact that *Sekiro* never got a full-fledged expansion might be explained by the fact that FromSoftware was working with a different publisher than usual, Activision. Previously, all of the *Souls* games—except *Demon's Souls*, which wasn't as well-known at the time—and their FromSoftware descendants had received one or more high-quality DLC expansions, which were often extensive and difficult. Truth be told, with Bandai Namco at the wheel, it was hard to imagine the future of *Elden Ring* without a proper expansion to add on to the already colossal adventure.

Still, players had to wait until the game's first anniversary, and even a few days after that, on February 28, 2023, for the *Elden Ring* DLC expansion to be revealed. It would be entitled *Shadow of the Erdtree*. The announcement was made with a superb piece of art holding all sorts of clues and raising many questions—FromSoftware's forte. In the image, we see what appears to be Miquella riding on a spectral steed—perhaps Torrent, perhaps not. In the distance, we see the Erdtree looking dark, ill, and seemingly injured. Glowing Grace trickles from its trunk. Fans, feeling more inspired than ever before, delivered a flurry of analyses. Even though it had been a full year since *Elden Ring*'s release, most players had been keeping an eye out for a DLC announcement.

In typical fashion, Bandai Namco held its cards close to its chest. Almost too much so given that the next bit of news about *Shadow of the Erdtree* didn't come until a year later, on the game's second anniversary on February 21, 2024. This time, the publisher put out a detailed trailer and announced a release date: June 21, 2024. In the meantime, a fascinating story trailer was shared on May 21. The video didn't end up appearing in the DLC itself and is actually quite important for understanding the lore. But we'll come back to that in later chapters.

When it was finally released, to fans eager to get their hands on it even two and a half years after *Elden Ring*'s release, *Shadow of the Erdtree* received acclaim from critics and players alike, selling 5 million units in just three days. That represented one fifth of the people who had played *Elden Ring*, as sales for the main game culminated at 25 million units, according to a FromSoftware press release in June 2024. The DLC's release was accompanied by a few interviews given by Miyazaki, who again declared his pride in the work of his teams and the results they achieved. At the same time, he announced that *Shadow of the Erdtree* would be the only DLC expansion for *Elden Ring*.

The content

In both form and function, *Shadow of the Erdtree* is very similar to its parent game, *Elden Ring*. The goal of the expansion was not really to create a feeling of exoticism or to make a paradigm shift, but rather to continue the experience of the original game for another few dozen hours. "It became obvious that there were elements in the big picture of *Elden Ring* that wouldn't fit into the main title, so we thought it would be good to release these to the world as DLC. However, at that point it was still just a general idea, as we were still focused on the main release. Actual development work on the DLC started after the release of the main title and after the initial patches settled down a bit," Miyazaki explains to the Japanese magazine *Famitsu* in early 2024, again according to a translation by Reddit user theangryfurlong.

The Realm of Shadow, where the expansion takes place, is actually separate from the rest of the game. It has its own map, which is again gradually revealed to the player, and while it is much smaller than the main map, the zones are so dense, especially thanks to their vertical dimension, that it takes a lot of time and observation to fully explore them. Still, the length of the additional adventure, although massive for a DLC, proves to be less taxing for players who may have gotten worn out or even exasperated by the end of the main adventure. So, spiritually, *Shadow of the Erdtree* remains very close to its predecessor; however, overall, it proves to be more condensed, with even greater interconnection between the various locations, especially around Messmer's castle—a real feat of level design. The DLC expansion includes legacy dungeons, vast plains to be traversed astride Torrent, ruins, and a few catacombs, but it also has some novelties, like the "gaols" and forges, mini-dungeons offering a few new subtleties in their design. Certain zones really stand out, like the Cerulean Coast on the south end of the map, strewn with blue flowers for a great effect; meanwhile, giant stone coffins the size of small apartment buildings regularly wash ashore there. The Abyssal Woods region is another highlight of the DLC. The woods are corrupted by the Madness of the Frenzied Flame, and the supposedly invincible creatures that roam the area are truly frightening, bringing back memories of the terrifying sequences in the prison known as the Tower of Latria in *Demon's Souls*. The game creates a powerful ambiance!

In terms of lore, the DLC gradually reveals the bloody past of the Realm of Shadow, connected to the war between Messmer, a new character who is particularly charismatic, and the people known as the Hornsent. We also discover, at the heart of the new adventure, Miquella's new plan. In an interview with *IGN* (February 21, 2024), Miyazaki says that George R. R. Martin had no involvement in the DLC, but the mythology that he developed during the pre-production phase of *Elden Ring* of course served as a base for the new story. It really seems that his collaboration with the studio ended quite early in the development of the original game. However, Miyazaki notes: "Mr. Martin and I have at least exchanged emails since the release of *Elden Ring*, but unfortunately we haven't been able to meet and speak in person. It's something I've wanted to do since the release and talk to him again and share in our joy for the game hopefully, but unfortunately he's just been so busy that we haven't had that chance yet. But I'll keep looking for an opportunity."

Toward new horizons?

After more than five years of production dedicated to *Elden Ring*, then two more for a very substantial DLC expansion, will FromSoftware continue to dedicate time to its new golden goose? Well, development of the *Dark Souls* saga was spread over a solid seven years; that said, it included three (big) games and six (excellent) DLC expansions. Seven years, in proportion to the 50 some odd years of history for the relatively young video-game medium, is a lot. The time spent on *Elden Ring* and its DLC demonstrates two things: first, that the game's ambition is at least equal to that of multiple other titles combined, and second, that production and development processes have gotten much longer and more complex in less than a decade. According to figures from *Moby Games*, over 200 people worked on the first *Dark Souls*, compared to over 1,600 for *Elden Ring*.

As such, when *IGN* raised the question of a sequel or another DLC expansion for *Elden Ring*, Miyazaki gave this reasonable answer: "We don't want to say this is the end of the *Elden Ring* saga for now. I think we said a similar thing at the end of *Dark Souls III*. We didn't want to flatten those possibilities or put a pin in them just at that time. [...] We don't have any current plans to make a second DLC or a sequel." We can't blame him for wanting to imagine other projects and try new things, like *Armored Core VI*, released in 2023 between *Elden Ring* and its DLC, which, while it didn't reach the sales of FromSoftware's biggest hits, still managed to draw around 3 million players.

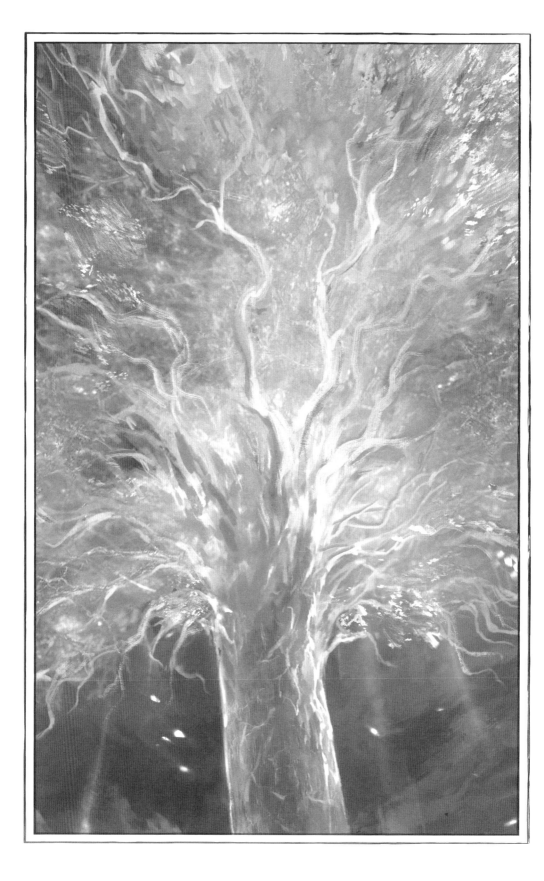

THE MONUMENTAL

ELDEN RING

FromSoftware's Magnum Opus

Part 2

Understanding Elden Ring

CHAPTER 1
AN OVERVIEW

"Brave Tarnished. Take the plunge. Of learning, and remembrance." These are the words of the strange, ghostly figure who greets the player after their defeat at the hands of the ruthless Grafted Scion. These spirits, unlike the other NPCs encountered throughout the game, are fixed in time and space, tirelessly repeating the same words to everyone they see. However, this encounter at the very beginning of the game is not entirely pointless. The words have meaning. The spirit invites you to literally plunge into the hole in front of him to begin an essential tutorial—one that went completely unnoticed for many players initially after the game's release. It's not easy to make the choice to plunge into the unknown, especially when you can't see how you'll get back safe and sound. Ultimately, taking the plunge means getting out of your comfort zone!

These few words from the spirit also resonate with how the player discovers the game's universe, which is as cryptic as can be. It's already been said, but the information forming the game's story and lore is scattered across numerous places that require a keen eye to find. While the game's objective is clear from the very beginning—to seize the throne and become the Elden Lord—the other factors at play in this game of thrones, if you will, sometimes remain unclear, even after dozens, or even hundreds, of hours spent playing and after the conclusion has finally been revealed. Who is Marika really? What happened to the Eternal Cities? Can the Two Fingers and Golden Order really be trusted? To answer these questions, along with hundreds of others that will arise as you investigate the game's universe, you need to "take the plunge." Again borrowing the words of the spirit cited at the beginning of this chapter, you also must immerse yourself in "learning and remembrance." Your immersion in the game's vast and complex universe is largely driven by observation and note-taking. However, there is no tutorial to present this aspect of the game to you. The arduous task of learning and remembrance depends entirely on the player's will. This really becomes evident to the player when they discover—often by chance and by reading between the lines—that certain events of the past may be more complex than initially suggested. The player then has to go back through their memory to reconsider everything they've discovered up to that point. Some elements that may have originally seemed unimportant might take on great meaning and shed light on certain gray areas. The game's storytelling is a jigsaw puzzle (though an incomplete one) to be pieced together–a game within the game.

This is all familiar territory for players of FromSoftware's past productions, as *Elden Ring* uses the very same peculiar rules of narrative design (a term you'll already know from the first part of this book).

How should you decipher the universe of Elden Ring?

◈ A Souls-like structure and themes

Demon's Souls, and even the *King's Field* series whose legacy it followed, offered a similar style of storytelling. At the same time, the adventure was divided into five distinct worlds, each one with its own puzzle-like universe to be put together. An overarching plotline connected the different worlds together and created stakes for the protagonist, who ended his odyssey in an incredible but incredibly cryptic place for any player who hadn't paid attention to the details.

From there, it was really *Dark Souls* that won audiences over to this storytelling approach, transposing its predecessor's concept into a semi-open world with greater ambitions. In addition to creating a coherent universe that's absolutely fascinating to discover, the first *Dark Souls* went as far as to offer a second–and well hidden!–path for the player to follow. To briefly describe this stroke of genius, it is an alternate route in the game's progression for which the player must follow specific instructions at certain moments in the game. When the player does this, a totally different side of the story unfolds, unveiling major forces that have shaped the universe since time immemorial. With that deeper understanding, once the game's final sequence arrives, in which the player finds a fire waiting to be lit in the center of a room, the well-informed player will pause to consider before providing the necessary spark. In the course of their adventure, the player will have lit dozens of fires–a recurring element of gameplay–but in this case, the player knows that this particular fire, the "final" fire, is different from all the others. The player has a choice to make. If they light the fire, a new cycle of the Age of Fire, belonging to the gods, will begin. If the player refuses and simply leaves the room, the Age of Dark, belonging to humanity, the main character's kind, will begin. Perpetuate the power of the gods, a group of manipulative tyrants, or give the little guy, the protagonist's own people, a chance? The answer is obvious, but the game's developers seem to have made a wild bet with the way they tried to shape the player's line of thinking in this atypical progression through the game (i.e., refusing to listen to recommendations). In adopting this approach, with *Dark Souls*, Miyazaki and his team placed a lot of faith in their audience, which would already be busy trying to understand the new game mechanisms (humanity points, blacksmith, covenants), studying strategies to defeat the wily bosses, and exploring the many nooks and crannies and vertigo-inducing vertical structures of the universe's different zones.

Thankfully, at the time, players came together on forums and social media to share their experiences, discoveries, and theories. The hazier points of gameplay were clarified, bosses' weaknesses were exposed, and hidden places were quickly revealed. The same goes for the famous alternative pathway, a secret that was quickly revealed as the official game guide was published shortly after the game's release. On the other hand, in spite of all the speculation surrounding the *Dark Souls* universe—i.e., its lore—it would take weeks, months, or even years for certain details to come to light. Indeed, to this day, there is a significant segment of the saga's community that continues to study the game's universe, with each member sharing theories and arguments, often backed up by specific knowledge (mythology, theology, symbology, etc.). Perhaps that's the true multiplayer mode of the series! On this subject, translator Ryan Morris comments on the website *Rock Paper Shotgun* (February 22, 2022) about how important this community collaboration has become for Miyazaki: "I know that he wouldn't want to define this or that—it's kind of a rabbit hole, I suppose, to start that conversation after the game is done. He also appreciates and enjoys the fact that players have taken so much time and energy, defining it [the lore] on their own terms and coming to their own conclusions."

Dark Souls laid the foundations for FromSoftware's particular style of story-telling, with the studio recycling the approach with varying levels of innovation for its subsequent productions. The two *Dark Souls* sequels each had their own unique elements. The second volume borrowed a handful of highly symbolic concepts from its predecessor and implemented them in a totally different universe that was almost impossible to tie back to the original story. The third volume, meanwhile, aimed to be a direct sequel to the first and offered fascinating explanations for certain questions that had long remained unanswered, particularly in its final DLC expansion, *The Ringed City*, undeniably a treasure trove for lore hunters. Between the latter two *Dark Souls* games, FromSoftware also put out *Bloodborne*, the absolute pinnacle of the studio's peculiar form of storytelling. In *Bloodborne*, the traditional dark-fantasy universe was replaced by a Victorian ambiance steeped in esoteric concepts and incredible violence, all on a backdrop of Lovecraftian divine forces, for a striking result. It is a true masterpiece. Finally, *Sekiro*, too, offered a different setting, more connected to real-world history, as the story takes place in Sengoku-period Japan. It was an eventful period shaped by provincial wars, from which the game's creators drew a lot of inspiration when writing the script. As for the rest of the game, the puzzle-like storytelling worked its magic again, while paired with characters and dialogue that were less cryptic than usual for the studio.

The various pieces of this unique narrative design can be found in many different ways. A significant portion of the information is found in descriptions of objects, from consumable supplies to even the humblest piece of equipment, as well as spells and smithing materials. Acquiring a weapon wielded by a character or a piece of armor that they've worn generally means learning more about their past or personality. Players also construct their knowledge through the game's dialogue, as well as, less obviously, by observing the backgrounds, bestiary, battle techniques used by enemies, the clothing worn by NPCs, the placement of dead bodies scattered hither and thither, along with the loot found on them, etc. Environmental story-telling, as it's called, is all over the place. It adds to the lore with each new zone explored and with each new vista.

All of these elements are found in *Elden Ring*. The principle is exactly the same, while being scaled to the game's large open world. In spite of the titanic under-taking for the development team and the usual (purposeful) omission of certain explanations, coherence was still the name of the game. And the team actually upped the ante: the macroscopic lore, at the scale of the entire Lands Between and even beyond, is blended brilliantly with microscopic lore, specific to each region.

The technical aspects and unique fragmentation of the storytelling were not the only items borrowed from the previous games of FromSoftware. The player is again faced with universal themes, full of symbolism and colored by some of the greatest myths of all time. Duality is a constant (life and death, order and chaos, twin relationships, etc.); we find syncretism of all kinds, dismal and fathomless stagnation, a hazy and abstract timeline of past events: this is all familiar territory for fans of the *Souls* games.

Elden Ring also borrows the concept of "ages" that is fundamental to the story of *Dark Souls*. Similar to the end of the first *Dark Souls*, by becoming the Elden Lord, you can choose to usher in a new age or extend the current one, the Age of the Golden Order. While the current age has been in decline since ancient times, this path to the throne appears to be the most natural for a novice or player who doesn't know any better. This insidious setup is reminiscent of the way *Dark Souls* incites the player to renew the cycle of the Age of Fire.

Still on the topic of similarities, *Elden Ring* puts us in the shoes of an anonymous Tarnished. In *Bloodborne*, it was a Hunter, and in *Dark Souls*, it was an Undead, and then an Unkindled. In each case, it's a unique term, but the idea remains the same: the player takes on the role of an anonymous character, just another person among the many. Like so many other players and so many aspiring to greatness before them; and that actually fits perfectly with the cyclical concepts of the games. However, within that anonymity, there is a detail that creates a slight difference between the main character and others of their kind. In *Elden Ring*, the Tarnished is guided by a "ray" of Grace—we'll come back to that!—and in *Dark Souls*, the player quickly finds themself at the heart of the prophecy of the "Chosen Undead."

The anonymous character—who it turns out is not so ordinary after all—always begins the adventure at the bottom of the ladder, in terms of both physical and magical strength, but also in terms of knowledge. The player must climb the rungs by acquiring experience, struggling through encounters with increasingly powerful adversaries (heroes, lords, gods, dragons, and an assortment of other creatures), and picking up certain key objects, before reaching the top and making the final push toward the conclusion, the final decision. By the end of the adventure, the player and their avatar have become all-powerful, armed with rare and effective equipment and, above all, unrivaled knowledge of things like the patterns of enemies and the geography of the places visited. With a bit of luck, the player will even know the impact that their decision will have on the world!

This structure was recreated flawlessly in *Elden Ring*. The game's objective is laid out from the very beginning, in the opening sequence. As for that, we find another constant, particularly inherited from the *Dark Souls* saga: much of the universe is introduced in the opening scene. In the first *Dark Souls*, all of the key elements of the plot appear in the introductory sequence, which is quite cryptic the first time you see it. Rewatching it regularly as you advance through the game allows you to better understand the universe and discern some of the unique characteristics of the major bosses, who are all present in the initial cinematic. We see the same principle in *Elden Ring*, whose introduction in still images—which are truly sublime illustrations!—presents all of the important characters in less than four minutes. It ends with the awakening of the player character, "a Tarnished of no renown," and assigns him an objective: to "become the Elden Lord." Shortly after that, we learn that we will need to collect "Great Runes," fragments of the Elden Ring that must be put back together so we can access the Erdtree and perpetuate the Age of the Golden Order. But there's a twist: in the end, we will need to burn the Erdtree and free the Rune of Death, which was taken and then sealed away long ago, to be able to seize the throne. And there you have it: that's all. The objective and progression of the game are no more obscure or complex than those few sentences. However, once you start delving into what actually happened in the past, you need to go off the beaten path to encounter—among others—more minor characters, who are absolutely crucial to the game's storytelling.

Collecting as many puzzle pieces as possible and trying to fit them all together is no easy task. And yet, that is precisely what we will try to do in this section of the book. In an interview with *IGN* (June 17, 2021), Miyazaki talks about the story-telling of his new game: "We hope that that level of understanding is easy to access, but then again there's a lot more depth there as they explore. And this depth, again, this idea of uncovering the world as you go, picking up its many little pieces, it's multi-layered, it's complex, it's very fascinating. This is something I myself enjoy a lot in these games, and in other RPGs I play. We had the greedy approach of wanting to make these two elements stand together, of wanting it to be easy to understand, but also give it a lot of depth."

As we've seen, *Elden Ring* is, from a storytelling perspective, a direct descendant of the *Souls* games. However, it distinguishes itself from its ancestors by using a slightly different creative approach for its characters. Indeed, most of the game's events revolve around family intrigue and rivalries between clans and regions. In fact, the first piece of the puzzle that I put down when I began writing this chapter was the creation of a family (Erd) tree. It was a fascinating exercise that reminded me of the convoluted diagrams connecting the different families in George R. R. Martin's *A Song of Ice and Fire*.

❖ The George R. R. Martin touch

At the start of the game, it's hard to discern the presence of the American novelist in the game's text and situations. After all, his taste for dark and painful stories, with lines between good and evil that are blurred or absent altogether, echoes the approach that FromSoftware has used in its productions for many years. However, as you progress through the game, you find more and more characteristic signs of his pen and his imagination.

One of the first "surprises" appears in the Roundtable Hold, when Fia betrays everyone by murdering D and revealing her desire to be a mother to Those Who Live in Death, cursed beings openly hunted by D and by the Golden Order more generally. This truly surprising sequence occurs after numerous interactions—mainly involving dialogue and searches for key objects—with several characters in the Roundtable Hold: Fia and D, but also Rogier, a secret ally to Fia. All of these actions set the scene, with the player unknowingly becoming an accomplice, for D to be caught in Fia's trap. While betrayals occur regularly in the *Souls* games, especially involving the recurring character of Patches, they are generally against the player. Plotting, treachery, and murder between NPCs is much rarer. There are examples—Lautrec in *Dark Souls*, who stealthily murders a Fire Keeper, or Eileen in *Bloodborne*, who hunts corrupt Hunters—but none of them involves a plan as devious as that of Fia and Rogier in *Elden Ring*. Theirs is a plot on par with the famous betrayals cooked up by Martin in his works. As Hidetaka Miyazaki developed all of the story set in the game's present, this dramatic turn of events is likely a vibrant homage to the American writer. Notably, it's the first moment in the game that clearly reminds us of their collaboration.

Much later, after a few dozen hours of play under their belt, the player discovers the family tree of the gods and demigods that reign over the Lands Between. On it, we find many family secrets, alliances, and relationships of all sorts; however, once again, we also find evidence of betrayals. We'll come back later to discuss in greater detail this blended family, which has had the goddess Marika standing at the heart of it since the beginning of time, but for now, I'd like to note that the theme of family ties plays a more important role in this title than in FromSoftware's previous games. This aspect of the game bears all the hallmarks of George R. R. Martin.

Finally, to finish by drawing a direct parallel with *A Song of Ice and Fire*, the main goal of *Elden Ring* is actually centered on a vacant throne and the identity of the person who will ascend to it. Well before the player's adventure begins, the Lands Between suffered a number of wars over that very throne. Ancient Dragons, Giants, and the great hawks of Stormveil faced off against Marika's troops. After that, Marika's own children fought amongst themselves to claim the throne and become the Elden Lord. And it was all in vain: as the game begins, the throne remains vacant...

Key concepts of Elden Ring

✦ Glossary and definitions

Now that we have a better understanding of how the story and universe of *Elden Ring* were developed, and above all, of how all of that is conveyed within the game, it's finally time to get to the heart of the matter. First, I feel that it's important to lay out and define certain terms and concepts that are particularly obscure.

Outer Gods: The Outer Gods have to be the most powerful and unfathomable forces in the universe of *Elden Ring*, with their dominion extending well beyond the Lands Between. While we know there are several Outer Gods, they remain both unseen and mysterious. No one knows what their true motivations are. Through emissaries and agents, they interact with more lowly creatures, promising them infinite power or any other hegemonic attribute. This is precisely the case for the Greater Will, the Outer God most frequently identified in the story. The arrival of the Greater Will, or at least of its emissary, in the Lands Between wreaked absolute havoc on the world's whole ecosystem. The Greater Will promised great power to the region's elites, known as the Empyreans.

Empyreans: There's a word you don't see every day! And it's far from being an isolated case. The game regularly borrows unusual terms from different fields: prelate, ascetic, apostate, consort, etc. This approach lends some additional cachet to the storytelling and adds to the mysterious ambiance, giving greater authenticity to the game's medieval setting. But let's get back to the term "Empyrean," which here has a very different meaning, unlike the unusual words mentioned above. In ancient Greek cosmology, the empyrean is the highest sphere of heaven, where the gods live. The term has also been used in Christian cosmology to describe one of the highest points of heaven, where God is found. In *Elden Ring*, an Empyrean is chosen by the Outer Gods; in the case of our story, that means the Greater Will. The criteria for selection are very vague, but it would seem that the Outer Gods always choose a powerful and influential woman. After the woman is chosen, a "Shadowbound Beast," also simply called a "Shadow"–in the case of Maliketh, he's even interestingly referred to as Marika's "half-brother"–is assigned to accompany her. The Shadow protects the Empyrean while guiding her toward her destiny. Nothing must distract the Empyrean from pursuing her objective: to find a consort, i.e., a husband worthy of her status, who will become the Elden Lord. Once she has accomplished her mission, she is elevated to the rank of a goddess. The most famous Empyreans are Ranni, Malenia, Miquella–who, while referred to as a man, is strikingly androgynous–and, previously, Marika.

Gods: First off, be careful not to confuse gods and goddesses with Outer Gods! Second, the gods possess great power and are supposed to guide the people of the world. Marika is a goddess, perhaps even the only one in the Lands Between when the adventure of *Elden Ring* begins. Other gods and divine beings are recorded in the annals of history, from an ancient time and probably taking on other forms and pursuing objectives different from those of Marika. Moreover, we can imagine that there might be other ways to become a god or goddess, but the most "common" way, according to the history of the Lands Between, involves an Empyrean finding a consort. The Empyrean's marriage to her consort seals this strange ritual, and so the consort, too, must possess great power. The consorts generally hold the title of "champion."

Champions: Here we have a perfectly ordinary word, but it's one loaded with additional meaning in the Lands Between. "Champion" is a rank that can be attained by warriors after demonstrating great feats, particularly on the battlefield. A champion can go on to become a consort, or even a lord, another fairly common term that here refers to the highest rank a mortal can achieve. I am, of course, referring to the title of Elden Lord, the highest distinction, a term often used in the sense of king or monarch.

Demigods: Quite logically, the demigods are the children of gods; in the game, that mainly means Marika's children. Children by marriage, i.e., the children of

Radagon, Marika's second husband and consort, also acquire demigod status after becoming part of the goddess's family. As such, there are quite a few demigods, including:

- Marika's children with Godfrey, her first husband, i.e., Godwyn and the twins Mohg and Morgott. Godrick is also considered a demigod, but he is supposed to be no more than a distant descendant of Godfrey, probably a son or grandson of Godwyn.
- The children of Radagon and Rennala, i.e., Radahn, Ranni, and Rykard, demigods by marriage.
- The twins born to Marika and Radagon, named Malenia and Miquella.
- The DLC *Shadow of the Erdtree* introduces Messmer as the son of Marika. The father is not specifically named, and Messmer has a sister, who also remains unnamed; we will theorize about their identities in the chapters to come.

Other strange terms, like "godskin," "Omen," "demi-human," "spellblade," and of course "Tarnished," will be explained later. The same goes for concepts specific to the game's universe, like the Erdtree and the titular Elden Ring. We will cover all of this in the chapters to come. We wouldn't want to spoil all the surprises now.

For the time being, just keep these few essential definitions in mind for a better general understanding. Before we dive into the archaeological excavation of the Lands Between, I'd like to briefly give a word of caution.

◈ Caution

First, it is important to pay (very) close attention to names. Just take a quick look at the list of demigods above. The names in each set of siblings are strikingly similar! Setting aside the fact that their starting letters are taken from the three distinct initials in the name of George R. R. Martin, their sounds are very similar and it's easy to get them confused. Godfrey, Godrick, and Godwyn are, indeed, three different characters. There is also a Godefroy (known as "the Grafted," the same epithet given to Godrick), a perfectly minor character whose very existence interferes with our understanding. There's also Rennala and Ranni, a mother and daughter duo. At the beginning of the game, Ranni even goes by the name "Renna," then comes to the aid of her mother during the boss battle between the player and Rennala. It's hard to keep it all straight! And that's not even mentioning Rellana, Rennala's sister, who appears in the DLC. Another example: Melina (the player's servant) is neither Malenia nor Miquella, and certainly neither Maliketh nor Millicent. Finally, Margit and Morgott are the same person, but they must not be confused with the demi-human Queen Margot, who you can find in a somewhat hidden optional dungeon.

This similarity between names makes it seriously difficult to keep track of each character, and often it's the character's epithet, like Margit the Fell Omen or Godwyn the Golden, that helps you keep everyone straight in the vast array of individuals. The game actually uses numerous nicknames, with the twins Malenia and Miquella, for example, each having quite a few. For Malenia, that includes Goddess of Rot, Scarlet Goddess, Blade of Miquella, and Malenia the Severed. For Miquella, it includes Lord Miquella, Miquella the Kind, and the Unalloyed. It's an aspect reminiscent of certain characters from *A Song of Ice and Fire*, with their unending lists of bynames. It's hard not to think of "Daenerys Stormborn of House Targaryen, the first of her name, Queen of the Andals, the Rhoynar, and the First Men, Protector of the Seven Kingdoms, Lady of Dragonstone, Queen of Meereen, the Khaleesi of the Great Grass Sea, the Unburnt, the Breaker of Chains, the Mother of Dragons."

Finally, a quick word of warning about the general haziness of the timeline of history for the game's universe. While such imprecise timelines could be found in the *Souls* games, in *Elden Ring*, the phenomenon is magnified to match the magnitude of the game's open world. With some of the gaping holes in the timeline, we'll have to make some assumptions, though always, of course, with evidence and reasoning to back them up. This is unavoidable if you wish to analyze the universes of FromSoftware's games: deciphering the chronology of events is no easy task, and as such, different people may reach different interpretations.

CHAPTER 2
THE PAST

"All that there is came from the One Great. Then came fractures, and births, and souls." These few words go further back into the history of the universe than anything else we learn in the course of the adventure. They come from a conversation with Hyetta, Three Fingers Maiden. Hyetta is reporting the message of the mysterious Three Fingers, the agent of an Outer God who we will return to later on. According to these beliefs, the game's entire universe came from the "One Great" and its initial fracturing. In other words, Hyetta is describing the Big Bang of *Elden Ring*'s universe. Or, to view the words through a more mythological or even cosmogonic lens, the One Great could be considered a primordial state. It makes me think, for example, of Chaos in Greek mythology, which was the origin of the world and the gods.

Here, we learn that the first, and maybe even all, of the Outer Gods were born from the fracturing of the One Great. The Greater Will, the Frenzied Flame, and the Formless Mother are mystical names that can be found in fragments of history hidden across the Lands Between. The Lands Between themselves, whose geographic location is as mysterious as its exact chronology, are also a result of the fracturing of the One Great. The souls that have inhabited the Lands Between did not all inherit the same attributes or strength. In fact, the dragons, with their mighty power, long reigned over the Lands Between.

Life in the Lands Between before the Elden Ring

Generally speaking, when it comes to the Lands Between and its history, the closer we get to the present, the more detailed the information becomes about the nature of events. However, as the period before the creation of the Elden Ring belongs to the distant past, a thick layer of fog continues to obscure our view of it. Thankfully, the *Shadow of the Erdtree* DLC expansion sheds some light on the remote era.

◈ Dragons, giants, and humans

The prehistoric era known as the Age of the Ancient Dragons, as its name indicates, was a period dominated by dragons–known as "Ancient Dragons" so as not to confuse them with the weaker and mortal dragons of more recent times. The Ancient Dragons wielded an ultra-powerful form of magic known as red lightning and used their indestructible granite scales to fend off all attacks. It is said that their scales made them immortal and that the dragons would protect their king by forming a literal living wall of rock around him.

The Ancient Dragons had many enemies. Among them were the formidable Giants. The Fire Giants even managed to defeat the Ice Dragons in the northern mountains, then forced them into exile, at least according to the description for the incantation Borealis's Mist[7]. The Giants then made their home in the newly conquered mountains, which were steep and hostile enough that they wouldn't have to face too many invaders.

Other peoples of the Lands Between preferred to defer to the supremacy of the Ancient Dragons. These included the humans, who, while much weaker than the Giants, were much more numerous and had enough ingenuity among them to begin laying the foundations for a budding civilization. Near the Siofra and Ainsel Rivers, they founded the cities of Nokron and Nokstella, respectively, which later were dubbed the Eternal Cities. The residents of the cities worshiped the stars and the Dark Moon, also known as the Moon of Nokstella. According to the description of the Moon of Nokstella talisman, "The Moon of Nokstella was the guide of countless stars." Astrologers began studying the night sky and derived from the stars the earliest forms of magic, later inspiring several different currents of sorcery. Waiting tirelessly for the coming of the Age of the Stars, the residents of the Eternal Cities prospered slowly but surely.

A third city was founded near the source of the Siofra and Ainsel Rivers. Sadly, its name did not survive the test of time, and today, the city's glorious buildings of old sit in ruin. The distinguishing feature of the nameless city is that it once stood near a sacred site, one that was even "considered a signifier of the divine" (Crucible Feather Talisman): the Primordial Crucible of Life.

---

7. I will occasionally add references to the descriptions of objects or to certain passages of dialogue to support a point or underscore an idea. That said, I won't provide citations in every single case. Unless otherwise noted, all of the information provided here comes from the game.

◈ The Primordial Crucible of Life

It seems that the Crucible may have manifested in several places across the Lands Between: within the nameless city on the Siofra and Ainsel Rivers, but also in the region of Rauh, whose ruins can be accessed in the present via the Land of Shadow. "In an age long past, before this land was enshrouded in shadow, the vitality of the Crucible flourished," states the description for Aspects of the Crucible: Bloom. The Crucible was venerated as a cradle "where all life was once blended together," according to the Aspects of the Crucible: Horns. That includes animals, beasts, and even the Giants, on whom supposedly grew the "mother of Crucibles" (Talisman of All Crucibles), i.e., an "intermingling [of] Crucible attributes": horns, fangs, feathers, thorns, knots.

Moreover, there were several major symbols associated with the Crucible. First and foremost horns, symbols of power, but also trees, representing life and regeneration, and finally the perfection of gold. Much later, the tree and gold symbols would live on after the decline of the Crucible. The two would be reclaimed and transcended by later forces. The horns, fangs, and all the rest, on the other hand, would forever remain symbols of the Crucible and would be used to enhance the attributes of the powerful Crucible Knights. These 16 knights sported the colors—a dull, reddish gold—and embodied the values of the Crucible. They also were known for their great strength, according to the description of the Crucible Gauntlets.

Ordovis, Siluria, and Devonia were the most famous of the Crucible Knights. By the by, these names are almost certainly references to the sequential Ordovician, Silurian, and Devonian periods of the Paleozoic era, the geological era when life first emerged from the oceans. Besides featuring the rise of more evolved living things, corresponding perfectly to the evolving primordial era of the Lands Between described here, the three periods spanned tens of millions of years, reminding us that the time scales of history can seem quite long in *Elden Ring*! In any case, Ordovis could be recognized by his greatsword "imbued with an ancient holy essence" and his impressive helm shaped like an axe. Devonia's favorite weapon was a hammer, while Siluria wore armor with a tree-like appearance. Her helmet featured "great tree ornamentation," with the roots pointing toward the heavens, and she wielded a great spear dubbed Siluria's Tree, designed to look like the Crucible tree. The colossal tree, a physical manifestation of the Crucible's ancient energy, was located not far from the nameless third human city. As they worshiped the Crucible and the stars, the people of the city had their beliefs completely shaken by the Greater Will, an Outer God that had remained unknown to all up to that point, when it decided to take an interest in the Lands Between.

The Greater Will's ambitions for the Lands Between

◈ Falling stars

The Greater Will did not appear personally in the Lands Between. Instead, it sent its first servant, Metyr, the "first shooting star to fall upon the Lands Between" (Remembrance of the Mother of Fingers).

As their name suggests, the Outer Gods do not actually exist in the same space-time as the inhabitants of the Lands Between. As such, they communicate and act through indirect means. Depending on the configuration and quality of those means, an Outer God's will may face significant inertia and take time to be enacted, or it might just be misinterpreted altogether by its vassals.

Metyr, Mother of Fingers, gave birth to all of the Two Fingers, strange emissaries of the Greater Will whose name literally reflects what they are: two giant fingers that twitch sporadically. "Fingers cannot speak, yet these are eloquent. Persistently they wriggle, spelling out mysteries in the air. Thus did we gain the words. The words of our faith," states the description of the Two Fingers Heirloom. So, the Two Fingers went about meeting the people of the Lands Between and spreading the good word of the Greater Will, as received by Metyr via her powerful receiver known as the "microcosm," a sort of ball of dark, pulsating energy. Thus, initial contact and communication were established.

"It is said that long ago, the Greater Will sent a golden star bearing a beast into the Lands Between, which would later become the Elden Ring," we learn from the description of the legendary Elden Stars incantation. This second falling star marked the next part in the Greater Will's plan: to convince the people of the Lands Between to serve it. We have no idea if the Outer God was familiar with the beliefs and customs of the Lands Between, but for the humans, stars and gold (i.e., of the Crucible) had divine meaning. Undoubtedly, they had to have noticed the golden falling star and would have taken it as a sign heralding a new era.

What's more, the previous quotation also mentions the Elden Ring, an item important enough that the entire game was named after it. Perhaps the golden star already contained the essential form of the Ring, or perhaps the Ring was forged at a later time by the mysterious beast mentioned with help from a few lackeys. Whatever the case may be, the Elden Ring contained exceptional power, a power never before seen in the Lands Between. It was capable of forcing any opponent into submission, of redefining the laws and basic ways of the world, and most likely of physically transforming the environment. Whoever controlled this miraculous tool, this Holy Grail, controlled all of the Lands Between.

The Greater Will knew the value of the Elden Ring and used it as leverage for negotiating with the various populations of the world. To prevent any one person or group from taking advantage of the Ring or abusing it, the Greater Will established another crucial concept: Order.

⬥ The Elden Ring and Order

The Elden Ring was made up in part of four interlocking circles, each one corresponding to a Great Rune containing massive power. The runes also represented high-level concepts, like life or death, a fact that would have great importance for later events. But in any case, the Elden Ring was the embodiment of Order, whose rules, a unique sort of law of nature, reshaped the face of the Lands Between.

For example, beasts "gained intelligence" (Bestial Vitality incantation) and thus gradually left behind their wild and uncontrollable state. "It is said that in the time before the Erdtree, stones were the first weapons of the beasts who had gained intelligence," we learn from the description of the Bestial Sling incantation. Naturally, we see in the symbol of the "stones" an analogy for our own human history and the rise of the Stone Age, the first stage in the development of human civilization. Thanks to Order and the gift of intelligence, the beasts of the Lands Between were able to join the other peoples of the world in civilization. The same was true for other minority species—who would soon suffer discrimination. These included the demi-humans, nimble creatures who, up to that point, had lived in caves; the Misbegotten; the Beastmen; and the giant hawks, who we will meet again very soon in our story.

Another example of a major shift brought about by the rise of Order, this one a subject with a lot more information in the annals of history of the Lands Between: beliefs surrounding death changed. Up to that point, funerary customs in the Lands Between were tied to another Outer God, represented by its emissary, the "twinbird" (Twinbird Kite Shield). The Outer God of Death was said to be evil, but even still, scholars were unable to determine its true intentions. Long ago, the twinbird gave birth to the Deathbirds, servants of death that look like tall birds with oversized, skull-like heads. Occasionally assisted by priests hoping to receive favors, particularly in the form of their "distant resurrection" (Death Ritual Spear) sometime in the future, as well as Gravebirds, "created to guard the spiritgraves built where all manners of Death ultimately drift" (Gravebird's Blackquill Armor), the Deathbirds were first and foremost the keepers of ghostflame. The spell Explosive Ghostflame explains that "death was burned in ghostflame" as part of a funerary ritual that would change with the rise of Order, particularly because of its rune dedicated to the afterlife, called Destined Death.

Meanwhile, the young Erdtree began its long growth as the Lands Between were transformed by the intentions of the Greater Will. The Erdtree, an absolute giant in the present day, standing taller than cities and mountains and visible from every region of the world, began sinking its roots deep into the ground from the nameless city that was built near the Crucible of Life, according to information from the Deeproot Depths Map. Some even say that the Crucible is "the primordial form of the Erdtree" (Crucible Gauntlets). The roots of the Erdtree began making their way into every underground space, no matter how far from the starting point. From then on, the dead were no longer burned in ghostflame; instead, their spirits would return to the Erdtree, guided by a golden light known as Grace.

◈ The Erdtree and the Two Fingers

"A proper death means returning to the Erdtree. Have patience. Until the time comes... and the roots call to you." A spirit tells the player this as they discover the first catacombs in the Limgrave region. In the early days of the Erdtree, many catacombs were built around its roots so that they could "feed" on the souls of the dead. These crypts were overseen by the "Erdtree Avatars" (Staff of the Avatar), who had incredible strength and endurance. To this day, we still find certain traces of mysterious entities that once guided the dead. There's the Black Steeple of the Helphen, erected to shine a light for warriors who died in battle to guide them in the spirit world. The Black Steeple of Helphen would later lend its name to a greatsword designed to look like a Gothic steeple, even featuring little gargoyles along its sides. There's also the "Usher of Death," named Rosus, who guided lost souls, and any other souls unable to find rest, to the catacombs. There are many statues of this strange shepherd scattered across the Lands Between. The gentle light that emanates from the statues always points to the nearest catacombs.

Certain individuals preferred to become "ash unreturned to the Erdtree" (according to Ranni the Witch) and thus became spirits, either wandering around or controlled by the Spirit Calling Bell, an important object that has survived through the ages to finally be used by the player. This refusal to return to the Erdtree, and more generally the refusal to comply with the Greater Will's authority, is as old as Order itself. However, the Outer God foresaw this and sent messengers to indoctrinate the people of the Lands Between and bend them to its will: the Two Fingers. As a reminder, the Two Fingers, secretly controlled by their mother, Metyr, were the emissaries of the Greater Will. They communicated their divine messages in various ways: either orally, with help from Finger Readers—old, immortal women with somewhat deformed bodies, easily recognized by their staffs topped with bells; or visually, via a language of light made up of shapeless symbols, indecipherable for common mortals. Their light-based messages were imbued with sacred magic and were studied using primordial forms of incantations. Incidentally, we can see examples of the Two Fingers' shining runes on the Coded Sword and the Cipher Pata.

The Church was also founded during this period to preach the good word of the Greater Will to the masses. As very few had access to the Two Fingers and were able to understand them, priests and other members of the clergy, which seems to have been quite limited, were given the mission of reaching out to the people, both within and beyond the Lands Between. The role and actions of the clergy long ago remain unclear; it wasn't until much later that the first real information on the Church was recorded, reflecting particularly cruel and violent acts. But we'll come back to that in due time.

For now, just know that the Church, the Two Fingers, and their Readers shaped the world according to the Greater Will's vision. The Erdtree continued to grow and became more majestic with each passing day, acquiring a golden light that would soon be compared to the sun of the Lands Between (Warming Stone). The Erdtree's first stage, which we might call its implantation, was complete. It became time to find a keeper of the Elden Ring, a being powerful enough to wield it and help the Erdtree prosper.

◈ The search for the Elden Lord

This period of searching for and crowning the first Elden Lords lasted an inestimable amount of time. Few details appear in the archives.

However, we do know that the four-headed Ancient Dragon Placidusax was, for a time, the Elden Lord, long before the Golden Age of the Erdtree. Perhaps he became a renowned champion when he confronted and defeated his rival, Bayle the Dread, another Ancient Dragon described as a "terrible harbinger of destruction" (Talisman of the Dread). Indeed, Bayle challenged Placidusax and the two battled almost to the death. Placidusax had two of his heads ripped off, which we can see to this day, the jaws still planted in the flesh of Bayle's wounded body.

The all-powerful Dragonlord Placidusax remained alive, but with only two of his heads. He continued to reign from the floating city of Farum Azula. Unfortunately, his goddess abandoned him. Placidusax "continued to await its return" (Remembrance of the Dragonlord), cutting himself off from the rest of the world indefinitely, hiding in the heart of the storm in Farum Azula. Left without its leader, occasionally being struck by meteorites (Ruins Greatsword), the floating city began to fall into ruin, notably crumbling over Limgrave and Liurnia, where fallen vestiges of the giant temple can still be seen today. Indeed, in those fallen vestiges, the player can find a good number of Sanctuary Stones and Ruin Fragments, relics of the "temple in the sky."

Placidusax became the Elden Lord when he married an Empyrean. Let me remind you, once the Empyrean married her champion, she would become a goddess, and her consort would earn the title of Elden Lord. After the departure of Placidusax's goddess, the contract between them was broken and he lost his title. At that point, the Elden throne became vacant once again, until the next lord was found.

No one knows how many Elden Lords there were over the centuries. The task of selecting Empyreans belonged to the strange Two Fingers. The hallowed individuals chosen by the Two Fingers would then have to find their champions in order to become deities and embody the Elden Ring, carrying forward its vision.

While few Empyreans became goddesses, they nonetheless all had histories and a fate that distinguished them from mere mortals. One of these Empyreans, whose actual name we don't know, is referred to as the "Gloam-Eyed Queen" (Godslayer's Greatsword). She was chosen by the Two Fingers, but then used her special status to conspire against the gods. Having a particularly close relationship with Destined Death, she drew energy from the rune to create Black Flames capable of killing the gods. She founded and led a squad of nimble warrior mages who were equally skilled at wielding rapiers and Black Flame incantations. They adopted the name "Godskin Apostles" or "Godskin Nobles," depending on their specialties, and began to actively hunt the gods.

Unfortunately for the Gloam-Eyed Queen, her power and plans were eventually annihilated by a man named Maliketh, the Shadowbound Beast—as a reminder, a sort of ultra-powerful protector destined to watch over its assigned Empyrean—of another of the Two Fingers' chosen ones: Marika.

Marika the Empyrean

◈ Her past

Even though she eventually became the central character in all of Lands Between history, there is much we do not know about Marika's past. We know that she descended from the Numen, a mysterious people from outside the Lands Between, and we also know that she grew up among a population of female shamans, who no longer exist. Her village was situated in the north of what is now the Land of Shadow.

Here, I'd like to posit a hypothesis about the Land of Shadow: while in the present it cannot be accessed by natural means, it is very likely that it was once part of the geography of the Lands Between. Much like the Eternal Cities before they were buried underground—we'll come back to that—the Realm of Shadow was probably accessible from the other regions of the Lands Between. It would have been located at the center of the present-day map, where we find the inland sea between Caelid and Limgrave to the south, and Leyndell and the Mountaintops of the Giants to the north. "The very center of the Lands Between. All manners of Death wash up here, only to be suppressed." These few words are engraved in the stone at the top of the Suppressing Pillar, a monument in the center of the Realm of Shadow.

As was said when talking about the region of Rauh, in the north of the Realm of Shadow, the Crucible was once venerated there. That worship was then fervently adopted by another people, one that's very important to this story: the Hornsent.

Like the humans, Giants, and dragons, the Hornsent had their own full-fledged civilization, with their own beliefs ("Horns are sublime artifacts to Hornsent, and their presence confirms the belief that they are a chosen people," according to the Clarifying Horn Charm +2), their own pride (dominated by vengeance), their own rituals ("Hornsent employed this to honorably end the suffering of a compatriot," notes the Blade of Mercy), their own curses (some transformed into man-flies, an insect-like creature), and lastly, their own fears (particularly of madness caused by the Frenzied Flame). Made up of both scholars and mighty warriors, Hornsent society exerted its power over most of the Realm of Shadow.

So, where does Marika fit into all of this? Well, the Hornsent persecuted her shaman people. The shamans were captured and locked up in jails in the Realm of Shadow, before being subjected to terrible experiments. "For pity's sake, your place is in the jar... Nigh-sainthood itself awaits you within. For shamans like you, this is your lot. Life were you accorded for this alone." These are the words of a spirit wandering around Bonny, a village where certain great Hornsent potentates still roam. The potentates, using giant meat cleavers, would butcher the bodies of the shamans to fill big jars kept in the jails. The shamans, whose flesh blended easily with that of others, were thus hunted and butchered to be elevated to this mysterious sainthood. No one knows if Marika herself was captured by the potentates, nor to what extent she witnessed these atrocious practices, but we know that she became aware of the massacre of her people and began to plot her terrible vengeance.

◈ Divinity

The seduction. And the betrayal.
An affair from which gold arose.
And so too was Shadow born.

These few phrases–taken from the official subtitles of the *Shadow of the Erdtree* story trailer–while mysterious and open to multiple interpretations, form the foundation of the story of how Marika became a goddess. The story trailer, a cinematic that sits apart from the game and its DLC expansion, shows Marika gathering golden filaments from an unidentifiable body. She stands atop Enir-Ilim, the tower of the Hornsent, more specifically at the foot of the Gate of Divinity, whose two massive columns allow a gentle yet powerful light to shine between them. It's said that an Empyrean who unites with her consort at this place will become a goddess. And yet, Marika stands alone. She brandishes the gold threads, which form a U shape. She looks almost Christlike, an aspect that will remain with her for the rest of her life. She is suddenly filled with the ultimate power.

At this point, unfortunately, we can only theorize about the answers to the many questions this scene raises.

Whom did Marika seduce and then betray? That could be the potentates, or the Hornsent more broadly, whom she would have betrayed to access Enir-Ilim and then the Gate of Divinity. She may have used her charms to achieve her aims–the Hornsent Grandam later calls her a "strumpet" several times. Another potential explanation, one more anchored in the lore surrounding Marika: the seduction and betrayal may concern the Two Fingers and the Greater Will. Indeed, before the sequence we see in the story trailer, Marika was chosen by the Two Fingers to become an Empyrean. As the shaman village was located right near the Finger Ruins of Dheo, Marika may have used her extraordinary passion to seduce the Greater Will's emissaries, promising to become the next standard-bearer of the Elden Ring. The Two Fingers would then have given her the strength needed to make her way to the Gate of Divinity, as evidenced by the hundreds of Hornsent bodies covering the ground and the two columns at the sacred gate. Moreover, Marika may have been assisted in the massacre by her Shadowbound Beast, Maliketh, although we have no evidence to confirm this. The betrayal of Marika, on the other hand, would come much later, in the era of the Golden Order, a subject that we will come back to.

With whom might Marika have had an affair? Because that's the other big mystery here, the "affair from which gold arose." Could it have something to do with the Two Fingers or the Greater Will? In any case, Marika presents herself to the Gate of Divinity without a consort. Later on, the story reveals to us that Marika and Radagon, her future husband, are in fact the same person. No one knows when Radagon became part of Marika, but it was likely the case at this particular moment in time, making him the secret first consort of the shamanic Empyrean. "The flesh of shamans was said to meld harmoniously with others," notes the description of the Tooth Whip. Radagon was probably a Fire Giant, given his red hair and his extraordinary strength, and he may have been absorbed by Marika sometime in the years before the scene at the Gate of Divinity. It's hard to confirm, but in the story trailer, when we see Marika brandishing the gold threads, her body appears androgynous, equal parts feminine and masculine. This styling was also present in the story trailer for the main game (another unique cinematic used only for promotional purposes), in which the first shots of Marika and Radagon appear one after the other, blending together; without a trained eye and deep knowledge of the game's lore, the illusion was perfect.

◈ Gold and shadow

"Marika bathed the village of her home in gold, knowing full well that there was no one to heal," states the description for the Minor Erdtree incantation. Shortly after obtaining divine status, Marika returned to her hometown, the shaman village, which had been decimated, and left a bit of her new power there, power based on "only the kindness of gold, without Order." Indeed, she was not yet serving the Order of the Greater Will. Additionally, she cut her braid, giving it as an offering to a mysterious "Grandmother," probably some belief of the people of her village, and left it there.

This kind and protective gold, a symbol of Marika's readiness to change the world, was soon joined by Shadow, as we learn from the line, "And so too was Shadow born."

This metaphorical shadow is none other than Marika's first child: Messmer. A cursed child, like others who would come later, as he was born of a single goddess. Indeed, it would make sense that Messmer is the first son of the fused being that is Marika and Radagon, Messmer's red hair being a major indicator, along with the presence of a curse, the pernicious influence of the Abyssal Serpent. The serpent in question used a torturous fire that made Messmer go mad. Later, the fire would seem to symbolize original sin. Marika ended up plucking out her son's right eye, behind which hid the serpent, and placed in the socket a powerful seal to contain the beast. Marika had extraordinary ambitions, and Messmer, or rather his imperfection, had to remain a secret from the rest of the world. Marika hid the central region of the Lands Between, where her son would live and grow, behind a veil to conceal her dark secret. Thus, the Realm of Shadow was created. The Remembrance of the Impaler description tells us that Messmer was "hidden away–keeping company with the original sin, and a hatred that would not be confined."

Marika's actions, cutting off the Realm of Shadow on an invisible plane that couldn't be accessed from the Lands Between, came with a number of consequences, notably the rise of the Scadutree. Growing out of forms of the Crucible found in the Land of Shadow, the Scadutree is considered to be the shadow of the Erdtree. Both trees would grow to epic proportions and inspire the people of their lands, who would become their faithful. While the Erdtree is golden and brilliant, the Scadutree is thorny and dark. The Scadutree actually has two trunks, one wrapping around the other in a deadly embrace. This symbol, a sort of spiral reminiscent of the natural tangles of the Crucible horns and knots, is seen often in the Realm of Shadow, especially among the Hornsent, whether in their magic or in their architecture. In spite of being cut off from the rest of the Lands Between, the inhabitants of the Realm of Shadow nonetheless remained close to the energy of the Crucible, developing their own beliefs and practices around it.

By placing the veil over the region, Marika brought about another notable consequence. Metyr, Mother of Fingers, who had been spending time in the depths of the earth in the center of the Lands Between, was also cut off from the rest of the world. "Despite being broken and abandoned, she kept waiting for another message to come," states the description of the Staff of the Great Beyond. As the Greater Will could no longer easily communicate with its emissaries in the Lands Between, changes of plan would henceforth take a lot longer to enact.

During this period of the distant past, Marika had another child: the description of Messmer's Kindling notes, "Messmer, much like his younger sister, bore a vision of fire." That younger sister is another character we'll meet much later on in this story: the red-haired Melina, whose body was ravaged by fire and who also lost an eye–the left one.

For the time being, the goddess Marika would begin her ascension to ever-higher spheres, toward power and prosperity that has remained unmatched to this day.

⬧ The start of her reign

Whether by force or by seduction, no one knows, Marika began by taking power as the queen of the region that's home to the city of Leyndell. At the time, the city wasn't the enormous capital we know today; still, it was likely a prosperous little city not far from the growing Erdtree.

We can imagine that Marika's royal power was similar to that of the House of Caria, ruling over the region to the west of Leyndell and the Altus Plateau. The House of Caria was led by Rennala, also known as the "Queen of the Full Moon." Rennala and her people owed their power and knowledge to the astrologers, figures from the Eternal Cities from whom they had descended. The Carian region of Liurnia, and later the Academy of Raya Lucaria, developed thanks to magic, with the Carians building a country and a culture around the teaching and practice of sorcery.

To the south, the Stormveil region was also governed by a monarch, known as the Stormhawk King. The proud Stormhawk King and his people, a race of giant hawks, lived in an extremely hostile environment, beaten by a perpetual thunderstorm with cutting winds, as we learn from the ashes of Stormhawk Deenh.

◈ Wars

The reasons for these first wars—there will be many more to come!—in the Lands Between are not very clear. Did they have something to do with the Erdtree and the favors it might have granted to the winners? Some sort of inscrutable conflict between Empyreans? Or could they simply have been wars between regions trying to gain territory and influence? Whatever the case may be, during this period, "faith and battle went hand in hand," according to the Erdtree Bow, and Marika came out victorious from a number of these conflagrations. Backed up by her faithful Leyndell Knights, a group of burly and skillful warriors, as well as a band of mercenaries led by a man named Godfrey—previously known to his soldiers as Hoarah Loux—Marika triumphed over the Stormhawks and the Fire Giants.

"The age of the Erdtree began amongst conflict, when Godfrey was lord of the battlefield," states the description of the Elden Lord Crown. The powerful warrior dueled with the Storm Lord and led the war against the Giants. The Fire Giants had for ages cut paths into the cliffsides at the Mountaintops of the Giants, far to the north of Leyndell. They decided to march on the Erdtree to burn it using the Giantsflame, also known as the Flame of Ruin. The eternal, diabolical flame was a power the Giants had borrowed from a "fell god," according to the description of the incantation Burn, O Flame! It's often said that with great power comes great responsibility: the Giants actually perceived the flame as a curse, as they were bound to serve as its keepers for all eternity. So, they tried to attack the Erdtree, but Marika and Godfrey counterattacked and challenged them on their home turf. In this battle, Marika and Godfrey were assisted by trolls (Troll's Golden Sword)—descendants of the Giants, according to the Troll's Hammer—as well as by the Knights of Zamor. These knights skillfully used ice magic that was particularly effective at countering the infernal flames of their adversaries. The Knights of Zamor had always been considered the sworn enemies of the Fire Giants, and their participation in this conflict sealed the deal. They were hailed as heroes once the Giants had been beaten into submission and the Flame of Ruin had been contained. Godfrey and his warriors also played a central role in the major victory. To mark the end of the war, Marika cast a curse on the most powerful of the Fire Giants, a colossus with almost godlike status because of his incredible strength and his reputation among his people. Cursed and defeated, from then on, he would have to guard the Giantsflame, contained in the Forge of the Giants, as the destructive fire could never be extinguished entirely, and thus would always pose a threat to the Erdtree.

In fact, after this event, "fire was prohibited to those who served the Erdtree," according to the description of the Spark Aromatic. The fear was so great that certain symbols were removed from emblems. This was the case for the Candletree, as some saw in the minimalist representation of the Erdtree an intolerable image of its branches on fire (Candletree Wooden Shield). In the same way that Messmer's flame came to be viewed as "original sin," people began to use the term "cardinal sin" for the idea of the burning of the Erdtree. We will return to this concept of "cardinal sin" much later in this story.

◈ Her marriage to Godfrey, her first Elden Lord

After seeing the champion Godfrey's feats on the battlefield, Marika asked him to be her consort. After their marriage, the warrior king wielded the Elden Ring and took his place on the throne of Leyndell. He began carrying Serosh, known as the Beast Regent, on his back to channel the beast's warrior impulses. Serosh also served as an advisor to Godfrey. It was official: Godfrey had become the "first" Elden Lord. First, according to the history written by the goddess-queen Marika, who began making many changes in the Lands Between.

She made Leyndell the capital, which developed into a majestic metropolis over the years. Next to it, the Erdtree also reached its zenith. It was the beginning of the tree's golden age. Troubadours and minstrels sang the praises of the Erdtree's champions (Harp Bow). All across the Lands Between, ritual battles "held to honor the Erdtree" (Ritual Sword Talisman) took place in arenas. Blood flowed for the glory of the Erdtree; the souls of fierce gladiators killed in battle helped it shine bright. The Erdtree also released sap. Like sacred tears occasionally raining down from its branches, the sap was blessed and was considered a godsend for the Lands Between. After hardening, the sap would turn to amber, "treasured as the most precious of jewels," according to the description of the Crimson Amber Medallion. Over time, a number of small Erdtree sprouts were found in various regions of the Lands Between. These saplings with extraordinary characteristics were dubbed

Minor Erdtrees and were thus venerated. The description of the Flask of Wondrous Physick states, "Basins are placed at the feet of Minor Erdtrees throughout the Lands Between in order to collect their crystallized tears." Guardians were assigned to protect the young sacred trees, being promised that "their deaths [would] lead not to destruction, but instead to renewed, eternal life" (Guardian Mask). Thus, driven by unshakable faith, an entire religious ecosystem developed around the divine golden Erdtree, as well as around Marika, Godfrey, and the capital city of Leyndell.

❖ The birth of the Golden Lineage

Godwyn the Golden was the first-born son of Godfrey and Marika. His long blond hair, inherited from his mother, fascinated people. He was a demigod admired by all. Godwyn, in turn, had his own children, who later had their own descendants. No one would be able to draw an exact family tree of the golden prince's bloodline, but it very well may include the characters Godefroy and Godrick. In any case, they were also considered demigods. However, their blood from the Golden Lineage was diluted over the generations, making them lesser members of the royal family, thus with less importance in the royal court.

But they weren't the only ones to be out of favor: things were much worse for Godfrey and Marika's two other children. The twins Mohg and Morgott were struck with the Omen curse. Born covered in horns, the Omens actually suffer from an incurable degenerative disease. Furthermore, as they are not touched by the Grace of the Erdtree, their souls are not guided there upon their death. Because of all this, the Omens were generally shunned. Even worse, the horns of most newborn Omens were excised, often leading to their deaths (Omen Bairn). In the royal family, they decided not to cut off the Omens' horns, but Mohg and Morgott were hidden away underground, imprisoned, even chained, for all eternity. Thus, from the time of their birth, Mohg and Morgott were kept in a dungeon below the capital. Undoubtedly, the Omens would have been worshiped by the Hornsent, who were also deprived of Grace and fascinated by the horns of the Crucible, but Marika saw the horns as a curse, an unfortunate reminder of her secret past. The Golden Lineage was cursed and the perfection of the goddess Marika had begun to show the first signs of weakness.

❖ The first signs of weakness

The Omen curse spread across all of the Lands Between and ravaged the population, even affecting the almighty royal family of Leyndell.

Almost certainly taking advantage of this moment of doubt and weakness, the Ancient Dragons suddenly reappeared to attack the royal capital. The assault was led by Gransax, armed with a giant spear several dozen meters long, who toppled for the first (and last) time the two fortified walls surrounding Leyndell (Bolt of Gransax). The Erdtree was once again threatened, and this new war brought terrible violence to the Lands Between. The old Crucible Knights lent their might to Godfrey's army, which took on the majestic winged creatures of the prehistoric era. To do so, the royal troops used the Giants' sacred art of smithing (description of the Hammer) to improve their equipment and boost their power. They also learned to use the Golden Lightning Fortification incantation, offering them strong resistance to the dragons' lightning. The Tree Sentinels—a small order of formidable knights wearing heavy armor and helms decorated with a golden blazon in the shape of a bush—also played a decisive role in the battle. The Ancient Dragons began losing their granite scales, and thus their immortality. They were driven back, with Godfrey once again proving his supremacy as a warrior. To this day, the capital bears the marks of the war against the dragons, as a giant dragon, in fact Gransax himself, remains petrified in the very heart of the city.

It was also during this battle that Fortissax, considered to be the most powerful of all Ancient Dragons, formed a friendship with Prince Godwyn, following a legendary duel. Out of their meeting and mutual fascination formed a new religious practice in the capital known as Dragon Communion. Fortissax's sister, Lansseax, took on a human form and played the role of a priestess in the cult of the Ancient Dragons. Initially driven by Prince Godwyn, the new beliefs became tolerated and accepted in the capital (Gravel Stone Seal). Knights even discovered in the religion new forms of attack and protection based on lightning. Certain Tree Sentinels joined the movement, believing "the only way to truly protect the Erdtree was to become dragons themselves" (Malformed Dragon Helm). Later, Dragon Communion came to be considered a "grave transgression," according to the description of the Magma Wyrm's Scalesword, particularly when members of this cult, known as Drake Warriors, pursued every means available to transform themselves into dragons. In doing so, they would gain greater power, vitality, and intelligence, but at what cost? Most of those cult members who subjected themselves to this experiment, sometimes even great war heroes, either perished or succumbed to madness. "Those who have performed the Dragon Communion will find their humanity slowly slipping away," says the description for the Magma Breath incantation. This marked a very dark chapter in Leyndell history.

Meanwhile, across the Lands Between, many prophets began to catch glimpses in their divine visions of the return of the Flame of Ruin. They saw the flame leaving the Forge of the Giants and burning the Erdtree, this cardinal sin thus bringing an end to the golden age of Marika, but also to the Order imposed long ago by the

Greater Will. The Flame Sling incantation's description recounts that prophets who announced this bad omen were banished from the Erdtree religion. They were forced to wear large blocks of wood around their necks so they could be easily identified. Thus, the people, blindly following the authorities, would be able to recognize them and would ignore their supposedly false prophecies.

And yet, these unfortunate prophets were not entirely wrong. In fact, the Fire Monks who had long assisted the Fire Giant in guarding the Flame of Ruin began to show signs of madness. After all those years of protecting the flame, some began to heed its siren call. A man named Birac, one of the highest ranking Fire Monks, "severed his own head as a lesson to the others" (Cranial Vessel Candlestand). Because of this act of faith, he came to be considered a saint among the Fire Monks who still had their sanity. However, his sacrifice failed to save those who had been corrupted by the Giantsflame.

◈ The fragmentation of the Rune of Death

With the deterioration of her power threatening her authority, Marika surprised everyone by doing something that would forever put her at odds with the original intentions of the Greater Will, the Outer God that had once turned the queen into a powerful goddess to serve its aims. She betrayed the Greater Will. As she carried out her plan, Marika almost certainly anticipated that the Greater Will would react very slowly, especially since Metyr, Mother of Fingers, had been trapped in the Realm of Shadow. "The Fingers remain still. Shaken by this turn of events, they are busy consulting the Greater Will. When they are finished, the Fingers will once again offer their guidance. But thousands, if not tens of thousands, of moons must first pass." These are the words of Finger Reader Enia. It would seem that the timeline of the Lands Between is fixed, beyond control, endless. But in this case, in the span of a few thousand years, as the Two Fingers conferred with the Greater Will to prepare a response, Marika had the opportunity to drastically change the face of the world.

The event that triggered this schism between the goddess and the Outer God was the theft and hiding of the Rune of Death, also known as Destined Death. The rune was removed from the almighty Elden Ring, and the very concept of death was erased from the Lands Between. Mortals became immortal. Their souls would no longer return to the Erdtree. Order and its perfect balance were corrupted. Life would henceforth prevail over death.

On the orders of Marika, her Shadow Maliketh defeated the Gloam-Eyed Queen and her Godskin Apostles and Nobles, who, I'll remind you, derived their god-slaying powers from Destined Death. Maliketh then recovered the Rune of Death and sealed it within his sword, Black Blade, from which he would later get his nickname. The Shadowbound Beast then made a vow to protect the rune with every fiber of his being for the rest of his existence.

◈ The Golden Order

As stagnation set in, and while the Two Fingers were busy struggling to confer with the Greater Will about what to do next, Marika established the Golden Order. "The Golden Order was created by confining Destined Death," states the description of the Mending Rune of the Death-Prince. At first glance, it would seem that the Golden Order was the logical successor to the Order established by the Greater Will and its vassals long ago, reworked and improved by the goddess to whom the Elden Ring had been officially entrusted. As such, from the outside, it would seem that there was nothing extraordinary about it. In reality, "The Golden Order is founded on the principle that Marika is the one true god," according to the wise words of Corhyn, a scribe who centuries after the founding would document—reluctantly—the true values of the Golden Order.

Notably, the organization was made up of religious fundamentalists guided by a search for knowledge, a universal but particularly vague objective. They aimed to gain "advanced mathematical and mechanical understanding" (Pulley Bow) as they conducted their precious research. "The fundamentalists describe the Golden Order through the powers of regression and causality. Causality is the pull between meanings; that which links all things in a chain of relation," states the description of the Law of Causality incantation. The description of the incantation's alter ego, the Law of Regression, states, "Regression is the pull of meaning; that all things yearn eternally to converge." Indeed, the fundamentalists of the Golden Order unlocked part of the mystery, as causality (the link between different things) and regression (fate) are two complementary facets of Marika. Going beyond the classic concepts of good and evil, which create balance in the universe, causality and regression are Marika's yin and yang. In spite of their learning and rigor, the fundamentalists of the past didn't really understand the full truth of these concepts, nor of Marika herself. In fact, causality and regression fed into two distinct—and secret!—personalities of the goddess. Causality for Marika and regression for Radagon, her masculine side who had been part of her at least since the events at the Gate of Divinity. Don't worry, we'll come back to this subject, as Radagon will play an important role later in the history of the Lands Between.

For now, just know that while Marika and Radagon's oneness remained a well-guarded secret, the fundamentalists correctly discerned these two concepts, and the Golden Order continued to grow around Marika's aura and dogma. Still, it's important to understand that the fundamentalists were true fanatics. "How easy it is for learning and learnedness to be reduced to the ravings of fanatics; all the good and the great wanted, in their foolishness, was an absolute evil to contend with," states the description of the Order Healing incantation. Later, they would find an ideal target: the strange beings known as "Those Who Live in Death." Still, we can easily imagine that others considered to be impure, like the Omens, Misbegotten, and demi-humans, all with links to the Crucible, would likely have been viewed with suspicion by the Golden Order at this time. It's possible that these people, too, were hunted by the Order. In any case, that's what's implied by the description for the spirit ashes of Perfumer Tricia, a "healer who dedicated her efforts to treating Misbegotten, Omen, and all those seen as impure."

◈ The exile of Hoarah Loux

Godfrey had become the most powerful of beings. He had triumphed over the Stormhawks, the Giants, and even the Ancient Dragons, the creatures who had reigned supreme since time immemorial. He had reached the pinnacle of his art and no battle was enough for him. But he had gone too far, and the Grace of the Erdtree abandoned him. "The hue of Lord Godfrey's eyes faded," as states the description of the Elden Lord Armor.

The first Elden Lord, cut off from the Erdtree, abdicated the throne and bid farewell to Serosh, the Beast Regent, to become a humble warrior again under his original name, Hoarah Loux. Becoming a Tarnished, which is to say, one without Grace, he led the other Tarnished to regions beyond the sea. The exiles embarked on a fleet of ships to travel to the Badlands. The Long March had begun, and it would be punctuated by terrible battles. Hoarah Loux even ended up breaking his axe during one of them. Meanwhile, one of his ships was damaged and had to be abandoned, according to the description of the Rusted Anchor. The army of Tarnished would not set foot again in the Lands Between for many long years.

Intrigue in Liurnia

With Godfrey gone, the Elden throne stood vacant once again. Marika had already drawn the ire of the Greater Will by stealing the Rune of Death, then founding the Golden Order for her own glory. As such, there was no way she could leave the throne without a lord, especially given the great upheaval happening in the world. She set her sights on the next region over from the capital, Liurnia, another place with a rich history, particularly thanks to a man named Radagon, who would go on to become Marika's second Elden Lord after agreeing to be her consort. Before we get into this next chapter in Lands Between history, let's go back in time a bit to really understand the inner workings of Liurnia and its royal family, the House of Caria, a rival at the time to the Golden Lineage of Leyndell.

Did Marika go to war with Liurnia to expand her influence? To gain territory? The reason for the confrontation might have actually been more subtle than that. Indeed, the description of the Monk's Flameblade indicates: "The monks came to the land of Liurnia in pursuit of a fugitive who stole their fire." So, we can see that there was a conflict tied to the role of the Fire Monks, a conflict that would have drawn a swift reaction from Marika, given her historical fear of seeing the Erdtree go up in flames. Marika would have dispatched to Liurnia a whole regiment of soldiers to put the thorny situation to rest. Still, this is just a theory, and in any case, relations between Leyndell and the House of Caria had likely already deteriorated by that point.

What's more, even within the Carian royal family itself, it seems that there was some division. Indeed, the Carian princess, Rellana, the younger sister of Queen Rennala, "disavowed her birthright" (Remembrance of the Twin Moon Knight) and allied herself with the Golden Order. Rellana took part in a ritual battle, "a demonstration of fidelity to the Erdtree," according to the description of the Carian Thrusting Shield. Queen Rennala didn't necessarily hold it against her little sister, as she gave her "a gift of lustrous black hair" (Rellana's Helm), but the schism within the royal family likely contributed to the conflict in the region of Liurnia.

◈ Radagon, Champion of Leyndell, versus Rennala, Queen of Caria

Two great battles raged across Liurnia during this period. Leyndell's army, led by Radagon, faced off against the smaller Carian army. Some even say it only had around 20 knights! However, the Carian Knights were enhanced by the powerful magic of glintstone, which enchanted their weapons and armor. They also gained an advantage from their swords, which served as catalysts helping them use sorcery in battle. The Carian Knight Helm's description indicates that they "were all heroes of the highest honors." The Carian army also had a few enchanted troll knights. The description of the Troll Knight's Sword tells us they were "called into service when the Queen invoked an oath they swore." With his enemies making heavy use of magic, Radagon relied on the Barrier of Gold incantation to make his troops more impervious to their spells. Radagon thus managed to pull off a victory in the first battle. Word of "Radagon's glory"–words that can be made out on a funerary monument in Liurnia–spread across the Lands Between.

From there, Leyndell's new champion took part in another battle against the Carians. This time, Queen Rennala was better prepared. She surrounded her manor with formidable magic traps that prevented Radagon's army from approaching the fortress.

Still, Radagon was not going to give up and tapped into the power of the Church of Vows, located atop a plateau in Liurnia. The one-of-a-kind blessing of the church—to this day—cleanses a person of their sins and can repair any broken bond between people. Using Celestial Dew, an ancient relic from the Eternal Cities, where "the stars of the night sky guided fate," Radagon invoked the blessing of the Church of Vows and brought an end to the war with Rennala, then boldly asked for her hand in marriage.

◈ Radagon's marriage to Rennala

The queen and the champion got married in the Church of Vows, giving it the reputation of having united Leyndell and Caria, the warm sun and the frigid moon. The site is even more symbolic as, from it, you can see the Academy of Raya Lucaria, Caria Manor, and the Erdtree. A Glintstone Kris was given by the Academy to Leyndell in a gesture of peace. Radagon, meanwhile, gave a gift of illustrious golden sewing materials, thus sealing the reconciliation between the two kingdoms. Other artisans took part in this peace-making event, including one who made the magnificent Full Moon Crossbow, whose two loading disks represent the moon overlapping the sun.

In spite of the rapprochement, Radagon continued to distrust Carian magic. He and Rennala moved to the Academy of Raya Lucaria, where magical research and teaching prospered. While the Carians derived their magic from the power of the moon, the historic emblem of Queen Rennala, the scholars at the Academy tended to get their power from the stars, following in the ancient heritage of the astrologers of the Eternal Cities. Most importantly, the Academy's teachers experimented with the magic of glintstone, a powerful and intriguing source of energy. Glintstone originally came from the Crystalian people, mysterious beings with bodies made entirely from minerals. With all this said, the Academy's rules and policies were subject to change.

For example, the pioneers of glintstone sorcery, masters Azur and Lusat, were banished from the Academy, in spite of their revolutionary research. Rennala felt that their powerful magic was too frightening, and they were forced to leave the Academy, even as their bodies began to transform into glintstone. While the students and scholars continued to study glintstone, Azur and Lusat's "primeval current," as it was called, was forbidden and was eventually forgotten. To give you an idea of the kind of rituals performed with the primeval current, the Primal Glintstone Blade tells us: "The old sorcerers would slice open their hearts with these blades to imbue a primal glintstone with their soul, and thus did they die." The Graven-Mass Talisman's description explains that "to those who cleave to [the primeval current's] teachings, the act of collecting sorcerers to fashion them into the seeds of stars is but another path of scientific inquiry."

So, the Academy's scholars began studying other glintstones. Some came from mines, but the fragments collected were "tinged with unstable magic" (Glintstone Scrap), and their quality was rarely suitable for experienced sorcerers. Other rarer and more prestigious glintstones were "formed from starry amber," according to the description of the Raya Lucarian Robe. This material from the stars was perfect for the school's needs.

Different curricula and approaches to magic developed at the Academy. Some were highly respected, like the Karolos Conspectus, based on the study of comets, and the Twinsage Conspectus, whose scholars "are the academy's elite," according to the description of the Twinsage Sorcerer Ashes. Other schools of thought became heretical, like the Lazuli Conspectus, whose scholars had the gall to consider the moon to be equal to the stars for the purposes of sorcery. In any case, the Academy's reputation was well founded. It was even talked about in Sellia, Town of Sorcery, located in the Caelid region, far away in the very southeast corner of the Lands Between.

Radagon and Rennala took advantage of the Academy's reputation to found a magical empire and expand their influence. They had three children together: Ranni, Rykard, and Radahn. As Rellana had left the Carian royal family, Ranni became the only Princess of Caria, taking up residence on the grounds of Caria Manor in one of the towers known as the Three Sisters. The historical archives mention Rennala and Rellana, but there is no trace of a third sister. We also find few details on the upbringing of Ranni, Rykard, and Radahn. They would, however, make history later in their lives, after the civil war that would tear apart the region of Liurnia.

✦ Civil war between the Raya Lucaria Academy and the House of Caria

To this day, we don't know what triggered this civil war, but undoubtedly it had something to do with Radagon's actions toward the House of Caria. For example, after marrying Rennala, he ordered that the Carian magic preceptors wear masks with the mouths sewn shut with golden thread, a symbol underscoring the fact that he expected them to keep their mouths shut (Mask of Confidence). And in fact, the stitching theme is typical of Radagon: it can be seen anywhere where he has exerted his influence. The symbol looks like an elaborate grille of diagonal lines.

Also, let's not forget that Radagon's initial goal, as champion of Leyndell, was to depose the Carian royal family. While his feelings for Rennala and choice to marry her were probably sincere, the House of Caria undoubtedly remained a target for him. He stoked existing rivalries between the Academy and the House of Caria, eventually leading to the outbreak of the civil war.

The Academy resisted the royal family's assaults using the Terra Magica sorcery. The way the spell works is that it boosts the magical power of the people located within its zone of effect. As such, it allowed even a novice sorcerer to gain the power of a master. The Terra Magica sorcery was cast from the Academy's highest belfry to cover the widest possible perimeter—actually covering the entire property. The House of Caria's troops were thrown off balance by the response from the army of powerful mages.

Meanwhile, at Caria Manor, the traps from the previous war were still in place. However, instead of Leyndell soldiers looking to seize the fortress, it was a group called the Cuckoo Knights. The knights had a sinister reputation and used a sort of "faux sorcery" from a type of glintstone; they followed no rules or code of ethics. The Academy gave them their magical power without actually teaching them how to use it; in exchange, the knights were expected to lead the assault on Caria Manor.

The Cuckoo Knights perished, but the House of Caria was left as a shadow of its former self. The Liurnian civil war ended up decimating both sides. It was at that point that Radagon surprised everyone. He abandoned his wife, Rennala, and returned to Leyndell, where he married the goddess Marika, thus becoming the second Elden Lord.

Marika and Radagon

◈ Queen Marika's second marriage

As Godfrey had gone into exile in the Badlands with other Tarnished, the Elden throne sat vacant, awaiting a new lord. Queen Marika, who had become known as "the Eternal" after the theft of Destined Death, began searching for a new consort. She set her sights on Radagon and called him back to her in Leyndell.

While it was hard to imagine Marika and Radagon being fused together as a single entity when she appeared at the Gate of Divinity, the concept is all the more extraordinary when you consider Radagon literally splitting off from Marika to go to war in Liurnia. And what should we make of the marriage between the two, with Marika recalling her alter ego to make him her consort and thus claim the Elden Ring? Just how far does this Machiavellian plan go?

The queen's dual identities became the Golden Order's most sensitive secret. However, a sculptor of great renown discovered the confidential information, and as he carved a noble statue of Radagon in the heart of the capital, he worked an enchantment into it. If you cast the Law of Regression incantation (as a reminder, "regression" is one of the two pillars of the Golden Order and is associated with Radagon) at the statue, it reveals the enchanted illusion created by the sculptor. Radagon's statue transforms into a statue of Marika. And a clear message is sent: "Radagon is Marika."

So, to summarize: Marika saw an opportunity, with the Elden throne vacant and the Two Fingers busy laboriously conferring with the Greater Will, and thus staying out of the intrigue in the Lands Between, and she swiftly took action. She took advantage of the widespread renown Radagon had gained as champion for his exploits since the war against the House of Caria and used it as an excuse to marry another version of herself. Their first two secret children, Messmer and Melina, had been afflicted by a curse, and that misfortune continued for their new progeny. Radagon and Marika had a set of cursed twins: Malenia and Miquella.

◈ The birth of the cursed twins Malenia and Miquella

With Radagon having returned to Marika, the children he had with Rennala were also recognized as demigods. Ranni, Rykard, and Radahn thus became part of the divine lineage by marriage, thereby getting mixed up in the intrigue between the Leyndell and Carian royal families.

The birth of the twins Malenia and Miquella added the final branches to Marika's family tree. "Miquella and Malenia are both the children of a single god. As such, they are both Empyreans, but suffered afflictions from birth. One was cursed with eternal childhood, and the other harbored rot within." With these few words, the description of the Remembrance of the Rot Goddess object paints a clear and accurate portrait of the twins. Miquella and Malenia were exceptional–being Empyrean by birth and not through selection by the Two Fingers–but were also cursed. Miquella would never grow up and Malenia suffered from the scarlet rot, a deadly disease that would soon spread across the Lands Between, especially affecting the Caelid region.

We have little information about the twins' upbringing. However, we do know that Miquella had a close relationship with his father, Radagon. Miquella gave his father, among other things, a unique incantation, the Triple Rings of Light, proof of the boy's exceptional spiritual strength. His twin sister, Malenia, admired her brother. The description of Malenia's Winged Helm includes a quote from her: "He possesses the wisdom, the allure, of a god. He is the most fearsome Empyrean of all." Malenia would assist him in pursuing his ambitions all throughout her life, earning herself the nickname "Blade of Miquella." Miquella, meanwhile, admired his half-brother Radahn. Because of his power and his unique aura as a formidable warrior, Miquella hoped that Radahn might one day become his consort.

However, the fate of the twins diverged from that of the Erdtree and Marika. As we'll see later. For now, let's take a few moments to examine one of the goddess Marika's initiatives that never made it into the official history of the Golden Order. And that was by design, as it concerned her mysterious past.

Marika's revenge

◈ Plotting

Marika never forgave nor forgot what the Hornsent had done to her shamanic people long ago. Her persecutors had been trapped in the Realm of Shadow for many years, but that wasn't enough for the goddess. She held onto an age-old thirst for vengeance. With the intention of massacring the Hornsent in the Realm of Shadow, she put together an army made up of soldiers bearing a Scadutree emblem on their armor, as well as fierce knights and Furnace Golems—enormous creatures that look like the embodiment of the Fire Giants' hellfire. The army was led by a commander named Gaius, a first-generation Albinauric. The Albinaurics are magical beings, originally created by humans, who are unable to use their legs. As such, they get around on mounts, their bodies becoming one with the creatures. Gaius rode a ferocious boar, and his almost sibling-like rivalry with Radahn, with the two competing in feats of strength and gravity sorcery, eventually propelled the Albinauric to become the commander of the queen's new army. Gaius, too, was considered to be cursed, and perhaps that's another reason why he was chosen for the task. In his role as commander, Gaius became the right-hand man to Messmer, who Marika had asked to lead the crusade in her name.

A quick aside here: the term "crusade" is used many times in the game to refer to this offensive, which has interesting implications, as the Hornsent are untouched by Grace and would thus have been considered heathens in Marika's view. What's more, a handful of priests were also sent to the Realm of Shadow, where "these keepers of the faith fought bitterly to spread their gospel," according to the description of the Battlefield Priest's Cookbook. Notably, they would use the Iris of Grace or the Iris of Occultation to either quell or intensify "the fears of their flock."

At the same time, churches dedicated to Marika were built in the Land of Shadow. It was a true crusade in the religious sense! End of the aside.

Up to that point, Messmer had lived in the Realm of Shadow, hidden away and constantly tortured by the fire of original sin, the fire of the Abyssal Serpent holed up where his right eye should have been. Thankfully, two winged serpents, depicted on Messmer's Helm (and on the Serpent Crest Shield), "were there through his eternity of suffering." Messmer despised the fire eating away at him, and yet he was unable to get rid of it. When Marika asked him to lead the crusade against the Hornsent, after the ages of waiting in isolation, Messmer agreed. He finally had an outlet for his immeasurable hatred.

✦ Massacres

And Messmer set out to massacre. By fire. Much of the Realm of Shadow was reduced to ashes, along with its inhabitants, whether Hornsent or not. Even Romina, Saint of the Bud, saw her ancient church destroyed in the Ruins of Rauh. All across the plains, the Hornsent were impaled, along with the Divine Beast Warriors, imposing lion-headed fighters respected for their strength and talent in battle. Messmer was nicknamed "the Impaler"; he inspired sheer terror in his enemies.

The description of the Messmer Soldier Armor tells us: "Though the chestpiece features a Scadutree motif, gold has been used for its engraving. A small consolation to those forced to wage a war without grace or honor." It paints a dramatic picture, one reflected in other descriptions as well, like that of the Crusade Insignia: "The warriors who fought in the crusade set aside both honor and mercy to wantonly impale and scorch those deemed impure. Those who felt invigorated by each cry of death were the same men who were certain of the sanctity of the campaign."

Among those warriors, the Black Knights were the most devoted and the most violent, using weapons imbued with powerful Erdtree incantations. However, their captain, Huw, and his father, Andreas, rebelled against Messmer. Sadly, they failed and were imprisoned in a crypt.

Discontent arose among the Fire Knights as well. Although Salza had "burned more villages and scorched more land than any other" (Rain of Fire incantation), he ended up refusing to take part in the crusade. The Fire Knights served as Messmer's bodyguards. They knew of his curse and actually sported his winged serpents on their armor. In addition to using his unique fire magic, the Fire Knights were fascinated by Messmer, his torments, and his rage. For example, Queelign—a name that references Quelaag from *Dark Souls*, the emblematic creature of the Chaotic Flame—wanted to become a second Impaler, just like Messmer.

Other knights joined Messmer's troops, including Godwyn's men belonging to the Leyndell religion of the Ancient Dragons. They had mastered lightning spells, considered in the present "a lost art in the Lands Between" (Knight's Lightning Spear).

The House of Caria also sent a battalion to the Realm of Shadow. They were led by the former princess Rellana, known as the Twin Moon Knight. Above all, she wanted to "save" Messmer from his curse, but Rellana also knew that "not even the brilliance of the moon could grant him succor" (Remembrance of the Twin Moon Knight). Still, she received the title of "Sword of Messmer" and even adapted her style of combat, fusing the lunar force of the Carian royal family with a sort of "golden flame" (Rellana's Twin Blades) from Messmer. Rellana went to the Realm of Shadow accompanied by her faithful chamberlain, the knight Moonrithyll, as well as a handful of trolls (friends of Moonrithyll), glintstone mages, and, of course, the Carian Knights with their emblematic spellblades. Rellana's preceptor, named Ymir, also known as the High Priest, rounded out the convoy from Liurnia, but his attention was quickly diverted to the study of the Finger Ruins. As such, he did not end up taking part in Messmer and Rellana's battle campaign.

They carried out the crusade against the Hornsent, and thus Marika's arcane plot for vengeance. However, they were stopped before they could finish the deed. The reasons for the stoppage remain murky, but it's very possible that Messmer, torn between his unconditional love for his mother and the feeling of abandonment that had been gnawing away at him for an eternity (when the player beats him, he says "Mother... Marika... A curse... upon thee..."), decided to not fully comply with Marika's orders. The character Leda tells us: "Queen Marika commanded Sir Messmer to purge the tower folk. A cleansing by fire." She's referring to Enir-Ilim, the tower of the Hornsent, where the Gate of Divinity is located. "The majesty of the white tower, stretching to reach the gods, even inspired a secret faith in the invaders, the people of the Erdtree," states the description of the Spiraltree Seal. Feeling torn, Messmer chose to plunge the tower into shadow. It was a way to make the place disappear without actually exterminating its inhabitants, much like Marika had done when she placed a veil over the Realm of Shadow.

In doing so, perhaps Messmer hoped to once again get his mother's attention, at least to get some answers, but he received radio silence from the Lands Between. Going beyond the stagnation that had already persisted for far too long because of Marika, a new event would overturn the (golden) order that had reigned up to that point. It was a twist of fate triggered by the princess and witch Ranni, the daughter of Rennala and Radagon, and thus Messmer's half-sister.

The Conspiracy of the Black Knives

◈ Ranni's choice

After a few thousand years spent in consultation with the Greater Will, the Two Fingers finally returned. Probably aiming to overthrow Marika, they chose Ranni to become an Empyrean. She then received her Shadow, by the name of Blaidd. Playing the same role that Maliketh played for Marika, Blaidd, known as the Half-Wolf, was tasked with serving and watching over Ranni to help her embrace her destiny as an Empyrean.

However, it seems that Ranni wasn't interested in becoming a goddess. She had no desire to take a consort in order to wield the Elden Ring and initiate a new cycle in furtherance of the Greater Will's aims. At some point in the past, the Carian princess had encountered an entity known as the Dark Moon, as noted in the description of the legendary sorcery Ranni's Dark Moon: "This moon was encountered by a young Ranni, led by the hand of her mother, Rennala. What she beheld was cold, dark, and veiled in occult mystery." The true nature of this Dark Moon, which is also described as "cold" (Freezing Pot), discovered by Ranni remains a mystery to this day. We know from the description of the Moon of Nokstella talisman that it "was the guide of countless stars," an important bit of information given Ranni's fate. But we'll come back to that in the next chapter. Could the Dark Moon be an Outer God like the Greater Will? Or is it some other force existing far above the scheming in the Lands Between? In any case, we know that it appears from time to time in the night sky, competing with the other moon—that is, Rennala's moon!

Ranni's secret mentor, an old snow witch she met in the forest, tried to teach Ranni "to fear the dark moon," as noted in the description of the Frozen Armament sorcery. It seems that there is a strong connection between ice magic and the Dark Moon. Although Ranni appreciated the old witch's lessons on cold sorceries, she was undeterred by her teacher's warnings and found herself drawn to the Dark Moon, especially at a moment in her life when her obligations as an Empyrean began to weigh on her.

At that point, Ranni wanted to give up her Empyrean status. But that was easier said than done. Thankfully for her, Blaidd, who was supposed to take action if Ranni tried to abandon her duties, had developed great affection for the princess. "In defiance of the fate he was born to, Blaidd swore to serve no master but Ranni," states the description of the Royal Greatsword, a weapon imbued with cold magic and wielded by the Half-Wolf. The Carian princess surrounded herself with people she could trust: Blaidd, of course, but also the troll Iji, the Carian royal family's longtime blacksmith and adviser, as well as

Seluvis, a preceptor of the occult arts who also created numerous puppets with eerily human-like appearances.

Still, her oath to the Two Fingers could not be broken easily. Ranni cooked up a plan to free herself from her bonds. A plan that involved killing herself. With the Golden Order having been shaken by the theft of the Rune of Death, Ranni knew that she could push things even further with her extraordinary mission.

◈ Stealing a fragment of the Rune of Death

Marika's Shadow, Maliketh the Black Blade, was completely caught off guard when a fragment of Destined Death was stolen from him. A piece of his sword—where the Rune of Death had been hidden since he killed the Gloam-Eyed Queen, just to remind you—was broken off and stolen by Ranni.

Using a sinister ritual, the Carian princess witch imbued the Black Knives of hired assassins with the power of Destined Death, as we learn from the description of the Black Knifeprint. The assassins in question were women descended from the Numen (like Marika) living in the Eternal Cities. They wore concealing veils and carried god-slaying weapons enchanted with the power of Death. Their blades were dubbed the Black Knives, hence the name of the great drama that followed: the conspiracy known as the Night of the Black Knives.

◈ The deaths of Godwyn (spirit) and Ranni (body)

On the night in question, the Rune of Death killed not just one demigod, but two, in a very clever plot. Indeed, Ranni's body perished, but her spirit lived on. The other demigod killed on the Night of the Black Knives was Godwyn the Golden, whose spirit was destroyed while his body was spared. It's an incredibly odd situation, but one with great consequences.

Ranni's soul was transferred to a puppet created by Seluvis, with the appearance of Ranni's former mentor, the old snow witch. Although her new body was much more fragile, it allowed her to save her spirit from her Empyrean destiny. After the Night of the Black Knives, Ranni hid for a time—particularly because of the events that followed—valiantly protected by her Shadow. However, she made sure to give her brother Rykard the Blasphemous Claw, a "slab of rock engraved with traces of the Rune of Death." The precious object would allow Rykard to take on Maliketh if the Golden Lineage ever discovered the truth of Ranni's plot.

As for Godwyn, his body remained. However, left soulless, he would forever be collateral damage of Ranni's plan. Why him, you ask? It's likely that Ranni wanted to make full use of the Rune of Death's power; but the rune would only be satisfied by the complete death of a being, with both body and soul returning to the Erdtree. Ranni's soul needed to remain to serve the Dark Moon, but her body needed to die so she could free herself from her Empyrean status and fate. Killing Godwyn was an option that suited Ranni's needs. Furthermore, the (partial) death of a demigod, especially one belonging to the Golden Lineage of Godfrey and Marika, would distract people enough to allow Ranni to go into hiding. Finally, hiring the Numen assassins would sow doubt about Marika's intentions, further undermining her.

However, the goddess's reaction was much more violent than expected. Upon learning of the death of her first-born son, who up to that point was her only child spared from any kind of curse, Marika shattered the Elden Ring. The explosion was so violent that it reverberated all across the Lands Between, and even deep in the Realm of Shadow.

The Shattering

◈ The Elden Ring is broken

Marika smashed her stone hammer down on the Elden Ring. The interlocking runes shattered, breaking Marika's weapon in the process. A few runes became lodged in fissures in the hammer; the rest of the Ring was scattered. The rune fragments symbolized the sudden and irreversible shattering of the Order established long ago by the Greater Will. What's more, the term "Shattering" came to define this important period of Lands Between history, with a whole series of wars following in the wake of the Elden Ring's destruction.

Most of the demigods, Marika's direct descendants and stepchildren, managed to get their hands on significant fragments of the Elden Ring, which became known as "Great Runes." With these Great Runes in their possession, they discovered immense power that completely blinded them. With that, each one wanted to seize the Elden throne and reign over the Lands Between.

Marika was sealed away within the roots of the Erdtree, probably forced there by her other half, Radagon, whose symbol—the lattice pattern—can be found on the entrance blocked by Impenetrable Thorns toward the end of the game. Radagon also tried to mend the Elden Ring using the same stone hammer that had broken it, but was unsuccessful.

A brief aside here: it's interesting to see how Radagon constantly tries to balance out Marika's actions. In this case, she breaks the Elden Ring and so he tries to restore it. Before that, after Radagon married Marika, he put an end to the violent ritual battles held in arenas in honor of the Erdtree. Finally, the two talismans dedicated to Radagon's and Marika's respective personalities complement one another. Radagon's Seal increases vigor, endurance, strength, and dexterity, while Marika's Seal increases mind, intelligence, faith, and arcane. When equipped together, they boost all of the player's characteristics, forming a whole.

As a last resort, Radagon sealed himself inside the Erdtree with his other half, Marika. In spite of her terrible offense, Marika remained a goddess and still continued to bear the vision of the Elden Ring.

With the exception of Rykard, who holed up in his manor on Mt. Gelmir and simply defended his territory, the demigods, armed with their Great Runes, went to war with one another over several decades, forever transforming the landscape of the Lands Between. Bandits and mercenaries proliferated across most regions. The Perfumers, ancient healers and apothecaries respected by all, were enlisted into the armed forces, "trading their aromatics for poisons and explosives" (Perfumer Hood). The perfumes that they had previously used to heal people were transformed into poisons and other malign agents to be used against enemy soldiers. Some clans stayed out of the wars, like that of Rennala and the Academy, which sealed its doors from the start of the Shattering to openly declare its neutrality: the Raya Lucaria mages would not interfere in anyone's battle. During this same period, the Erdtree Avatars, tree-like giants with incredible strength, emerged. They were determined to protect the Minor Erdtrees, offshoots of the sacred tree which had begun to decline. All across the Lands Between, danger was everywhere.

❖ The Grafted clan

Back in Leyndell, the capital, a fierce battle raged. Godrick led an assault alongside Godefroy. Both were nicknamed "the Grafted." Grafting is a practice that involves taking body parts from others and attaching them to one's own body to gain greater power. Godrick and Godefroy both had atrocious, chilling appearances, with various members and growths sticking out from their bodies.

These descendants of Godwyn, and thus of Marika's Golden Lineage, attacked Leyndell with the intention of claiming the Elden throne. They had a large army behind them and managed to break through Leyndell's first perimeter wall. However, they did not make it through the second wall, harboring the city itself. To this day, we can see major scars of this war in the expanses between the two ramparts, signs of the unspeakable violence that ravaged both Godrick's army and the golden troops of Leyndell. The capital was protected by Morgott, who had emerged from the depths of the city where he had been imprisoned since his birth. After breaking free, he declared himself the Omen King and Lord of Leyndell.

Morgott possessed extraordinary strength, and there's no doubt that his presence and determination played a decisive role in the battle.

Godefroy the Grafted was captured by a warrior named Kristoff, "an honorable knight of Leyndell who was also a devout worshiper of the Ancient Dragons," according to Kristoff's ashes. Godefroy was then imprisoned in an evergaol. The evergaols, prisons existing outside of time and space, were created to hold the Golden Order's most formidable enemies. For example, under other circumstances, Bols, a troll in service to the Carian royal family, was imprisoned in one, as was Alecto, Black Knife Ringleader, who assassinated Godwyn.

Meanwhile, Godrick ended up facing off against Malenia. A tomb in Limgrave evokes his painful memory: "Godrick the Golden, humiliated. Having tasted defeat by the Blade of Miquella. Now on his knees, begging for mercy." As he left Leyndell, Godrick took with him many treasures, notably the Mimic's Veil, which allows the user to hide from view by mimicking nearby objects. All it took was for Malenia to be distracted for a second and Godrick managed to flee to Stormveil Castle, whose throne had been vacant since Marika's victory over the Stormhawks. However, the people of Limgrave were not especially happy to have him as their king. Godrick was unpopular and his penchant for grafting disgusted the locals. His soldiers who has escaped Leyndell with him terrorized everyone, remorselessly seizing property from anyone they could. They took many slaves and sent them to Stormveil Castle, including a man named Gostoc who, much later, would help the player character topple the Grafted—but not without robbing the player of a whole bunch of runes.

◈ The scarlet rot ravages Caelid

In the Wilds east of Limgrave, another battle raged that would go down in history. For years, the Cleanrot Knights, led by Malenia, relentlessly fought Radahn's soldiers. Known as the Redmanes, in honor of their general, Radahn, and his long red hair inherited from his father, Radagon, the soldiers of Caelid had no weaknesses and were first-rate warriors.

The war between the two clans stretched on and on, until the fateful Battle of Aeonia. The Swamp of Aeonia was situated next to Sellia, Town of Sorcery, in the heart of Caelid. Radahn's men, led by Commander O'Neil, faced off one last time against the Cleanrot Knights before Malenia invoked a "scarlet flower" (a term used in the description of the Scarlet Aeonia incantation), a giant bulb that exploded, spreading scarlet rot across the whole region. From then on, the land would be forever cursed, tainted by the terrible disease. Even the dragons who lived in Caelid had to migrate to the highlands to the north, giving the place the name Dragonbarrow. They built walls there imbued with eternal fire to protect them from the scarlet rot. The Redmane Fire Pot's description recounts that, to this day, the surviving Caelid soldiers, still tormented by the disease, continue to fight the spread of the scarlet rot using fire. However, the "abandoned children of the goddess" (Pest Threads incantation), easily recognized by their insect-like form, roam around the region as well, and each side continues to fight desperately for control of the territory. A hopeless situation. The use of the word "abandoned" to describe these servants of the scarlet rot is significant, as their goddess, Malenia, disappeared after the explosion of the scarlet flower. The description of the legendary ashes of Cleanrot Knight Finlay tells us: "Finlay was one of the few survivors of the Battle of Aeonia, who in an unimaginable act of heroism carried the slumbering demigod Malenia all the way back to the Haligtree. She managed the feat alone, fending off all manner of foes along the way."

◈ The Haligtree

The Haligtree: another important landmark of the Lands Between, even though its very out-of-the-way location in the far north of the country makes it no match for the omnipresent Erdtree. Indeed, the Haligtree is supposed to be a competitor for the Erdtree. While both can claim divine status, the concepts that the Haligtree represents are more welcoming than those of its rival, in the sense that the weakest individuals, including certain victims of the Golden Order's persecution, have found refuge with the Haligtree. This is the case for the Albinaurics. Because they were untouched by Grace, making them incompatible with the values of the Erdtree, they were hunted and killed.

The Haligtree was planted and cultivated by the demigod Miquella with help from his sister Malenia. Together, they took on the massive project when Miquella came to the realization that the Golden Order and its strict fundamentalism were powerless to do anything about the curse eating away at Malenia (Radagon's Rings of Light incantation). They also founded the citadel of Elphael, known as the Brace of the Haligtree, essentially equivalent to the capital city of Leyndell. The citadel prospered, as did the Haligtree—at least for a time. Miquella played an important role in growing the tree, watering it with his own divine blood from the time it was just a small sapling, according to the Haligtree Crest Surcoat's description. The Erdtree and its shadow, the Scadutree, had grown with help from the primordial force of the Crucible; it seems that this was not the case for the Haligtree. As such, the undertaking became too much, even for the legendary Empyrean duo.

However, Miquella got an idea: he would boost his power by becoming a god, to save the Haligtree, of course, but also, above all, to usher in a new age, an "Age of Compassion" (Circlet of Light). No one knows how Miquella learned of the existence of the Gate of Divinity in the Realm of Shadow, a well-kept family secret, but in any case, that was the next stage of his plan. As an Empyrean, he needed a consort to attain divine status. He had long wished for his half-brother Radahn, the ultimate warrior, to fill that role. Sadly, the Red Lion General was not interested in becoming Miquella's consort. All that mattered to him was fighting.

And so, tasked with conveying to the Lord of the Battlefield her twin brother's intentions, and possibly for other, more official reasons, given the context of the Shattering, Malenia went to war with Radahn in the Caelid region. "Miquella awaits thee, O promised consort" (Young Lion's Greaves), Malenia whispered into Radahn's ear before exploding the rotflower blossom in the Swamp of Aeonia.

In addition to his consort, Miquella also needed to find a way to get to the Realm of Shadow. To achieve that aim, he cooked up a plan in which he would manipulate his half-brother Mohg and use the blood magic of the Formless Mother to teleport from one plane of existence to the other.

◈ The Mohgwyn Dynasty and Miquella's plan

Unlike his twin brother Morgott, who had taken control of Leyndell and defended his family as it was weakened by the Shattering, Mohg fled to get far away from all the machinations. No one knows how, but he encountered another Outer God known as the Formless Mother, or Mother of Truth. The Formless Mother drew her power from blood, particularly tainted, cursed blood. The description of the Cursed-Blood Pot tells us that Mohg was drawn to cursed blood from childhood—which, I'll remind you, he spent imprisoned below the capital. That fascination included his own blood, that of the Omens. When he encountered the Formless Mother, he was smitten with the merciless Outer God and became her vassal. He adopted the title Lord of Blood and began to form the Mohgwyn Dynasty to worship the Formless Mother. He built a palace on the ruins of an ancient civilization overlooking "a swamp of festering blood" (Swarm of Flies incantation).

It was at this point that he became determined to become Miquella's consort, repeatedly inviting Miquella into his bedchamber. The Formless Mother promised that if Mohg united with the Empyrean, she would grant them both immense power. Miquella would rise to godhood while Mohg would become a lord, truly earning the title of Lord of Blood that he so craved. Unfortunately for Mohg, Miquella never responded to his invitations. Reacting to the refusals, Mohg and his henchmen went to the Haligtree and cut the branches in which Miquella had embedded himself, slumbering as he fed the tree with his own energy. The Lord of Blood captured the childlike demigod and confined him to a cocoon in his palace, allowing Mohg to regularly draw Miquella's divine blood.

However, Miquella had actually orchestrated all of this. He possessed the power to enchant people and bend them to his will. He used his powerful charms on Mohg so that the Lord of Blood would kidnap him and take him to Mohgwyn Palace. Thanks to certain blood rituals of the Formless Mother, Miquella would be able to find his way to the Realm of Shadow. Indeed, on the other side of Marika's veil, there was an active tribe of blood demons, and Miquella anticipated that they would heed his call, as we learn from the description of the Bloodfiend Hexer's Ashes. "Long ago, a subjugated tribe discovered a twisted deity amongst the ravages of war, and they were transformed into bloodfiends. The Mother of Truth was their savior." Confined to Mohg's cocoon, but free to take action in the Land of Shadow—yet another strange concept of *Elden Ring*'s world!—Miquella's story would continue later, and we will come back to it in the next chapter.

As for the palace of the Mohgwyn Dynasty, it continues to exist to this day, located in the depths of the Lands Between, hundreds of meters below the Caelid region. Not far from the abominable palace, we find the Eternal Cities, once prestigious places now hidden from the outside world and lit by the diffuse light of a false night sky affixed to the cracked dome of the underground space.

◈ The Eternal Cities

Long before the Shattering, as the Erdtree was quickly growing, the Eternal Cities were struck by a true catastrophe. Astel, Naturalborn of the Void, or sometimes called the Stars of Darkness, a mysterious being formed from "many-colored star debris" (Bastard's Stars), struck the Eternal Cities with meteorites, and even a much more powerful piece of a star. Astel destroyed countless buildings and plunged what remained of the Eternal Cities, Nokron and Nokstella, into the depths of the earth. In particular, this story is recounted by the description of the Remembrance of the Naturalborn: "A malformed star born in the lightless void far away. Once destroyed an Eternal City and took away their sky. A falling star of ill omen."

A band of soldiers—slaves, according to the Inverted Hawk Heater Shield—was then dispatched to the Eternal Cities to assess the extent of the damage. Known as the Fallen Hawks, they got lost while exploring the underground space and were condemned to wander the labyrinth of caverns forever. No one knows who sent them. However, what we do know is that the inhabitants of the Eternal Cities did not embrace the plans of the Greater Will, and they flat out rejected the propaganda of the Two Fingers (Nox Mirrorhelm). They worshiped the stars and, to a lesser extent, the Dark Moon, the very same one secretly admired by Ranni. As such, we have to wonder: did the Greater Will send Astel to annihilate this resistance movement? After all, the Greater Will had already sent other fallen stars–first Metyr, Mother of Fingers, then the golden star bearing the Elden Beast. The description of the Night Maiden Armor tells us: "Long ago, the Nox invoked the ire of the Greater Will, and were banished deep underground. Now they live under a false night sky, in eternal anticipation of their liege. Of the coming Age of the Stars. And their Lord of Night." Moreover, the Shattered Stone Talisman, a "shattered linchpin stone" that can be found in the underground ruins of the village of Moorth in the Realm of Shadow, might also shed some light on the strange "fall" of the Eternal Cities: "Linchpin stones are spiritual anchors said to hold the ground in place and quell the fury of earthquakes–when this one shattered, the surrounding town fell into the broken earth. One account claimed that the moon itself had come tumbling down." Could this story symbolically represent the fall of the Dark Moon?

For now, let's return to the Lord of Night. This is an important element in the mythology surrounding the now-buried Eternal Cities. It represents the hope that one day, astrology would return to its former glory and bring about the Age of Stars. The Dark Moon and Age of Stars: two terms that echo Ranni's destiny–but we'll come back to that in due time. The people of the Eternal Cities conducted numerous experiments in pursuit of their ambitions. For example, the Dragonkin Soldiers, not to be confused with Godwyn's Drake Knights, used a unique ice lightning incantation, even though they had not seen the sky for a very long time. Other experiments aimed to craft the legendary Lord of Night. This was a novel approach, nothing like the process of champions going to war to become lords happening on the surface of the Lands Between. To forge the Lord of Night, scholars studied Mimic Tears, materials capable of mimicking various forms, including the human form. With these experiments, they aimed to "forge a lord," according to the description of the Mimic Tear Ashes. The description of the Silver Tear Husk adds: "The Silver Tear makes mockery of life, reborn again and again into imitation. Perhaps, one day, it will be reborn a lord..."

Inhabitants of the Eternal Cities also forged a Fingerslayer Blade. The name describes quite literally the weapon's purpose and is reminiscent of various "godslayer" weapons. The Fingerslayer Blade was created to kill the Two Fingers, and thus to silence the Greater Will. The weapon would undoubtedly be invaluable for the Lord of Night. It was hidden in Nokron under the throne of a giant, myste-rious skeletal statue. Could the statue in question be an imagined depiction of what the Lord of Night might look like? Or could it actually be the result of the scholars' experiments?

◈ Decline

While more minor movements, like those supporting the Haligtree, the Mohgwyn Dynasty, and the Eternal Cities, were gaining steam to one extent or another, the Erdtree religion was beginning a great decline. The shattering of the Elden Ring was a decisive and irreversible act that brought stagnation and madness to the Lands Between. The demigods, whether siblings or children, battled one another for power. The blessings of the Erdtree began to lose their sanctity, as highlighted by the descriptions of the Blessed Dew Talisman and Blessing of the Erdtree incantation. The Golden Order was no more than a shadow of its former self.

However, the hardcore members of the Golden Order found a new target amid the general chaos: Those Who Live in Death. These creatures began to appear shortly after the Night of the Black Knives and the theft of the Rune of Death, along with deathroot. The plant's description states: "The Rune of Death spread across the Lands Between through the underground roots of the Greattree, sprouting in the form of deathroot." Thus, as evidenced by Those Who Live in Death, death was returning bit by bit to the cycle of the Lands Between, which had been stagnant up until that point. Considered to be impure, sullying the Grace of the Erdtree and contradicting the truth of the Golden Order's fundamentalists, Those Who Live in Death were hunted and killed, with the hunters extracting deathroot from them. To restore the imagined sense of order, the deathroots were returned to Maliketh, and thus to the fragmented Rune of Death.

◈ The return of the Tarnished

Initially, the Two Fingers had counted on Ranni to replace Marika, but the Carian princess got away from them, seemingly having been killed at the same time as Godwyn on the Night of the Black Knives. So, the mouthpieces of the Greater Will turned to another solution: the Tarnished. While the Tarnished had followed Hoarah Loux on a pilgrimage when Marika married Radagon, they were finally returning to the Lands Between.

"Tarnished–O, Tarnished! Seek the Erdtree and stand before Marika, its Queen. Become the Elden Lord!" These are the words in the description of the Lord's Heal incantation, "bestowed by the Two Fingers upon the Tarnished deemed worthy of becoming a lord." The former pariahs of the Lands Between began to receive the Grace of the Erdtree, an interesting paradox given their name, which would soon have real weight to it given the world's situation. The light returned to the Tarnished shortly after the destruction of the Elden Ring. A gift from the Greater Will, according to the official story from the Golden Order and the Two Fingers.

However, I should note that the clergy, the Church mentioned in the section on the early days of the Erdtree, played a role in the spread of Grace. Missionaries traveled to the Badlands, where the Tarnished had gone. According to the description of the Confessor Armor, the missionaries gave the Tarnished Grace and sent them back to the Lands Between to overthrow Marika.

While this plan was underway to take down Marika and seize the Elden throne, war was never openly declared between the Two Fingers and the goddess. In fact, the Two Fingers had embraced the name of the Golden Order and wished to use it for their own purposes. The future Elden Lord would simply restore the Golden Order's shine. And it would keep the name. After all, the Golden Order was connected to the plans of the Greater Will, particularly through the golden Erdtree, the shining sun of the Lands Between. However, all of the fundamentalist aspects of the Golden Order would be reviewed and corrected to make a clean break with the cycle and structures established by Marika, who had taken far too many liberties with her vision for the Order.

So, the Two Fingers were fairly subtle about enacting their new plan. The demigods had been repudiated and the Two Fingers needed new candidates for the Elden throne. The Tarnished were returning to the Lands Between—"The call of long-lost Grace speaks to us all," we hear in the game's introduction. Thus, called by Grace, the Tarnished were to encounter their maidens in the course of their journey, and the maidens would guide them to the Elden throne and teach them the wisdom of the Two Fingers (Traveling Maiden Robe). To provide structure to this new scheme, the Two Fingers and the Church created a new haven: the Roundtable Hold.

The Roundtable Hold

⬧ A home away from home

The Roundtable Hold could only be accessed by Tarnished who had united with their maidens. The maiden would show the Tarnished the way to this ethereal, otherworldly place. A similar structure, now in ruins, could be found in Leyndell. Perhaps it was the place in the capital where high-ranking members of Marika's Golden Order would make decisions, and the Two Fingers decided to reproduce it in order to impress anyone entering the space?

One of the first notable characters to enter the Roundtable Hold was Sir Gideon Ofnir. Originally, he had wanted to personally stand before the Elden Ring and become the first Tarnished Elden Lord. However, in the course of his quest, he had a long conversation with the Two Fingers—a rare occurrence given their declining vigor and increasing silence—which led him to understand just how broken the world and the original Order were. His quest for power evolved into a quest for information—for the truth. He adopted the title of "the All-Knowing" and became the head of the Roundtable Hold. From then on, he would welcome in newcomers and would probe and test them to assess their ability to withstand the despair that would await them on their quest.

Dozens, or even hundreds, of other Tarnished either stayed at or passed through the Roundtable Hold. Among them, a few names would go down in history. Seluvis, for example, an ally of Ranni, worked for a time with Gideon before returning to Caria Manor. A certain Fia also made her way to the Roundtable Hold; her embrace gave reassurance to valiant warriors. And in fact, it turns out that she is the "Deathbed Companion" for the assassinated Prince Godwyn—but we'll come back to that later. Vyke the Dragonspear was a renowned knight of the Hold, perhaps the person to get closest to the Elden throne before embracing a much darker fate, as he was consumed by an entity we haven't yet discussed in depth, but which will play a crucial role later in the story: the Frenzied Flame. Finally, the awful Dung Eater also stayed for a time at the Roundtable Hold before being jailed in the depths of Leyndell. In spite of his power worthy of a champion, and thus of becoming a lord, his unhealthy penchant for curses and filth earned him a vile reputation. And rightfully so!

◈ Lost sheep

Of course, not every Tarnished is destined to be a champion, nor do they all have the ambition of ascending to the Elden throne. Some lost their Grace as they wandered the Lands Between. A branch of the Church whose members are called "confessors" became dedicated to eliminating those Tarnished who had strayed from the straight and narrow path. They also, of course, hunt opponents of the Two Fingers and of the Greater Will.

Wearing black leather so as to blend into the shadows, the confessors are also skillful assassins. They use both dark magic, in spite of it being considered heretical in the Erdtree religion, and more subtle poisons. The head confessor Crepus even used crossbow bolts coated with lethal doses of scarlet rot. The description of the Darkness incantation tells us these "assassins were themselves once Tarnished who had strayed from guidance, and they pursued their duty in the darkness that is without Grace."

◈ The Two Fingers' challenge

To test the strength and bravery of the Tarnished, the Two Fingers developed a sort of challenge that also happened to serve their purposes nicely. Indeed, the Tarnished could not enter Leyndell unless they had collected at least two Great Runes from the bodies of demigods. So, the Tarnished would have to take on the demigods, who remained formidable in spite of being weakened and worn out from years of war, and acquire from them the runes giving them their great power—certainly a challenge capable of identifying the champions most worthy of the Elden throne.

Sadly, time passed and no Tarnished managed to complete the quest to reach the Elden Ring. They gradually descended into madness, fled, went into hiding, or were killed by the confessors. Most of the chosen ones were eventually abandoned by Grace. The Roundtable Hold became nearly deserted and began to fall into a state of disuse. The Two Fingers' master plan was put in jeopardy, until the arrival of a new hope, one last Tarnished touched by Grace: the *Elden Ring* player's avatar.

CHAPTER 3
THE PRESENT

The fallen leaves tell a story.

The great Elden Ring was shattered.

In our home, across the fog, the Lands Between.

Now, Queen Marika the Eternal is nowhere to be found,

and in the Night of the Black Knives, Godwyn the Golden
was the first to perish.

Soon, Marika's offspring, demigods all,
claimed the shards of the Elden Ring.

The mad taint of their newfound strength triggered the Shattering.

A war from which no lord arose.

A war leading to abandonment by the Greater Will.

Arise now, ye Tarnished.

Ye dead, who yet live.

The call of long-lost Grace speaks to us all.

Hoarah Loux, chieftain of the Badlands.

The ever-brilliant Goldmask.

Fia, the Deathbed Companion.

The loathsome Dung Eater.

And Sir Gideon Ofnir, the All-Knowing.

And one other. Whom Grace would again bless.

A Tarnished of no renown.

Cross the fog, to the Lands Between.

To stand before the Elden Ring.

And become the Elden Lord.

The introduction to *Elden Ring* perfectly lays the foundation of the story and universe. In a handful of lines, it presents many of the things we've just examined over many pages–the intro really packs it all in!–while describing the player's ultimate objective–i.e., *your* ultimate objective.

You are a Tarnished who has crossed through the fog and just set foot in the Lands Between. Your first objective is to find a maiden to guide you and to pull you out of the symbolic fog, i.e., your ignorance.

Melina

Varré, a deceitful manipulator in service to Mohg, Lord of Blood (but you don't know that yet), is the first person to greet you in the Lands Between. His white mask appears dirty and he seems like an odd character, but nonetheless, you lap up his words of reassurance. According to him, finding a maiden isn't all that important, especially as you are guided by Grace, which is pointing you in the direction of Stormveil Castle and its lord who you must defeat: Godrick the Grafted. So, there you have a concrete task to complete. Not far from Varré, in a church further down the way, you meet the merchant Kalé, with his stringed instrument and his unusual Santa Claus-like outfit, who seems much nicer. You buy a few things from this quintessential utilitarian character and then get back on the road. Although memorable for being the first people you meet at the start of your journey, these two characters are ultimately inconsequential. Later on, Varré will try to get you to join the Mohgwyn Dynasty, and Kalé is really just another traveling merchant.

The first truly important encounter of the adventure occurs a bit farther on, at a Site of Grace where you rest for a moment before taking on the immense troll terrorizing the region. It is here that Melina comes to you. This is not the first time she's seen you, as she found you unconscious a few hours earlier. Let's just say that she's been keeping an eye on you since your arrival in the Lands Between–literally just the one eye, as her left eye is sealed shut and has a strange scar across it, like a talon-shaped tattoo. Melina offers to become your maiden, or at least to act like it since she doesn't actually have the official status. She wants to guide you in your quest for the Elden Ring and help you gain power by acquiring runes. She also gives you the Spectral Steed Whistle, a magical ring that allows you to summon Torrent, your trusty steed who will help you explore the Lands Between. In exchange, you will accompany Melina to the foot of the Erdtree, where she will discover her destiny. "Me, I'm searching for my purpose given to me by my mother inside the Erdtree long ago, for the reason that I yet live, burned and bodiless. [...] I am no maiden. My purpose was long ago lost." It appears that Melina has no memory of her past, of her brother Messmer or of the fire curse that connects the two of them.

So, she tells you her scattershot story and reveals to you her doubts, sitting at this Site of Grace not far from your first big battle, against Margit the Fell Omen.

A test for the Tarnished

It turns out that Margit is actually none other than Morgott, the cursed child of Godfrey and Marika's Golden Lineage, and the self-proclaimed Omen King since the Shattering. While his true form remains in Leyndell, ready to defend the capital against all attacks, Morgott also inhabits the body of a less remarkable avatar, the aforementioned Margit the Fell Omen, which he uses to test future champions like yourself. Above all, Morgott aims to snuff out the ambitions of those who are attracted by the power and tragic fame of the Elden Ring, as noted in the description of the Fell Omen Cloak. When in his Margit form, he positions himself strategically. He "welcomes" Tarnished at the entrance to Stormveil Castle, where Grace guides them at the beginning of their quest. Being quite weak and inexperienced, most of them haven't even met their maiden yet. When they meet Margit in the battle arena, he summarily destroys them as if it were nothing. Again with the goal of testing the strength and will of the Tarnished, and perhaps even getting them to abandon their quest—in your case, your session of *Elden Ring*—Margit is also the leader of the Night's Cavalry, a group of very powerful knights dressed all in black who prowl around the Lands Between. It's said that they hunt champions and great warriors, but they often attack the first person they see.

With the help of spirit ashes and weapons improved at Kalé's forge, you finally manage to defeat Margit. You are now a seasoned fighter, ready to explore the world and take on even more hostile adversaries. Melina opens the Roundtable Hold for you. There, you meet various characters who seem to be allies. Finger Reader Enia, who's as old as sin, occasionally gives you instructions from the Two Fingers, the "thing" that stands next to her and randomly wriggles about. Very strange. The mysterious Fia resides in her bedchamber and grants you a blessing with her embrace. The veteran soldier Sir Gideon Ofnir is there too, and he may have even been there since the Roundtable Hold was created. From the time of your arrival, he takes you under his wing, but still considers you a good-for-nothing novice. However, he reassesses that opinion once you finally get your hands on one of the Great Runes, the pieces of the Elden Ring held by the demigods. The enigmatic Ensha protects Sir Gideon, and the equally cryptic Twin Maiden Husks serve as merchants. In another room, a large man whose body seems to be half made of stone tirelessly strikes his anvil. Hewg, as he's called, is the smithing master and offers to improve your weapons. He is chained at the foot—he has been a prisoner in the Hold since time immemorial. Long ago, he was condemned to forge a weapon capable of killing a god or goddess. A seemingly impossible mission—but you will undoubtedly need that weapon in the course of your adventure. It would be a good idea to give him a bit of your time. You will occasionally hear him pray: "So please, grant me forgiveness, Queen Marika." He is a decidedly intriguing character with expertise that's crucial for your quest.

Many others will appear in the Roundtable Hold as you travel across the Lands Between. Roderika the Spirit Tuner will improve your spirit ashes. The sorcerer Rogier, afflicted by the curse of Those Who Live in Death, stands not far from D, a hunter for the Golden Order who can be easily recognized by his Twinned Armor. Brother Corhyn is a devotee of the Golden Order, but he will leave the Roundtable Hold to travel with Goldmask, another Tarnished who has come to the Lands Between to study the values of the Golden Order. Finally, a man named Diallos can be found in the Hold upon your arrival, but his dark fate will take him far away, and even far from the Elden throne. From time to time you will cross paths with Nepheli Loux, a powerful warrior who lives up to the name Loux, an homage—or actual marker of relation?—to the man who once guided the Tarnished on a pilgrimage out of the Lands Between: Hoarah Loux. While she's Gideon's adoptive daughter, she isn't particularly important to the main story and is instead connected to more minor plotlines, which we will cover in the next chapter. The Dung Eater also makes a few appearances in the Roundtable Hold. His unsettling presence is actually an apparition, as his physical body is held in a jail below Leyndell.

So, Margit the Fell Omen guarded the entrance to Stormveil Castle; Godrick the Grafted guards the exit. As we've already learned, the demigod Godrick long ago got his hands on a piece of the Elden Ring and then attacked some of his fellow demigods in the capital, before falling back to Stormveil, where he used his tyrannical power to seize the throne. While your battle against Margit was tough, the battle against Godrick promises to be even more arduous. Your victory over him earns you his Great Rune, a powerful and coveted piece of the Elden Ring. It entitles you to an official audience with the Two Fingers in the Roundtable Hold.

"The Greater Will has long renounced the demigods. Tarnished, show no mercy. Have their heads. Take all they have left." These instructions from the Two Fingers, communicated by Enia, couldn't be any clearer. Sir Gideon begins to see potential in you. He tells you about the other demigods who hold Great Runes: Rennala, Radahn, Rykard, and Morgott. For the time being, the Two Fingers has made the capital unreachable for you; your test is not yet finished.

Once you have the second Great Rune in hand, you have successfully completed the Two Fingers' challenge. Gideon informs you that the path to Leyndell and the Erdtree is finally open to you. "Marika's trespass demanded a heavy sentence. But even in shackles, she remains a god, and the vision's vessel. Confer Great Runes to become Elden Lord, and join Queen Marika as her consort." These words from the

Two Fingers don't necessarily disparage the reigning goddess, but it's time to take back the reins of the Golden Order and to restore the Erdtree to its primary function as planned by the Greater Will: to collect souls.

Cardinal sin

Back in Leyndell, it turns out that the powerful Morgott is not actually the last line of defense before Marika's living prison inside the Erdtree. Rather, an impenetrable barrier of thorns blocks all looking to enter—or exit—the goddess's presence. The Erdtree is sealed shut.

You find Melina, who had slipped away upon your arrival in the capital city to try to "ascertain the purpose [she] was given," according to her own words. It would seem that her murky fate is clearer to her now. She tells you: "The thorns are impenetrable. A husk of the Erdtree's being that spurns all that exists without. The only way to stand before the Elden Ring... and become the Elden Lord... is to pass the thorns. My purpose serves to aid in that very act. So I'd like you to undertake a new journey, with me. To the Flame of Ruin, far above the clouds, upon the snowy Mountaintops of the Giants. Then I can set the Erdtree aflame." Set the Erdtree aflame, undertake a new journey—these are unexpected words given that you believed you had reached the end of your quest.

Finger Reader Enia calls the burning of the Erdtree a "cardinal sin," the end of the iconic symbol of the reign of Marika, but also of the Greater Will. What's more, the Two Fingers in the Roundtable Hold have gone silent, they "remain still." According to Enia, they are again busy consulting the Greater Will, beginning a new conversation that may last a few thousand years, like when Marika had Maliketh steal the Rune of Death, plunging the Lands Between into inexorable stagnation.

Upon hearing of your plan to commit the cardinal sin, Enia is troubled. However, her measured words do not call into question your destiny: "The realm, and all life, in ruins. Impossible events transpire, beyond the ken of the Fingers. Who is to say that the cardinal sin must be cardinal forever? Go on. Finish the job. Take the course you deem most worthy." This last statement bears more wisdom and perspicacity than it first seems: indeed, at the end of your quest, you will have to make a choice among a number of options. You probably don't realize it yet, but there are no less than six distinct outcomes that have been developing since the start of your adventure.

For now, it's time to climb the mountain, following in the footsteps of Marika and Godfrey, who long ago took on the Giants and beat them into submission. The Fire Giant is still there in the mountaintops, and he tests your strength in a fierce battle.

The titan constantly watches over and protects the Forge of the Giants, where the Flame of Ruin has long laid dormant. With the Giant defeated, Melina finally channels the sacred flame capable of setting the Erdtree ablaze. She sacrifices herself, using her own body as fuel to commit the cardinal sin. As the branches of the giant tree above you begin to glow red, you lose consciousness.

The end of the world as we know it: the return of the Rune of Death

You are surprised to awake in the floating city of Farum Azula. How did you get here, to this place seemingly of another world and time? A sinister character lurks in the city. Long ago, Maliketh took refuge here to keep the Rune of Death out of reach from the rest of the world. The witch Ranni had stolen a fragment of the rune from him by breaking off a piece of his sword, the extraordinary blade that earned him his nickname, Maliketh the Black Blade. After that, he hid his sword, and therefore the Rune of Death, inside his own body. He once again became a beast, as before, with his terrible claws as his only weapons.

After the Rune of Death was sealed inside his body, Maliketh developed an insatiable taste for deathroot. He would send agents of the Golden Order out to look for Those Who Live in Death possessing the plants, which contain within them a bit of the Rune of Death. Maliketh adopted another identity, Gurranq the Beast Clergyman, and waited hungrily for his doses of deathroot in a Caelid temple that resembles the stones of Farum Azula. You will already have met Gurranq on the quest assigned by D in the Roundtable Hold. You may have given him enough deathroot in your encounters with him for him to mutter a few confused words intended for Marika. You may have encountered the formidable guardian protecting his temple, one of the Black Blade Kindred. Finally, you may have noticed the red jewel on top of Gurranq's left hand. You will find that same jewel on Maliketh: it is a stone placed over a seal that contains the power of the Rune of Death. During your battle with him in Farum Azula, Maliketh plunges his dagger into the seal to extract his Black Blade imbued with Death.

Maliketh's defeat releases Death into the Lands Between. Taking the form of a red smoke, Death envelops you and knocks you out. You lose consciousness, probably for quite some time, because when you finally open your eyes again, you see the capital city buried in ashes. Thanks to Melina, the Erdtree glows red: it has been burning ever since you released the fire from the Forge of the Giants. The cinders have covered Leyndell and Death has spread through its neighborhoods and the surrounding area. The barrier of thorns that blocked access to Marika's prison is now open, having been consumed by the fire of cardinal sin.

After a couple of incredible battles on the path to the Erdtree, first against Sir Gideon and then against Hoarah Loux, both of whom came to make one last attempt to seize the throne, you finally meet Marika in her tree prison. However, her masculine alter ego, Radagon, challenges you to a duel. Armed with the hammer that long ago shattered the Elden Ring, he is the last thing standing in the way of you taking the throne. Or so you think. After defeating Radagon, you come face to face with the majestic creature sent by the Greater Will: the Elden Beast. "It was the vassal beast of the Greater Will and living incarnation of the concept of Order," we learn from the description of the Elden Remembrance. This fight is highly symbolic: you are there to overthrow the concept of Order and shape the fate of the Lands Between according to your own will as the new Elden Lord.

Choose your own ending

The ability to choose your own ending has been a constant in the *Souls* games. *Elden Ring*, continuing to honor its heritage while being much more ambitious than its predecessors, offers a multitude of different endings. Six of them, to be precise. One of them is automatic, and we will get to that one last, but as for the other five endings, the options are clearly presented after you defeat Radagon and the Elden Beast. The options will be offered to you depending on your completion of the various quests and the special runes you've collected from them. Indeed, each of these special runes, received from key characters in the story, embodies a fundamental concept. As you reforge the Elden Ring, you have the opportunity to add one of these runes, shaping the kind of Elden Lord you wish to become.

◈ Melina: the *Age of Fracture*

Let's start with the most "logical" ending, or at least the one that you will automatically unlock by finishing the game after following a straight line laid out by Melina. Unlike the *Souls* games, in which the basic conclusion always followed the will of the being manipulating the player, *Elden Ring* offers a more open default ending. When you become the Elden Lord by selecting the main option, "Mend the Elden Ring," you usher in the Age of Fracture. As its name indicates, in this age, you will not continue the work of either Marika or the Greater Will. Fracture symbolizes the abandonment of the Golden Order, and even of the original Order, which, in any case, disappeared long ago. The only relic of the former era is that the

Erdtree remains standing. It no longer burns, but remains dried up. Dead wood rising above the landscape. But no matter, the Elden Ring is yours and you are now free to chart the course that you want for the Lands Between.

Without Melina and her mysterious plans, the cardinal sin wouldn't have been committed and you wouldn't have freed the Rune of Death. She liberated you from the manipulation and plotting of the Two Fingers, offering you a true destiny. And what did she get out of all that? Why did she guide you on this path? The game doesn't offer many clues to answer those questions. We know that Melina watched you from the very beginning, when she found you unconscious. At that moment, she tells Torrent, the spectral steed: "Don't worry Torrent, fortune is on his side. We found him here, after all. One of his kind is sure to seek the Elden Ring. Even if it does violate the Golden Order..." Melina already knows that you will have to defy and confront the precepts of the Golden Order.

At bit later, when Melina comes to you at the Site of Grace, she offers you, in her own words, "an accord." In exchange for her providing the services of a maiden—which she clearly explains she is not—you will have to take her to the foot of the Erdtree. She needs you. She cannot get around on her own as she possesses no physical body. She can only materialize at Sites of Grace. In spite of her ethereal form, she takes your hand, an exceedingly rare sign of affection in the game's hostile universe.

Over the course of the adventure, Melina appears at several Sites of Grace, specifically those located at churches. She shares with you the words of her mother, Marika, echoes that she hears resonating in the houses of worship rather than words spoken directly to you by the goddess through Melina. Marika's words concern past events, like Godfrey's great feats or certain tensions with Radagon, but also more private thoughts. "The Erdtree governs all. The choice is thine. Become one with the Order. Or divest thyself of it. To wallow at the fringes; a powerless upstart." Are Marika's words, conveyed by Melina, actually directed at the player?

To interpret Melina's aims, we need to make a few assumptions. What if Melina was actually enacting a plan conceived by her mother, Marika? The goddess is trapped inside the Erdtree, but perhaps she found a way to restore her daughter's body (burned long ago by Messmer's flame?), to have her form and voice materialize at various Sites of Grace across the Lands Between. After all, Grace is an instrument of the Erdtree. Moreover, on the Altus Plateau, Melina says: "I was born at the foot of the Erdtree. Where mother gave me my purpose. [...] I... have to ascertain for myself. The reason for which I live, burned and bodiless." Naturally, "mother" refers to Marika, and indeed, Melina finds an answer to her question about her purpose after visiting the capital. She finds it's impossible to enter the Erdtree; the barrier of thorns is impenetrable. Melina's destiny is to serve as fuel to commit the cardinal sin, to burn the Erdtree in order to open the way to Marika's prison. Once again, because of her ethereal form, Melina cannot do it on her own. So, she counts on you to take her to the Forge of the Giants.

As such, could Melina embody Marika's determination to bring an end to the current age, in which her children have torn each other apart since the Shattering? There's a good chance that's the case. Finally, it's interesting to note the parallel between the old Finger Readers, most notably Enia in the Roundtable Hold, acting as the mouthpieces of the Two Fingers and thus of the Greater Will, and Melina, who conveys the words of Marika, even if only through echoes. Goddess versus Outer God: a battle that plays out—and is won—through the manipulation of the one who will wield the Elden Ring.

✦ Fia: the Age of the Duskborn

This next conclusion is tied to the quest assigned by Fia, Deathbed Companion. Her duty as a Deathbed Companion is to absorb the heat and vitality of valiant warriors by embracing them, and then to pass that energy on to a dead person, always a high-ranking noble. The Deathbed Companion lies patiently next to the "exalted" noble's body, "to grant him another chance at life." The description of her Deathbed Dress says, "The touch of the fabric is exceedingly soft, so as not to harm even the most withered corpse, while still sharing her warmth." This process was considered a sacred art back in Fia's homeland. However, she decided to leave her country. Indeed, as a Tarnished, she felt herself drawn to the Lands Between. She moved to Leyndell for a time, where she became close with a man known as Lionel the Lionhearted, an intrepid and chivalrous knight who took her under his wing. Unfortunately for him, she drained his vitality to the point of his death. You can find a dessicated Lionel inside their humble abode in the heart of the capital.

Fia then caught wind of the tragic fate of Godwyn, the first of the demigods to perish, who became known as the Prince of Death. She also learned that after his demise, Those Who Live in Death appeared in the Lands Between. Convinced of her destiny in exile, she later tells you: "I choose to lie with Godwyn of my own will. Not the remains of one chosen for me." She also decided to become a protector of Those Who Live in Death, who are relentlessly hunted by the Golden Order. For that very reason, she infiltrated the Roundtable Hold, gathering energy from the warriors passing through as she waited for the right moment to destabilize the Golden Order.

Indeed, the first time you meet Fia in the Roundtable Hold, she embraces you, a rare sign of affection in the game, like when Melina holds your hand at one of the first Sites of Grace. The only difference is that Fia's embrace discreetly siphons off a few of your health points. It's a cunning scheme, fitting for her character. With the help of Rogier, a sorcerer you encounter at Stormveil Castle who is secretly afflicted by the curse of Those Who Live in Death, Fia manipulates you into helping her trap another character in the Roundtable Hold, a man known simply by his initial, D. He is one of the infamous killers of Those Who Live in Death, collecting deathroot for Maliketh. Thanks to the bait you collect, items connected to the Night of the Black Knives, on which Godwyn was killed, Fia ends up luring D into her trap and killing him in a remote room in the Hold. She then reveals to you her true intentions: "I am Fia, Deathbed Companion. Hark, Roundtable. Disturb not the Death of Godwyn, the exalted. We, who humbly live in Death... Live in waiting, to one day welcome our Lord. What right does anyone have to object? Our Lord will rise. The Lord of the many, and the meek." After that, she disappears from the Roundtable Hold. You will cross paths with her again much later in your adventure.

At the end of the game, you find Fia under the Erdtree, in the area known as the Deeproot Depths. She sits at the base of a gigantic, misshapen mass, which must be Godwyn, who has been kept going since time immemorial by the vitality of warriors embraced by the Deathbed Companion. Interestingly, the location's Site of Grace is called the "Prince of Death's Throne." After you battle Fia's guardians, Rogier and Lionel the Lionhearted, she meets with you again. Along with giving you her habitual embrace, she charges you with a quest: to find the missing half of the mark on Godwyn's flesh. The incomplete mark has a shape reminiscent of a curled-up centipede.

The other half of this Cursemark of Death can be found on Ranni's body. I'll remind you, Ranni perished at exactly the same time as Godwyn on the Night of the Black Knives. "Ranni was the first of the demigods whose flesh perished, while the Prince of Death perished in soul alone," explains the description of the Cursemark. Indeed, the mark was supposed to be circular, but it was broken in two when the two demigods perished at the same time. So, you go on another quest to collect the other half of the Cursemark from Ranni's charred body at the top of the Divine Tower of Liurnia.

When you give Ranni's half of the Cursemark of Death to Fia, she makes you a champion: the champion of the Deathbed Companion, of Godwyn, and of Those Who Live in Death more broadly. With the mark made whole, Fia lies down with Godwyn's giant body. She then produces the Mending Rune of the Death-Prince, which she considers to be her child, a symbol of the future that she foresees for the Lands Between. According to its description, the rune "will embed the principle of Life within Death into Order. [...] Thus, this new Order will be one of Death restored." It's an ambition that goes far beyond collecting souls in the Erdtree, as desired by the Greater Will. Marika had sealed away Death, plunging the world into stagnation; Fia hopes to restore Death, to reintegrate it back into the natural cycle of existence.

"Please, do one thing for me. Brandish this child, my rune, and take for yourself the throne. Stay the persecution of Those Who Live in Death. By becoming our Elden Lord." These are among the last words Fia speaks to you as she hands you the precious rune. At the end of the adventure, you can usher in the Age of the Duskborn by adding the centipede-shaped rune to the Elden Ring. A rune created from the sudden deaths of two powerful demigods and enchanted by the gentleness and warmth of the Deathbed Companion until she breathed her last breath.

◈ Goldmask: the Age of Order

The quest of the strange character known as Goldmask begins with one of his followers: Corhyn. He calls himself "Brother" Corhyn, meaning that he's a cleric, but he wears a blindfold over his eyes and a massive wheel around his neck, symbols of the prophets of the Lands Between. At one point, Corhyn was one of those prophets. "Even after exile, Corhyn refused to recant his prophecies. And for this, he was blessed with the guidance of Grace," explains the description of Corhyn's Robe. As such, he was one of the Tarnished guided by Grace to the Erdtree, and thus to the Elden Ring. The sacred light has since abandoned him, and he now aims to unlock the secrets of the Golden Order.

You meet Brother Corhyn when you arrive at the Roundtable Hold. He remains there for a time, teaching you the incantations of the Two Fingers. "I'm thinking of leaving the Roundtable Hold. Do you know of the noble Goldmask? Though he was a Tarnished, living outside the Lands Between, he was a great scholar who foresaw the coming guidance of Grace. And now, I hear he has come to the Lands Between alone to contemplate the Golden Order... I wish nothing more than to seek his instruction, and perhaps even help him in his research." Not long after confiding in you with these words, Corhyn leaves to search for Goldmask, traveling to the Altus Plateau.

Indeed, Goldmask is located northwest of Leyndell. He stands immobile, pointing a finger toward the capital and the Erdtree. You easily recognize him by his massive golden headpiece resembling the sun. The description of the headpiece, known as the Radiant Gold Mask, notes that its owner is "a staunch pursuer of Golden Order fundamentalism." As a reminder, the concept of fundamentalism is inextricably tied to the Golden Order founded long ago by Marika, and the fundamentalists studied the Order through two major lenses: causality (Marika) and regression (Radagon). "The noble Goldmask lamented what had become of the hunters. How easy it is for learning and learnedness to be reduced to the ravings of fanatics," says the description of the Order Healing incantation. Goldmask became disillusioned with what the Golden Order had become since the Shattering, a pack of killers who go about hunting Those Who Live in Death. Still, he continues his research on the organization's distant past, the origins of its fundamentalism.

With information you provide, Corhyn goes to Goldmask, who becomes his new master. Corhyn tells you, "I frantically attempt to record his wisdom; the movement of his finger." Goldmask's finger movements are both subtle and complex, laying out and solving equations, among other things, in line with the pure fundamentalist spirit of the original Golden Order. And while Brother Corhyn does not yet know how to decipher Goldmask's reflections, we can again see a parallel with the way the Finger Readers interpret the motions of the Two Fingers. More than just a mouthpiece, Corhyn considers himself a "documentarian" for the Golden Order. He is not the first person to become a disciple of the (very) solitary Goldmask, but unlike others, Brother Corhyn persists in following him and recording his strange reflections.

"The master's reflections had heightened as we neared the Erdtree. While still a precise calculus, the rhythms grew increasingly wild. Until he simply ceased. Now the master is facing quite the puzzle," Corhyn tells you while standing with Goldmask at a location overlooking the capital. Goldmask is stuck on something concerning Radagon. It is time for you to unveil the secret of Marika and Radagon's shared identity, which, I'll remind you, is hidden in the statue of Radagon. The Law of Regression incantation reveals to you the famous line: "Radagon is Marika."

The secret is broken. You reveal the information to Goldmask, whose finger immediately begins to move again. The puzzle is now solved, but it leaves Goldmask and Brother Corhyn all the more perplexed. "The Golden Order is founded on the principle that Marika is the one true god," Corhyn tells you before the secret is revealed; now, Radagon, who was supposed to be "just" a champion, has been added to the equation. Marika can no longer be seen as a flawlessly pure goddess; instead, she is a blend of two distinct personalities. Feeling troubled, Goldmask and Corhyn leave Leyndell for the Mountaintops of the Giants, a destination forbidden by the Golden Order as it contains the Flame of Ruin.

In spite of that prohibition, Corhyn follows his master, torn between the Golden Order's precepts and this flaw they have discovered in the Church's dogma. With the revelation of Radagon's secret, Goldmask now questions the unity and perfection of the Golden Order, as well as of its creator, Marika, which does not at all please Brother Corhyn. He even sees it as blasphemous. Because of this ideological dispute, they end up parting ways.

After the Erdtree is set ablaze, you find Brother Corhyn deep in prayer, lambasting his former master and praising the Golden Order, just like when you first met him. Then, you stumble upon the body of Goldmask. On it, you find the Mending Rune of Perfect Order, which you collect to incorporate into the Elden Ring. And thus begins the Age of Order. "The current imperfection of the Golden Order, or instability of ideology, can be blamed upon the fickleness of the gods no better than men," states the rune's description. After becoming aware of the weaknesses of the goddess Marika and her Order, Goldmask followed his reflections and his quest through to the end, giving his life and putting his legendary wisdom into the creation of this unique rune, whose only purpose is to perfect the Golden Order, the ideology that he studied for so many long years.

✦ The Dung Eater: the Blessing of Despair

The last of these four "conventional" conclusions–the ones that share a nearly identical final cinematic–is centered on a vile character called the Dung Eater. He has no actual name, being known only by his repugnant status–a being that feeds on excrement. You first encounter him fairly late in the adventure, after you reach the Altus Plateau, and at that point, it's hard to imagine buying into his point of view and carrying forward his actions to usher in a new and sordid age for the Lands Between!

The Dung Eater worships filth and curses. He kills and then defiles his victims as a way of cursing their future lives and even entire generations to come. Acting like a gardener, he plants his foul seed in the corpses of those he murders and cultivates it to prevent their souls from returning to the Erdtree. The Dung Eater's objective is to contaminate literally all life in order to overthrow the Golden Order. He considers himself "a scourge upon the living." "Must eat more! Defile more! Everything that matters to you!" These are his own words. He has big plans for the world.

Roderika the Spirit Tuner is the first person to detect the oppressive presence of the Dung Eater in the Roundtable Hold. She feels it and immediately warns you about the sinister individual. However, it turns out that he is not physically inside the Roundtable Hold; rather, it is a projection of him. His actual body is held prisoner below the capital, in the labyrinthine network of sewers that stretches out across the city. For a time, the Dung Eater simply ignores you, but when you return to the Roundtable Hold with a Seedbed Curse, he finally deigns to give you some consideration. He then tells you the location of his physical body.

After a few visits to his prison and a battle with his projection on the outskirts of the capital, the homestretch of this unpleasant quest finally comes into focus. The Dung Eater sits bound in his cell. He asks you to bring him the Seedbed Curse that he had long ago planted in numerous corpses. "Defile my flesh with the seedbed curse. Again and again. Until it is done. Until a cursed ring coalesces, that may one day defile the Order itself." The ring in question is none other than the Mending Rune of the Fell Curse, to be added to the Elden Ring. The Seedbed Curse can be found on bodies scattered across the Lands Between. They are all bound to chairs, implying that the individuals were subjected to unimaginable torture and suffering. Once you bring the Dung Eater five of the seeds, he dies of his own defilement, generating the rune with its gangrenous appearance.

There's really nothing surprising about the Blessing of Despair–the title for the ending you get if you complete the Elden Ring with the Dung Eater's rune. His curse is everywhere, inevitably infecting all future generations. "They'll be born cursed, all of them. Along with their children, and their children's children, for all time to come." The Dung Eater's words continue to resonate and usher in this new, particularly sinister era. But at least the Golden Order has now been deposed!

♦ Ranni: the Age of Stars

Now, this probably has to be people's favorite ending for *Elden Ring*. It is also the most interesting conclusion in terms of lore, as it is centered on a key character from the game's past. A character, moreover, responsible for the Shattering and thus for the game's present state of affairs. This notable ending is not, like the previous four, triggered by the mending of the Elden Ring, but rather by summoning the witch Ranni after defeating the final boss. Indeed, if you see Ranni's quest all the way through, a summon sign will appear. If you use it, an ending scene different from all the others will play. To really understand this conclusion, we need to take stock of Ranni's motivations and the actions taken to further her cause.

The last time we saw Ranni, she had challenged the Two Fingers and rejected her status as an Empyrean in favor of becoming a devotee to the cold Dark Moon. The Carian princess then disappeared after orchestrating the Night of the Black Knives and destroying her physical body, later replacing it with a doll resembling the snow witch. Since that day, she has actually been hiding in a tower behind Caria Manor, well protected by the fortress's many traps, but also by the faithful knight Loretta, or at least a projection of her. Finally, at the foot of Ranni's tower, the Glintstone Dragon Adula, defeated long ago by the Carian princess and now sworn to be a defender of the Dark Moon, stands guard. After you've overcome all of these obstacles and discovered the secrets of the Conspiracy of the Black Knives with the help of Rogier, Ranni's quest can finally begin.

With the goal of finding Ranni's original body and thus getting your hands on the Cursemark of Death that Rogier and Fia seek, you decide to enter into her service. The witch sees you as an opportunist, but no matter, she has a very important–and mysterious for now–task for you. She introduces you to her inner circle, which consists of Preceptor Seluvis, War Counselor Iji, and the warrior Blaidd. You meet up with Blaidd in the depths of the Lands Between, at Nokron, the Eternal City.

Unfortunately, you cannot access the main neighborhoods of the city, which are located higher up at the tops of some impassable cliffs.

From here, the information you need can be learned from either Iji or the sorceress Sellen, an old acquaintance of Seluvis. In either case, the next step is the same: you need to travel to Caelid to defeat General Radahn, also known as Starscourge Radahn. Indeed, long ago, Ranni's brother had defied and halted the cycle of the stars using his gravitational magic. However, his reasons for doing this remain unclear. Perhaps it was simply to intimidate and flex his power? Or perhaps it was to prevent other falling stars from coming to the Lands Between, after those sent by the Greater Will, as well as Astel, who destroyed the Eternal Cities? Unfortunately, those very same stars were crucially important for Ranni and the Carian royal family. They guided, or even altered, their destiny. "If General Radahn were to die, the stars would resume their movement. And so, too, would Ranni's destiny," concludes Sellen. Unblocking the stars, and thus Ranni's fate, could also offer you a solution for exploring more of Nokron. Or in any case, that's what Blaidd tells you. Blaidd heads off to Redmane Castle, where a peculiar festival is taking place. Many champions of the Lands Between go there to take on Radahn, the most powerful of the demigods.

After you defeat the Starscourge, following a supremely epic battle, the stars' cycle starts back up as expected. What's more, a shooting star immediately strikes the Limgrave region. "I can't fathom how Radahn was holding back something of that scale," says Blaidd. The impact opens up a new way into Nokron, and Ranni's quest, as well as her destiny, can continue.

As you explore the Eternal City, you finally discover the mysterious object that Ranni seeks. The secret treasure of Nokron is none other than the Fingerslayer Blade, mentioned in the previous chapter. The description of this singular weapon says that it "cannot be wielded by those without a fate, but is said to be able to harm the Greater Will and its vassals." Well, with the death of Radahn, and thanks to the movement of the stars, Ranni again has a fate, and she holds a terrible grudge against the Two Fingers for having chosen her and dragged her into the drama of the Empyreans.

"It is in thy possession, is it not? The hidden treasure of Nokron? My thanks. Finally, all the pieces are in place. Soon must I begin my journey. Upon the dark path only I may tread," declares Ranni when you return to her tower to give her the Fingerslayer Blade.

The seal that had blocked access to Renna's Rise, a tower located right nearby, has now disappeared. Renna was the name that Ranni used when you first met her under the moon in Limgrave. She has since apologized for having used the false name. Renna could have been her mentor, the snow witch, whose gear you find in Renna's Rise, or it could have been the name of a former Carian princess—maybe a sister or ancestor of Ranni given that the name is quite similar to Ranni, Rennala, and Rellana—for whom a tower was once built. Or, Renna could simply be a pseudonym used by Ranni, as Iji seems to suggest: "Lady Ranni has departed on her journey. Along the dark path of the Empyrean, from Renna's Rise, as she calls it." Whatever the case may be, at the top of this tower, a teleporter takes you underground, where the Ainsel River flows. There you find a small doll made to look like Ranni.

From that point on, the quest takes a turn to paint a more intimate portrait of Ranni. While the doll is initially lifeless, it eventually speaks to you when you arrive in Nokstella, the second Eternal City, after Nokron, where the Dark Moon was once worshiped. The doll tells you Ranni's story, including how she rebelled against the Two Fingers over her Empyrean status. Feeling inspired and confident, she also tells you about Blaidd, who was assigned to watch over Ranni, or, truth be told, to ensure that she would embrace the fate laid out for her by the Greater Will. However, Blaidd had pledged his allegiance to Ranni. As such, he found himself torn between his duties as a Shadow and his more personal promise to the princess. The description of Blaidd's Gauntlets describes him as he "who would defy destiny itself if it would have him turn upon his Lady." That said, the Two Fingers decide to take advantage of his ambivalence and send out an assassin, a Baleful Shadow resembling Blaidd. In spite of that troubling resemblance, you defeat the assassin. "Now I can finally stand before them [the Two Fingers]. This is farewell, my dear. Tell Blaidd, and Iji... I love them." These are the doll's last words, after which she becomes inanimate once again.

Your journey takes you beyond Nokstella, deeper into the depths of the Lands Between. You cross a lake of scarlet rot, for example, and keep going down. At the deepest level, you encounter—and battle—Astel, Naturalborn of the Void, who long ago partially destroyed the Eternal Cities. Ranni is not there. The moonlight doesn't penetrate that far down into the earth. An interminable elevator ride takes you back to the surface. There, on the broad plateau overlooking the southern end of Liurnia, you spot two moons next to each other in the sky. The normal one belongs to Rennala, and the dark moon belongs to Ranni. Not far from there are the ruins of the Cathedral of Manus Celes—seemingly meaning something like the "Divine Hand," an idea belonging to the same lexical field as the Two Fingers. Glintstone Dragon Adula makes one last appearance to keep you out, but fails. Below the cathedral, you find Ranni, sitting in front of the Two Fingers, which has been eviscerated by the Fingerslayer Blade. The messenger lies dead and there's blood everywhere. The scene is quite striking. You take Ranni's hand and give her the Dark Moon Ring: "Symbolic of a cold oath, the ring is supposed to be given by Lunar Princess Ranni to her consort."

"So, it was thee, who would become my Lord," says Ranni, satisfied with your recent feats. The witch disappears and you won't see her again until the end of the game when you activate the sign that says "Summon Ranni." She then materializes before your very eyes and picks up Radagon's head as if she's going to restore the Elden Ring herself. But she stops and declares: "The battle is over, I see. To every living being, and every living soul. Now cometh the Age of the Stars. A thousand-year voyage under the wisdom of the Moon. Here beginneth the chill night that encompasses all, reaching the great beyond. Into fear, doubt, and loneliness... As the path stretcheth into darkness. Well then. Shall we? My dear consort, eternal." The cinematic ends as you take her hand, the same delicate gesture seen in a number of key scenes in the game. Fingers and hands—an incredibly important motif in *Elden Ring*!

In the end, Ranni succeeded in challenging the Two Fingers. While she transforms into a sort of goddess with you at her side as her champion, her consort, her lord, which is to say, according to terms identical to those of Marika's reign, she nonetheless frees herself from following the same destiny as Marika, who was bound to serve the Greater Will for many thousands of years. Ranni speaks of a "thousand-year voyage under the wisdom of the Moon"; perhaps the Dark Moon is actually another Outer God, guiding the stars across the night sky. While we have no other indication to suggest that, in any case, the Age of Stars will unfold in its honor. "As it is now, life, and souls, and order are bound tightly together, but I would have them at great remove. And have the certainties of sight, emotion, faith, and touch... All become impossibilities. Which is why I would abandon this soil, with mine order. [...] Mine will be an order not of gold, but the stars and moon of the chill night."

◈ The Three Fingers: the Age of Chaos

The last in this long list of possible conclusions to your adventure is quite different. Indeed, it is the only ending that gives you no choice, even if you completed the other questlines. Once you have been touched and forever marked by the Frenzied Flame of the Three Fingers, you will have no other option than to follow the path of chaos. Well, that's not quite true. With an object that's quite difficult to find, Miquella's Needle, you can thwart destiny and refuse the title of Lord of the Frenzied Flame.

The Three Fingers, Frenzied Flame—these are terms we encountered earlier in this story, but they still remain unclear. The Frenzied Flame is actually the manifestation of an Outer God, and we can consider the Three Fingers to be its mouthpiece, much like the Greater Will and the Two Fingers. While the golden sparks of the

Frenzied Flame cause the Tarnished to go mad—an unpleasant and even fatal side effect—the evil entity is also, more broadly, the embodiment of chaos.

So, why would you embrace the path of chaos when it is so "easy" to mend the Elden Ring or to take Ranni's hand and enter the Age of Stars? Actually, at least initially, you can follow this path purely with good intentions. Indeed, obtaining the Frenzied Flame is the only way to set the Erdtree ablaze on your own to avoid Melina having to sacrifice herself. Perhaps you just want to save her from her tragic death by taking on the crucial role that she plays for the end of the adventure? Unfortunately, Melina knows all about the Frenzied Flame and she will warn you about it several times before immediately abandoning you if you are touched by the Three Fingers. So, you find yourself bound to serve the Frenzied Flame—you were fairly warned.

The quest that leads you to the Three Fingers begins quite early in the adventure. After a visit to Castle Morne at the southern end of the map, and after a few encounters that end with the death of a blind woman named Irina, you meet Hyetta. You find her in the highlands of Liurnia, far from Castle Morne and Irina's body. However, the two women look a lot alike. You can even say that they're doppel-gangers, but with different personalities and objectives. Hyetta, who is also blind, is looking for a path through the darkness. A "distant light," as she calls it. "It will lead me to my true duty as a Finger Maiden." So, the young woman declares herself to be a "maiden" and is looking for a Tarnished to guide to the Elden throne.

The distant light only appears to her when she eats a Shabriri Grape, a sort of yellowish, swollen eye with a sweet taste that fills the eater with an intense heat. Going from one distant light to the next, Hyetta makes her way to the capital as you give her more of the eye-like fruits.

One of them, the Fingerprint Grape, is taken from Vyke the Dragonspear, a knight who was once the hope of the Roundtable Hold. He was even the Tarnished to get closest to becoming the Elden Lord. However, he became very attached to his maiden and turned to the Frenzied Flame to save her from her sad fate. Sound familiar? Perhaps he too chose to save his maiden from the flames of the Forge of the Giants by taking her place in the inferno. Sadly, his quest for the Elden Ring ended when he found the Three Fingers and the Frenzied Flame. The Three Fingers' fingerprint marked both his body and his soul. Even his gear—his weapon and pieces of armor—was marked by the being's red-hot fingerprints, which deformed and melted the metal. The description of Vyke's War Spear states, "Like Vyke himself, it has been tormented by the yellow Flame of Frenzy from within." Vyke was overcome by madness and abandoned his quest for the Elden Ring as he was neither able to help his maiden, who was left with no one to guide, nor save himself.

Once Vyke's glowing eye is given to Hyetta, she finishes her pilgrimage into the depths of Leyndell, beyond the underground prison of the Omen and the cell of the

Dung Eater. She eventually found the distant light, which turned out to be the embers of the Frenzied Flame. Her fate was to serve a Tarnished in order to further the aims, not of the Two Fingers, but rather of the Three Fingers. "May the Flame of Chaos find purchase within you," she tells you. She adds that if you want to meet the Three Fingers, you will need to remove all of your gear and present yourself in your birthday suit before the strange, grimy-looking metal door located not far away.

Melina warns you: "Please put a stop to this madness. The Lord of Frenzied Flame is no lord at all. When the land they preside over is lifeless." Shabriri, of Shabriri Grape fame, also gives you a warning, in his own way, while appearing as Yura, another character killed in the course of the adventure and who is easily recognized by his headwear, a sort of iron *kasa*, a traditional Japanese hat. Just as Hyetta adopted the appearance of Irina, Shabriri uses Yura's body to achieve his own aims. He appears to you late in your adventure, on the path to the Mountaintops of the Giants. Armed with a nice speech perfectly crafted to make you feel guilty about having Melina serve as fuel to burn the Erdtree, he tells you about the Frenzied Flame and the possibility of saving your maiden. "If you inherit the Flame of Frenzy, your flesh will serve as kindling and the girl can be spared... setting you on the righteous path of lordship. The path of the Lord of Chaos. Burn the Erdtree to the ground, and incinerate all that divides and distinguishes. Ahhh, may chaos take the world! May chaos take the world!" His voice gets increasingly shrill as he repeats his mantra; at the same time, there's something chilling in his voice that puts a damper on your enthusiasm.

This emissary of the Three Fingers is a mysterious character. He has no real body and seems to have very extensive, almost omniscient, knowledge. "It is said that the sickness of the Flame of Frenzy began with Shabriri, the most reviled man in all history," we learn from the description of the Howl of Shabriri incantation. Meanwhile, the description of Shabriri's Woe tells us: "It is said that the man, named Shabriri, had his eyes gouged out as punishment for the crime of slander, and, with time, the blight of the Flame of Frenzy came to dwell in the empty sockets." So, "it is said" all these things about him, and yet no one knows who he really is. In any case, it would seem that he was the first person to fall victim to the Frenzied Flame's torments. Ever since, he has dreamed only of madness and chaos. Above all, he aspires to convince someone to become the Lord of Chaos, as he tried to do with Vyke, and now you.

Below Leyndell, standing in front of the repulsive-looking door, you remove all your gear. The entrance finally opens, with the door literally melting before your eyes. You enter a dark, sinister, empty room. The only thing inside is the Three Fingers. The monster grabs you with its red-hot appendages. Its fingerprints are burned into your flesh, and the Frenzied Flame now lives within you.

Hyetta, your new maiden since Melina abandoned you, shares with you the wisdom of the Three Fingers: "All that there is came from the One Great. Then came fractures, and births, and souls. But the Greater Will made a mistake. Torment, despair, affliction... Every sin, every curse. Every one, born of the mistake. And so, what was borrowed must be returned. Melt it all away, with the yellow Chaos Flame. Until all is One again." She finishes this speech with: "No more fractures... No more birth..."

These few sentences may be the key to understanding the origin of all the elements and events that make up the universe of *Elden Ring*. In the era of the primordial gods, the Greater Will apparently substituted something–an early form of the Elden Ring?–for the original Oneness, resulting in imbalance and fracture. The Outer God then seemingly hid its treasure somewhere in the Lands Between. Being the pure embodiment of Order, the Greater Will organized its plan around that concept. The plan was supervised by the Two Fingers, serving as both mouthpieces for and representatives of the Greater Will. Then, the Three Fingers and the Frenzied Flame came to the Lands Between. Chaos. Order and Chaos. Good and Evil. Yin and Yang. Together, the five fingers of a hand. Balance had been disrupted since time immemorial, and so the forces driving the universe took action to restore it, "until all is One again," as Hyetta says.

As such, you may merely be the puppet of divine forces you know nothing about. By becoming the Lord of Chaos, the Lord of the Frenzied Flame, you can unleash fire on the Lands Between and spread chaos to replace the established Order. However, you'll need to watch out, as your old maiden is apparently looking for you and plans to kill you.

Indeed, in the final sequence of this conclusion, we see Melina, this time with an actual physical body. She looks into the camera with a truly unsettling gaze and announces: "I will seek you, as far as you may travel... To deliver you what is yours. Destined Death." We find similar words earlier in the adventure in the description of Melina's weapon, the Blade of Calling: "The one who walks alongside flame shall one day meet the road of Destined Death." Now that we have a better understanding, the double meaning appears evident. The first interpretation follows the normal course of the adventure, with the flames of the Forge of the Giants consuming the Erdtree and opening the way to Farum Azula and Maliketh's lair. The second interpretation is a warning about the Frenzied Flame, cautioning you that you will face bitter vengeance if you ever succumb to it. Choose carefully!

An alternative path

The *Shadow of the Erdtree* DLC does not offer a new opportunity to finish the game and become the Elden Lord. Instead—and this is quite clever—the expansion pits you against another character who wants to overthrow Marika and her established order. Remember, sometime long ago, Miquella figured out a way to get into the Realm of Shadow with help from his half-brother Mohg and the Formless Mother. The Empyrean went there in search of the Gate of Divinity to elevate himself to god status. He wanted to usher in an Age of Compassion.

✦ The followers of Miquella

You know absolutely nothing of Miquella's extraordinary objective when, after defeating Radahn and then Mohg, you touch the Empyrean's hand—which is to say, the hand of the old corpse wrapped in a cocoon at the top of Mohgwyn Palace—and enter the Realm of Shadow, a place you did not previously know existed. A new world, new peoples, new rules, and, of course, a new batch of memorable characters, most of whom have also traveled to the Land of Shadow to follow and help Miquella.

Needle Knight Leda is the most devoted of this group of followers. She initially guides you through the Realm of Shadow, first in person and then through messages, serving as a sort of shepherd for the DLC's main quest. The needle is one of the symbols of Miquella, and the various needles that you find throughout the game, objects produced by the Empyrean, can be used to counter curses, such as the scarlet rot, and more generally to ward off the influence of the Outer Gods. Adopting that symbol in their name, the Needle Knights were devoted servants of Miquella. Leda is now the last of her order, according to the description of the Lacerating Crossed-Tree talisman.

Redmane Freyja, who was an elite knight in service to General Radahn, is also a follower of Miquella. Radahn first noticed her during a gladiator fight and he soon enlisted her to join his army. "A hideous scarlet wound was once hewn into the center of her face. Later, Miquella gently put his lips to it and the unfading scar became the compass that Freyja would thereafter follow," the description of Freyja's Helm tells us. Freyja herself also tells you this story, which took place in the Swamp of Aeonia when Malenia's rotflower blossom exploded. We don't know how, but Miquella somehow sucked out the poison of the scarlet rot. "Now, I consider this wound my compass," Freyja tells us.

The Hornsent, an anonymous member of his race who thirsts for revenge against Messmer and, more broadly, against Marika and the Erdtree, is another member of the group of followers. Indeed, he is convinced that Miquella will save his people and redeem them. "I believe Miquella's apologies, when he says our delivery will come," are his exact words.

Ansbach, Pureblood Knight, who served the Mohgwyn Dynasty, is the oldest of the group. He was once a formidable warrior for the Dynasty but is now dedicated to scholarship.

Moore, who strikes an imposing figure in his heavy armor made of "verdigris"—a rare metal said to be a gift from an Outer God, according to the armor's description—is a merchant. He maintains a close relationship with the Forager Brood. The Forager Brood is a group of insect-like creatures spread across the Land of Shadow, distributing objects and provisions. There's a fair chance that, under his armor, Moore is one of them; or perhaps he is "their savior, whose name was unknown," as it says in the description of the Forager Brood Cookbooks.

Thiollier is another merchant, and a close associate of Moore. In spite of his lack of self-confidence, Thiollier considers himself an expert on poisons. And he has plenty of them in his inventory!

Finally, Dryleaf Dane is a mute warrior monk with a powerful set of legs. Dane belongs to the Dryleaf Sect, a group of spiritual seekers who "reject dependence on others in all matters of faith, seeking self-discipline and self-sufficiency above all else" (Dryleaf Robe).

✦ Miquella's plan

So, there you have a small collection of vastly different profiles, leaving you to wonder what could have brought them all together in the Land of Shadow. Miquella is well aware of the fragile connections holding them together. So, he simply enchanted each of the characters!

As Leda has historically been the Empyrean's most devoted follower, she's probably not as influenced by the enchantment as some of the others, and Miquella once saved Freyja's life, so she definitely believes in his actions. However, the demigod most certainly enchanted Ansbach while the two battled; the Pureblood Knight had wanted to free Mohg from Miquella's influence. The same goes for Thiollier, who is absolutely obsessed—"I would sacrifice everything, just to gaze upon her, one last time"—with Saint Trina, an entity who was actually part of Miquella. It's a strange concept, though seemingly similar to the oneness of Marika and Radagon, which we will discuss in the next chapter, as it is not of direct importance to this story. While doing research on Saint Trina, Thiollier fell under the spell of Miquella, forgetting even his deepest desires. As for Moore, of the Forager Brood, Dane, who advocates for the independence of the mind, and the Hornsent, who is obsessed with Messmer, nothing else could have brought them together around a common goal. Miquella enchanted all of them.

"[Miquella] knew that his bloodline was tainted. His roots mired in madness. A tragedy if ever there was one. That he would feel compelled to renounce everything," you learn from Ymir, a former Carian preceptor who has moved to the Realm of Shadow, when you ask him about the Empyrean. Indeed, as you make your way through the Land of Shadow, here and there you will find Miquella's Crosses, marking parts of his body and spirit that he discarded in order to sever ties with his past and thus offer the purest version of himself to the Gate of Divinity. "Miquella set off for the tower enshrouded by shadow, abandoning everything–his golden flesh, his blinding strength, even his fate," states the description of Miquella's Great Rune. He even ended up breaking and detaching from the rune, the main source of his power of enchantment.

After Miquella abandons the rune, his charms no longer work on his band of followers. A divide begins to form within the group. Thiollier, again haunted by thoughts of Saint Trina, quickly exits the main questline to search for the abandoned half of Miquella; meanwhile, conflict begins to arise between the other characters. Leda, Freyja, Moore, and Dane versus the Hornsent, Ansbach, and the player character. Indeed, Ansbach finally remembers his past with Miquella: "I believed that with sufficient mastery, even an Empyrean would be within reach of my blade. I could not have been more mistaken... Miquella the Kind... is a monster. Pure and radiant, he wields love to shrive clean the hearts of men. There is nothing more terrifying." The Pureblood Knight then discovers that Miquella intends to use Mohg's body as a host for his king consort. And while he doesn't hold it against you for killing his master–"His Eminence was felled in an honorable duel, and such are the risks of seeking Lordship"–he finds the humiliation inflicted by Miquella to be intolerable.

Before you confront the Empyrean, you will have to take on Messmer at the Shadow Keep. Marika's son turns out to be ancillary to the main story. He has been abandoned in the Realm of Shadow for a long, long time and is consumed by hatred and the curse of the Abyssal Serpent. Still, the battle with Messmer is one of the most interesting and intense of the DLC. For defeating him, you get Messmer's Kindling, which you can use to burn the sealing tree that has shrouded the true form of the tower of Enir-Ilim.

Miquella is with Radahn at the top of the tower, at the Gate of Divinity. Radahn, who was previously vanquished by the player in the Caelid region, somehow found his way to the Realm of Shadow, where "all manners of Death wash up [...] only to be suppressed." We don't know exactly how, but Miquella used Mohg's remains to reincarnate Radahn in the Land of Shadow to stand at his side, younger and more powerful than ever. However, you notice on Radahn's body, particularly his arms,

Omen horns, indicating a sinister connection with Mohg's corpse. Eventually joined by Ansbach, who is enraged, and Thiollier, you battle with Miquella and Radahn.

◈ Two possibilities

If the Empyrean and his consort are defeated, you can continue on your quest for the Elden Ring. The Age of Compassion will not come. After all, you are a Tarnished and Leda was right about your intentions: "It was never Kindly Miquella, was it? The Erdtree was leading you all along. So that you might ascend to lordship. Why come to these lands to begin with? I suppose it must be what his Eminence, or perhaps the Erdtree, desired all along?"

However, there is a unique side to this battle with divine stakes. One that results in a game-over, inviting you to redo the battle; however, it can offer an alternative to the different fates presented in *Elden Ring*. Indeed, during the battle, you can be embraced by Radahn. It's a technique like any of the extraordinary warrior's other battle patterns. However, the second time Radahn grabs you, you bow down to your adversary, fully under the demigod's charm. "Lord of the old order. Let us go together," Miquella says to you from his perch on the shoulders of his consort. The words "heart stolen" then appear in yellow on the screen, instead of the usual "you died" in blood red. When you pledge allegiance to Miquella, supporting his Age of Compassion instead of fighting to usher in an age in which you will be Elden Lord, the game treats this as if you failed in your quest and thus makes you start over, just like you would any other time you die. However, this conclusion to the adventure in the Lands Between could be perfectly satisfying, from a storytelling perspective.

The Age of Compassion could be a benevolent one. Miquella himself appears to be benevolent. His actions speak for him—for example, his attempt to make the Haligtree a sanctuary. He understands the inner workings of the Lands Between, of his family that has been torn apart; he sees the corruption and hopes to put an end to it. However, his methods are questionable. Enchanting a whole bunch of people in the name of doing "good," depriving them of their free will and beliefs because they don't quite see eye to eye with him—those are some pretty extreme measures.

Ever since the first *Souls* games, FromSoftware's titles have always asked us to examine the notions of good and evil, and more broadly, our perception of the "other." Someone who is a stranger to us. Using a lot of universal symbolism, but occasionally changing the rules or the meanings of words we know—here, I'm thinking in general of the ambiguous timelines or, for a more specific example, of the concepts of Fire and Darkness that are pitted against each other in *Dark Souls* and which actually represent the conflict of the gods versus the humans—the game designers push us to reflect on what we accomplish in their games. They encourage us to try to understand what good or evil means in their universe, to revise our own moral standards. The answer is never obvious because the worlds depicted in FromSoftware's games are never simplistic. Of course, neither is our own world, and understanding concepts of good and evil, both in thought and in action, remains one of the big philosophical themes present in our daily lives.

Miquella, with his problematic beliefs and methods, quietly fans the flames of such reflections. He is a "monster," in the words of Ansbach, even though he himself previously served the Lord of Blood, the demigod and his dynasty based on particularly atrocious and bloody rituals. Thus, it's all a matter of perception. The characters and universe of *Elden Ring* prove to be truly fascinating in light of these philosophical questions. Going beyond the writing, the designers brilliantly used their game design to push their ideas as far as they could go. Using the language of video games, they pushed their title to the next level with novel artistic and philosophical mechanisms. They could have simply offered a different ending when you go to reforge the Elden Ring, a conclusion centered on the Age of Compassion, and it would have worked, even if the surprise factor would have been lacking. Instead, they chose to integrate this alternative ending into a "death" that's a bit different from usual, with the player character giving in to Radahn's embrace. And what if this were the true ending to *Elden Ring*? What if the game of good versus evil was rigged, making you redo the battle until you win, thus extinguishing all hope for an Age of Compassion, which cannot be founded on the principle of domination that comes with a victory in battle? I'll let you be the judge.

CHAPTER 4
ADDITIONAL LORE AND THEORIES

This chapter is dedicated to all of the elements that are secondary to the story recounted in the previous chapters. However, note that when I say "additional" or "secondary," I don't mean that these elements are insignificant. In fact, they are essential for fully understanding the rich and complex universe of *Elden Ring*. This chapter will also offer the opportunity to return to certain points and characters previously discussed, and I will offer various theories and analyses concerning them.

Now, it's time to examine one of the major characters in the Lands Between, related by marriage to Marika's royal family. His name has been mentioned a few times already in this book, but his retreat during the Shattering meant that he was sidelined from the story of the player's quest for the Elden Ring. And yet, the plotlines surrounding Rykard—as I am, of course, talking about him—are particularly fascinating.

Rykard's madness

◈ Intrigue and blasphemy on Mt. Gelmir

Rykard is the son of Rennala and Radagon, and thus the brother of Ranni and Radahn. Those four characters all played more or less important roles in the main story of *Elden Ring*; Rykard, on the other hand, always steered clear of their drama, in his manor perched high up on Mt. Gelmir. However, he was not entirely spared by the war, as some of Leyndell's troops were dispatched to a battlefield not far from Rykard's volcano. "It was the stage of the most appalling battle in the entirety of the Shattering," recounts Sir Gideon Ofnir. However, we don't know the full story of that battle. Only the outcome of the conflict remains visible to this day. We see numerous bodies hanging along the side of the mountain, and we catch sight here and there of former Leyndell soldiers, recognizable by their golden tunics, left to their own devices and devouring the bodies of their comrades lying on the ground. There are two possible explanations for the presence of the capital's soldiers on Mt. Gelmir. The first, corroborated by Gideon, has to do with Rykard's blasphemy, a "grave sin" that forever marked him as an enemy of the Golden Order. We'll come back to that blasphemy in just a bit. The second explanation may be tied to his sister, Ranni.

As we know, shortly after murdering Godwyn, Ranni gave Rykard the Blasphemous Claw, a relic imbued with the Rune of Death that gives the user a certain advantage in a direct battle with Maliketh. So, with Ranni giving Rykard the claw, proof of her involvement in the Conspiracy of the Black Knives, it would seem that she had a stronger affinity with and greater trust in her brother Rykard compared to her other brother, Radahn. Moreover, Radahn impeded the stars, putting a block on Ranni's destiny and likely putting an end to any solidarity they may have had between them. Rykard is also called the Praetor—a term that refers to a magistrate with judicial functions in ancient Rome—and enjoyed a reputation as a worthy sovereign. As such, he would have been seen as the right person to trust with such an important secret, one that led Marika to destroy the Elden Ring.

However, with the outbreak of the Shattering wars, Rykard's trajectory diverged from that of his peers. The wars spread all across the Lands Between, with the expectation that a new Elden Lord would emerge from the chaos. As a demigod, Rykard got his own Great Rune from the Elden Ring, but he decided to seek the ultimate power through means other than the throne of Leyndell and the Erdtree.

While widely known for his noble and heroic virtues, an aspect of his personality and leadership respected by his soldiers, Rykard also directed a group of inquisitors operating in the shadows, hunting down and torturing his opponents. Feeding his hunger for power, the Praetor embraced the dark side of his authority and turned in a much more radical direction to go down the road of blasphemy. The Remembrance of the Blasphemous quotes him: "I understand. The road of blasphemy is long and perilous. One cannot walk it unprepared to sin." It turns out that Rykard became acquainted with the Serpent King—the serpent being a Judeo-Christian symbol of sin that can also be tied back to Messmer's Abyssal Serpent—which consumed him, becoming one with him and his Great Rune, and granting him tremendous power.

The description of the Serpent-God's Curved Sword mentions an "ancient serpent deity" of a religion once practiced on Mt. Gelmir. While the religion has since been forgotten, we still find traces of sacrifices made long ago to this mysterious Serpent King. The god may have been named Eiglay as there's a temple bearing that name located not far from Volcano Manor, the home of the Praetor. The player also does battle with a Godskin Noble in the Temple of Eiglay, with the warrior probably having come to the volcano to kill the serpent god with his god-slaying Black Flame. In short, no one knows how Rykard met the serpent, but in any case, he committed a grave sin by giving himself over to it. The former demigod, on the verge of death and half devoured by the giant reptile, thus became the Lord of Blasphemy. Quite the evocative title. So, we have the Lord of Blood (Mohg), the Lord of Night (Eternal Cities), and, of course, the Elden Lord: each one an ultra-powerful position with its own distinct objective. Rykard chose blasphemy as the distinguishing feature of his lordship.

Unfortunately, by giving himself to the serpent, he was absorbed, body and soul, by the god. It took control of Rykard's body and used his fragment of the Elden Ring to boost its own influence. When the player finally gets their hands on Rykard's Great Rune, they discover that it has the power to absorb life—just like Rykard's sword, the Blasphemous Blade, and like the Serpent-God's Curved Sword mentioned above. As such, we have to wonder if the Serpent King influenced the power of the rune and bent it to its own will or if the rune already contained that life-draining power, with Rykard thus appearing to the serpent as the ideal vessel for deploying that power.

After eating the Praetor, the serpent didn't stop there. It devoured all those who presented themselves for an audience with Rykard, from his most insignificant subjects to the most valiant of war heroes. We can still see them writhing about on the surface of the Blasphemous Blade... Looking far beyond the kingdom on Mt. Gelmir, the Serpent King wanted to swallow the entire world and all the gods with it. Rumor of Rykard's depravity spread far and wide across the Lands Between, and Volcano Manor became the center of all kinds of sordid theories. The Praetor's former followers went out in search of a spear—or greatsword, depending on who you ask—called the Serpent-Hunter, supposedly the only weapon capable of wounding and killing the serpent god.

◈ Lady Tanith

Following Rykard's transformation, which prevented him from being able to appear in public or even from governing his dominion, Lady Tanith took charge of Volcano Manor. According to the description of the Consort's Mask worn by Tanith, she was once "a dancer in a foreign land"—perhaps a Dancer of Ranah, like the one we meet in *Shadow of the Erdtree*. When Rykard met Tanith, he was immediately smitten with her and chose her to be his consort. Surprisingly, Tanith really developed feelings for him much later on, after her husband was eaten by the Serpent King. She was also the only human that he could bear to have by his side—or at least she was the only person he didn't devour.

Tanith made the manor her home and founded the movement known as the Recusants, a group of powerful warriors who hunted the Tarnished of the Roundtable Hold, i.e., those who had pledged themselves to the Two Fingers. Rykard had always seen the Golden Order and the Erdtree as targets to be deposed, and the Recusants were recruited to pursue those ambitions. And the group was never particularly scrupulous in its methods: they followed the philosophy that might makes right. For example, a member named Anastasia, known as the Tarnished-Eater, disguises herself as a Finger Maiden in order to trap unwitting Tarnished. With her giant Sacred Butchering Knife—so much for being discreet!—she easily kills her prey and then butchers it, before gobbling it up like an ogress. Hence her nickname, "the Ogress."

For years, Tanith and her Recusants thus carried on with Rykard's plans. After the player infiltrates Tanith's group of warriors, she explains to them: "The Erdtree blessed the Tarnished with Grace. But it was all too meager, in the face of the enormity of their task. The Tarnished were forced to scavenge, squabbling for crumbs. Like the shardbearers, vying for power in the wake of the Shattering. Our Lord, indignant, had refused. To scurry about, fighting over what miserly scraps they allow us. If the Erdtree, and indeed the very gods, would debase us so, then we are willing to raise the banner of resistance, even if it means heresy." More resistance fighters challenging the Erdtree—they could have had their own conclusion to the adventure!

The path of Rykard, which we might otherwise call the Praetor's justice, is thus embodied by this strange character named Tanith, whose name shares sounds with that of Themis, a Greek goddess. Themis was the personification of divine law; she was equivalent to *Iustitia*, or Justice, in Roman mythology, and I'll remind you that the term "praetor" comes from ancient Rome. But the reference goes deeper than the name, as Themis was one of the wives of Zeus, the almighty god of Olympus, reminding us of the immoderate ambitions of Rykard and the Serpent King. In addition, as an allegory for justice, the goddess is represented by certain symbols that we also see in Tanith: the blindfold can be compared to the Consort's Mask; the unsheathed sword can be represented by the massive sword held in front of Tanith's Crucible Knight bodyguard (his presence at the manor can probably be explained as a gift long ago from Marika to Rykard); and finally, there's the obvious parallel of the serpent regularly depicted at the feet of the Greek goddess, even though she is supposed to be symbolically crushing the snake to stop it from spreading its venom. However, while the depictions of these two figures seem to be similar, the interpretation of their symbols and their own interpretations of justice vary greatly between Tanith and Themis. The false impartiality of the Recusants and the targets of their judgment can in no way be viewed as objective justice. They detest the Golden Order and all its followers must be executed!

The Recusants' quest ends, however, when the player kills Rykard by stabbing him with the Serpent-Hunter. Then, the next time we see Tanith, she appears to have collapsed to the floor, lying beside her husband's remains. And she's eating them! "Dear Rykard, please find purchase within me, I wish to be your serpent; your family. One day, let us devour the gods together." Immediately after the player puts an end to her horrifying trance with a coup de grâce from their sword, Tanith's Crucible Knight bodyguard suddenly intervenes. After the fierce battle, Rykard's story arc comes to an end.

But what a strange love story between the Praetor and Tanith! While there's the couple's morbid fascination with the old serpent-god religion, eventually leading to their terrible fate, we also have to wonder about how the two first met, when Tanith was a dancer. The description of the Consort's Mask says that Rykard immediately fell in love with Tanith, at first sight, as if hypnotized. It's hard not to make the connection with the legendary hypnotic snake that uses its power to charm its prey and then devour them. Was Tanith a follower of the ancient Serpent King religion? Could she have enacted a plan when she first met Rykard to eventually restore power to her serpent god? These are just theories, of course, but behind her Consort's Mask, no one knows what her face actually looks like. Speaking of which, masking her true appearance: a technique used by another character at Volcano Manor to incite the player to join the Recusants.

◈ Daedicar's secret

Rya, whose actual name is Zorayas, travels across the Lands Between in search of champions among the disillusioned Tarnished, inviting them to come to Volcano Manor to join the Recusants. Beneath her human appearance, there actually lies an anthropomorphic serpent. Rya believed herself to be Tanith's daughter. "I am told I was born by the grace of a glorious king," she tells us. However, she later discovers that the origin story she was told was a lie. Indeed, like the other serpent-like creatures in the region, she was created through some sort of sordid ritual at Volcano Manor.

At the end of her quest, whether she dies or leaves the manor, Rya leaves behind a talisman called Daedicar's Woe, made from flayed skin: "It is said that this woman, named Daedicar, indulged in every form of adultery and wicked pleasure imaginable, giving birth to a myriad of grotesque children." Daedicar was apparently flayed in punishment for her actions, this torture symbolizing the shedding of snake skin in ancient rituals. While it seems that Daedicar is a character of some importance to the history of Volcano Manor, her name is mentioned nowhere else. We might even draw a link between Daedicar and Tanith. Could Tanith be hiding her face behind a mask because her skin was flayed? What's more, Tanith always considered Rya to be her daughter and she was fascinated like no one else with the manor's serpents, first and foremost Rykard. This could also support the theory about Tanith mentioned in the previous section.

The other residents of Volcano Manor have no close ties to Rykard's family or to his greedy plan initiated with his blasphemy. They are just Recusants following their own motivations. Among them, the one closest to Rykard is Bernahl.

◈ The two Bernahls

The first time you meet Bernahl is in a little wind-beaten shack in the Stormveil area of Limgrave. A devotee to the art of war, Bernahl aims to teach others everything he knows and to travel around learning new techniques. At first, he seems affable, presenting himself as a kind and helpful knight, with a handsome face and well-kept hair. However, your later encounters with him are quite different. Indeed, you meet him again at Volcano Manor many hours later. He's wearing a heavy helmet covering his entire head and carries an imposing mace instead of his two-handed sword. He doesn't introduce himself, at least not at first, and all signs of kindness have disappeared when he talks to you. "But know that the path you walk is blasphemy, and leads only to a miserable death," he tells you at Volcano Manor. The truth is, he's virtually unrecognizable, unless you have a keen eye and recognize a piece of his armor or a particularly good ear and recognize his voice. Now that he's wearing his helmet, Bernahl is plunged into a sort of anonymity; he's just another Recusant, revealing a totally different personality from what we saw earlier when we first met him in Limgrave.

We really don't know how he ended up at Volcano Manor or why he joined the Recusants. However, we can understand that he didn't like the Golden Order. According to the description of the Beast Champion Armor, at some point in the past, Bernahl lost his maiden. She threw herself into the fire at a time when everything seemed to be going the knight's way, when he was a renowned champion of the Lands Between, on his way to becoming a lord. It is heavily implied that Bernahl's maiden sacrificed herself–in vain–to pave the way for him to wield the Elden Ring. Just like for the tragic champion Vyke, the death of a loved one was too much for him. Bernahl turned away from his quest and the Grace that had motivated him. In hindsight, his first words to the player have more meaning, as he questioned the player about their beliefs as a Tarnished: "Does your faith in the guidance of Grace hold firm, despite the collapse of the Golden Order?" It's likely that Bernahl went on to meet Rya on his journey, and she enlisted him to join the Recusants. A new beginning for him among the band of murderers, for whom strength and the art of war mattered more than all other virtues and beliefs in the world.

There are several clues that Bernahl was close to Rykard. First, his mace, given the charming name Devourer's Scepter, depicts a snake wrapped around a sphere, "devouring the world," according to its description. Rykard had such a vision before being consumed by the Serpent King, and the legendary weapon could have been a gift from the demigod to the knight. Interestingly, after you defeat Rykard, Bernahl doesn't seem to be particularly affected. "I harbor you no ill will. The strong take. Such is our code," he tells the victorious player. "O Greater Will, hear my voice. I am the Recusant Bernahl, inheritor of my brother's will, and you will fall to my blade," are the last words he speaks. It goes without saying, his "brother," which can be interpreted as his brother in arms, is none other than Rykard.

As Bernahl no longer has any reason to remain at the manor, he leaves to fight the Recusants' enemies. We later see him again in Farum Azula, where he is continuing his previous quest. After a ferocious duel, the knight perishes, leaving behind a strange object: the Blasphemous Claw. It's the infamous artifact that Ranni gave to Rykard at the start of the Shattering. It can be used to fend off some of Maliketh's most devastating attacks. As such, Bernahl was in on the secret of the Conspiracy of the Black Knives, proof of his particularly close ties to Rykard and his family.

◈ House Hoslow

Among the other residents of Volcano Manor, besides the grotesque recurring character that is Patches, who we will talk about later, there's a man named Diallos. He is a nobleman belonging to House Hoslow, whose motto is: "The tale of House Hoslow is told in blood." This saying is repeated several times throughout the game, reminding us of some of the catchphrases of the families in *A Song of Ice and Fire*, like "A Lannister always pays his debts," for House Lannister, and the famous "Winter is coming," for House Stark. As another nod to the work of George R. R. Martin, Diallos Hoslow looks strikingly similar to Kit Harington, the actor who played Jon Snow in the TV series *Game of Thrones*: similar face and hair, and even the voice actor, Peter Caulfield, sounds like Harington!

Diallos does not begin the adventure on Mt. Gelmir, but rather in the Roundtable Hold. He is one of the characters hanging out there when the player arrives for the first time. He soon leaves the Hold to look for his servant (not maiden) Lanya, who has looked after him "since childhood," according to the young nobleman. The Hoslows' slogan proves to be true when we next meet Diallos in Liurnia. Lanya is dead, lying at his feet. She is the victim of a Recusant attack. Diallos swears on the name of his family that he will exact revenge.

"The Recusants sent a lackey. Can you believe they invited me to join them? Now! After what they did... I can scarcely believe it myself. Do they think me a fool? You might be surprised to learn I took them up on the offer. Then I only had to ask. The location of the Recusant hideout," Diallos tells us. Driven by an unquenchable thirst for vengeance, an irrepressible rage, a bloodthirsty furor, the young knight makes his way to Mt. Gelmir... and does absolutely nothing other than join the ranks of the Recusants.

It turns out that Diallos is a weak and cowardly man, and in spite of his family's adage, he has never known blood, nor battle, nor suffering. In the end, he's all talk but no action; he succumbs to the charms of Tanith's flattery, becoming convinced that he has "the stuff of champions." Part of the reason why her praise works on him is that Diallos has an inferiority complex due to his own history with his family. Throughout his life, he was chaperoned by a servant who wasn't particularly devoted to her duties—he states at the beginning of the game that she is "fickle" and disappears as soon as she gets the chance—while watching his older brother Juno be groomed to be a leader.

Juno Hoslow is now the head of their house. He wears Hoslow's Helm, whose impressive crest of silver flowers is the "symbol of the head of the revered House of Hoslow." He skillfully wields Hoslow's Petal Whip, whose many sharp barbs inflict "devastating blood loss"—a weapon passed down from generation to generation that likely gave the family its famous motto. Word of Juno's exploits spread across all of the Lands Between, reaching Tanith, who invited him, too, to become a Recusant champion. However, he "discreetly refused," according to the description of Hoslow's Armor.

As such, it's no wonder that Diallos always felt like he was disappointing and dishonoring his family when he was compared to the perfection of his illustrious brother. Sadly, there is no winner in this story. Juno ends up being hunted by the Recusants and is executed by the player; meanwhile, Diallos leaves Volcano Manor after Rykard is defeated, with no goals, no home, and no organization to latch onto.

Later in the adventure, we meet Diallos again one last time. He has moved to Jarburg, the hidden village of the Living Jars. We will come back to these singular beings later; anyhow, Diallos has become the Potentate of the village. The use of this term for a sovereign or one who wields great power is amusing because the Potentate of the Living Jars is really just a guardian warrior. Indeed, the Living Jars are hunted by poachers—Perfumers looking for resources to add to their concoctions—and their village is regularly raided. Diallos ends up facing off with one of the raiders. While he manages to kill the man, many corpses of Living Jars are left strewn about the village. And Diallos is also injured.

His quest ends with an interesting question, as he asks the player if, as the village's Potentate, he succeeded in defending and saving the Living Jars. The player can respond either yes or no, depending on how much they like Diallos, who remains decidedly pathetic until his final breath. To his credit, he fought and won the only battle he ever had to face in his life, and it was for an honorable cause. On the other hand, the poacher was able to decimate a good portion of the village's population, and as such, Diallos's victory is not a resounding one. In any case, the player's response has no effect on the outcome of the quest. It's merely about giving either a few moments of redemption or of total dishonor to this poor wretch who has spent his whole life being pushed around and crushed by powerful and complex forces of society.

Duality

Bernahl possesses two opposite personalities, and we can easily know which one we're about to encounter, depending on whether or not he's wearing his helmet. Diallos and Juno, in spite of belonging to the same family and harboring similar ambitions, grow in very different directions. Rya changes her appearance and name depending on who she's talking to. Finally, Rykard, in spite of becoming one with the Serpent King, still has his own face on the back of the giant reptile's neck, and the snake turns one way or the other to either let the former demigod speak or to sideline him. Two different natures can coexist and interact with one another: this is the very definition of duality.

Here, I've only mentioned these very clear examples of duality from Volcano Manor because we've been discussing its residents, but the concept is seen everywhere throughout the universe of *Elden Ring*. Duality is everywhere, from the small details to the big, overarching themes.

◈ Duality, duality, everywhere

The Erdtree and the Haligtree; the warm, solar light of the Erdtree versus the frigidity of the moon; Rennala's moon and Ranni's Dark Moon; the Two Fingers; the two heads of the Twinbird, tied to ancient burial rites; Miquella and Saint Trina; Marika and Radagon; the Golden Order's fundamental forces of causality and regression; the Spirit Jellyfish Aurelia and Aureliette; Gurranq and Maliketh; the two medallions that must be assembled to use the two Grand Lifts of the Lands Between, Dectus and Rold; Godfrey with his violent impulses and Serosh who channels them; the two forms of Astel: Stars of Darkness and the Naturalborn of the Void. I'll stop there, but the list goes on and on. The examples of duality are so numerous and interconnected, cementing together the already rich universe of the game, that undoubtedly, on your next spin around the Lands Between, you might find new ones, perhaps even some not mentioned in this book. It is a real strength of the monumental work that is *Elden Ring*, so let's get into it!

Moreover, as I've discussed previously, at the very highest level of the game's universe, we have the conflict between Chaos and Order. It's yet another example of duality, and a particularly interesting one as it really comes down to the balance between all things, a sort of unity (the opposite of duality) forgotten long ago. I'll remind you that everything in the game's universe came from the "One Great"—a name with more meaning than it initially seems, when you think about it. Out of the fracturing of the One Great arose countless forms of duality, each pair of forces constantly opposing or responding to one another.

At a much smaller scale than the great forces shaping the world, each living thing possesses a body and a soul. The story of *Elden Ring* often draws on this particular duality.

✦ Body and soul

In the world of *Elden Ring*, the body and the soul are two different vectors for a single individual. While this may remind you of dualism in religion or philosophy—the distinction between material and spiritual existence—the people of the Lands Between experience this separation in a very real way. Upon their deaths, at least when all goes according to the Greater Will's plan, their souls nourish the Erdtree, while their uninhabited bodies decay down in the catacombs. The player very clearly sees this, the piles of bodies clinging to the Erdtree's roots, after defeating the catacomb guardians.

There are also cases, under extraordinary circumstances, where a spirit dissociates from its body; the body and soul then each carry on their existence in a state of semi-life or semi-death, each one detached from the other. The game even uses specific terms for those affected by this dissociation: "bodyless" and "soulless." The most obvious example for this phenomenon comes from the Night of the Black Knives, when two demigods each partially perished, with Ranni losing her body and Godwyn losing his soul.

The Prince of Death

Deprived of his soul, the one who would become the Prince of Death still continued to live, or perhaps better put, continued to exist. However, he underwent a surprising physical transformation. When his body and soul were still connected,

Godwyn had a perfectly normal appearance, that of a burly man with long blond hair inherited from his mother, Marika.

But after losing his soul, taken from him by Destined Death, his body mutated and continued to get bigger and bigger. Marks of Death Blight began to appear all over his flesh. The black spines of Death Blight are usually fatal. The Tarnished, at least, die instantly when afflicted with them. However, they don't seem to affect what remains of Godwyn. His body is able to tolerate them. It's interesting to note that resistance to Death Blight comes from the character stat Vitality, and the Prince of Death possesses exceptional Vitality, as we know from the various talismans associated with him, made up of pustules and cysts taken from his face and which greatly boost the user's Vitality. Fia the Deathbed Companion also plays a role in the great Vitality of Godwyn's body, as she transmits to him that which she has taken from warriors by embracing them.

Beneath the fearsome spikes of Death Blight is a mass of flesh with an appearance not unlike that of certain sea creatures. A fish tail and a head that looks sort of like a cross between a squid and a shellfish dominate Godwyn's new look. This unsettling physiognomy doesn't initially seem to bear any meaning. However, we see a similar squid-like appearance in the Wormfaces of the Altus Plateau. These enemies, one of which serves as a boss, are remarkable for their usage of Death Blight to trap and kill their adversaries, much like Fia and her formidable mist sorcery. Besides these sea creature-like beings, most followers of the Prince of Death seem to have a connection to water. Indeed, the largest gatherings of Those Who Live in Death can be found near bodies of water, where the Tibia Mariners pass in their boats. The Tibia Mariners: now there's a very odd handful of bosses. They steer their boats among Those Who Live in Death, seemingly to guide or protect them. The Tibia Mariners possess Deathroot, the precious relics sought out by Gurranq—who, I'll remind you, is actually Maliketh—because they contain fragments of the Rune of Death. In short, the Tibia Mariners are among the emissaries of the Prince of Death, and water seems to connect Godwyn to Those Who Live in Death. Water is also a strong symbol: it both gives life and wreaks destruction, such as in the Biblical story of the Great Flood. Water also, importantly, evokes regeneration, renewal, and purification. The last sentence in the description of the Mending Rune of the Death-Prince, the rune that brings about Fia's ending and the Age of the Duskborn, becomes all the more meaningful in this context: "Thus, this new Order will be one of Death restored."

So, Godwyn's soulless body has transformed into an entity that has inspired a whole race of persecuted people, Those Who Live in Death, who also unintentionally arose from the tragic Night of the Black Knives. It is a trajectory very different from the glorious destiny one might have expected for a demigod of the Golden Lineage.

Wandering Mausoleums

There are other soulless demigods in the Lands Between who belong to a particularly enigmatic segment of lore. Their bodies lie within Wandering Mausoleums, singular structures sitting on four powerful legs of stone and wandering all over the place. "The mausoleum prowls. Cradling the soulless demigod," one of the game's spirits tells you. We cannot open the tombs found inside of the mausoleums, but it is possible to draw on their power in order to replicate the Remembrances of other demigods—only in mausoleums that have bells—or of other very powerful characters.

Who are the soulless demigods entombed in these Wandering Mausoleums? The spirit quoted above also mentions an "unwanted child" of Marika. It could be that the mausoleums, of which there are seven, contain some of the goddess's progeny. The Japanese version of the game uses a more specific term meaning "bastard" to refer to the soulless descendant. Later on in the adventure, during a stop in one of Marika's churches, Melina repeats the words of the goddess's echo she hears: "Hear me, Demigods. My children beloved. Make of thyselves that which ye desire. Be it a Lord. Be it a God. But should ye fail to become aught at all, ye will be forsaken. Amounting only to sacrifices..." Behind this somewhat vague declaration, which can be interpreted in multiple ways, perhaps hides the secret of the bodies in the Wandering Mausoleums. Could the demigods inside be the imperfect children of Marika, sacrificed sometime during or before her reign? This theory may be corroborated by the term used by the Hornsent Grandam in the Land of Shadow, calling Marika a "strumpet." It's possible that from dalliances not recorded in the history of the Lands Between, Marika may have given birth to several unwanted children, who she sacrificed within the Wandering Mausoleums. However, that doesn't entirely make sense given the birth of the twins Mohg and Morgott, who were afflicted with the terrible Omen curse and locked away for part of their lives.

It could also be that the demigods in the mausoleums don't actually belong to Marika's lineage, and are instead the children of other gods. Indeed, among the headless soldiers and knights serving as guardians of the mausoleums, some of them sport Deathbird emblems. As a reminder, the Deathbirds were servants of the Twinbird, an emissary of an ancient Outer God tied to burial rites before the rise of the Greater Will.

Other symbols appear on the armor and weapons of the headless knights, like the bell "which rings in constant mourning for the soulless demigods" (Mausoleum Surcoat) or the solar eclipse, the "protective star of soulless demigods" (Eclipse Crest Greatshield). The solar eclipse is a symbol rarely seen throughout the adventure, but it is all over the place in the area of Castle Sol, in the far north of the Lands Between. The castle's banners feature an eclipse from which the sunlight appears to drip down, an image strikingly reminiscent of certain events in *Dark Souls III*. At Castle Sol, there are two spirits who make some interesting remarks. Here's the first: "Ohh great sun! Frigid sun of Sol! Surrender yourself to the eclipse! Grant life to the soulless bones!" The second, although sounding disappointed, is more specific: "Lord Miquella, forgive me. The sun has not been swallowed. Our prayers were lacking. Your comrade remains soulless..." Both of these spirits were counting on an eclipse to restore life to a soulless body, probably one kept in a Wandering Mausoleum, and furthermore, someone close to the demigod Miquella. Perhaps they were one of the undesired members of Miquella's family, deprived of a soul and sent to a mausoleum?

It's interesting to note that Miquella is himself imprisoned, half-asleep, in a cocoon inside the Mohgwyn Dynasty Mausoleum. And that name is no surprise, as Miquella's body was captured by Mohg to steal his blood. Miquella's spirit, on the other hand, is off exploring the Realm of Shadow. And truth be told, Miquella may also have transferred part of his body there, as he abandons along his path a few bits of his spirit, but also of his flesh!

So, soulless bodies are rare, but they do indeed exist in the Lands Between. The reverse is even more extraordinary, as Ranni appears to be the only case of a person whose spirit has lived on after their body was destroyed.

◈ Twins

We can't talk about the concept of duality in *Elden Ring* without mentioning the various sets of twins throughout the story. Besides the mute and unmoving Twin Maiden Husks found in the Roundtable Hold, the most discreet pair are named Darian and Devin.

D and D

Darian, who is supposedly the elder of the twins, if we're to believe the letter left behind by Rogier after his death, is particularly memorable for the exceptional design of his armor. The Twinned Helm and Armor feature two "entwined twins of gold and silver." The effect is striking, especially as Darian, who we first know only by his initial, D, constantly keeps his hand up to protect the silver twin emerging from his armor. Using either his left or right arm, depending on his posture, he holds the twin as if it were his child.

"The two known as D are inseparable twins. They are of two bodies and two minds, but one single soul. Not once do they stand together; not one word do they speak to one another," the description of the Twinned Armor tells us. It seems that these two characters have a singular bond. Two bodies sharing one soul–a unique situation in light of what we learned in the previous section!

The player collects the armor belonging to D (Darian) from his dead body, which has been consumed by the spines of Death Blight inflicted by Fia after she ensnared him in her trap. According to the armor's description, it "longs to find its way to the other D." You finally meet the other D (Devin) much later in the adventure, high up in one of the Eternal Cities, near the location where Fia sits with Godwyn's giant, misshapen body. Lying on the ground, Devin is barely able to string two words together. After handing him his brother's armor, you meet him again a bit later on next to Fia's body: Devin has just killed her. He is wearing the Twinned Armor and has recovered his ability to speak, along with enough strength to stand and carry out his quest for revenge, as if the singular breastplate wrought in gold and silver gave him new life and even restored his soul.

Indeed, the armor could be the vector of their shared soul, perhaps even carrying memories of each–for example, memories of Fia's face and actions. However, the two Ds prove to have different personalities, with Darian being calmer than his younger brother. Devin, driven by his rage, doesn't bother to support the silver twin head on his armor as his brother did.

"See the wrath of the Golden Order! The Order's justice, writ in blood!," he yells at the lifeless body of the Deathbed Companion, before finishing his speech: "Honeyed rays of gold, deliver my spirit." Indeed, D and D were once members of the Golden Order, "the only institution not to revile them as accursed beings," according to the description of the Inseparable Sword. They would hunt Those Who Live in Death, probably while taking turns wearing the Twinned Armor, for the Golden Order, and particularly on behalf of Gurranq, Beast Clergyman, who would greedily consume the Deathroot taken from the victims.

The strange name, D, and the official title "Hunter of the Dead" are references to the series of novels *Vampire Hunter D* by Hideyuki Kikuchi, whose main character, as you might have guessed from the title, is named D and... hunts vampires.

The other main sets of twins in the story of *Elden Ring* are descendants of Marika. They are all cursed in their own way, and while we've already examined them briefly in previous chapters, it's now time to take a closer look at the connections between them.

The Omens M and M

Morgott and Mohg, the Omens locked up for the first part of their lives below the city of Leyndell, bound by magical shackles, follow two completely opposite trajectories.

After the Shattering, Morgott became the Lord of Leyndell, the Omen King, and even became known as "the Grace-Given," as Sir Gideon Ofnir tells you. The Omen curse, in addition to causing horns to sprout all over the affected person's body, leaves the victim untouched by Grace, which is to say that they are cut off from the Erdtree. As such, Morgott managed to overcome his curse and even "took it upon himself to become the Erdtree's protector," according to the Remembrance of the Omen King. The description of Morgott's Cursed Sword, with its superb multi-colored blade, tells us: "The accursed blood that Morgott recanted and sealed away reformed into this blade." So, he eventually "recanted," a term typically used for a person who gives up a belief, religious or otherwise, and transferred his cursed blood into his sword.

His brother Mohg also succeeded in breaking out of his prison by means of blood. However, unlike Morgott and his transcendence, Mohg was always fascinated with his cursed Omen blood and eventually decided to worship the Formless Mother, an Outer God tied to accursed blood.

The twins Morgott and Mohg mirror one another in their actions, but also in their Great Runes. The two are similar, but Morgott's is more straightforward and better defined, while Mohg's "is soaked in accursed blood."

The Empyreans M and M

Miquella and Malenia are also on the list of cursed twins (though are there any twins at all in *Elden Ring* free of curses?). Their connection is very different from that of Mohg and Morgott, who were locked up together below Leyndell for ages and ages before going their separate ways to follow their own destinies. Indeed, Miquella and Malenia have always worked together to overcome their curse. For example, Miquella developed his needles to keep his sister's scarlet rot in check; meanwhile, Malenia made a commitment to use her power to protect and elevate her brother, even adopting the title "Blade of Miquella." So, after the Shattering, she waged war against Radahn to communicate a message from her brother: that he wished for the great warrior to become his consort. In any case, while we already know much of their story, each of the twin Empyreans also possesses an interesting duality with regard to their own curse.

Malenia is the Scarlet Goddess, or the Goddess of Rot. The description of her blade, the Hand of Malenia, states: "Through consecration it is resistant to rot." In other words, her sacred sword protects her from her own curse. As we'll see later on, it is not the only object to confer this type of protection. However, the powerful connection between Malenia and the scarlet rot has caused all sorts of alterations to the Lands Between, particularly in the Caelid Wilds.

The Battle of Aeonia in the eponymous swamp forever changed the face of Caelid, which fell victim to the scarlet rot. To this day, the abandoned children of the goddess Malenia, anthropomorphic insects that use the Pest Threads incantation, battle with the remainders of the Redmane army.

Gowry the Great Sage is one of Malenia's abandoned children. Bearing a human form, the old man lives in a cabin located near the Swamp of Aeonia and Sellia, Town of Sorcery. The idea of "abandoned children" actually comes from Gowry himself: he says that Malenia disowned them when she withdrew from the battle. I'll remind you, Malenia caused a scarlet flower to erupt, destroying the swamp, before Cleanrot Knight Finlay took her back to the Haligtree. Malenia was half-dead after pulling that stunt. "The rotting sickness erodes one's memory," Gowry tells us, and it seems that he's right, given the fidelity of his memories of Malenia's departure...

Anyhow, after the battle, the Sage found several infants in the swamp, five sisters who he raised as his own children: Mary, Maureen, Amy, Polyanna, and Millicent. The player follows the last of these, Millicent, to discover her story and her connection to the Goddess of Rot. That connection is actually quite tenuous, as the first stage of her quest involves finding and repairing an Unalloyed Gold Needle, the famous magical object once crafted by Miquella for his sister to "forestall the incurable rotting sickness." More generally, Miquella's Needles are relics of incredible power, "crafted to ward away the meddling of Outer Gods." There are few of them in the Lands Between, with one having been abandoned by Malenia during the Battle of Aeonia. When you give the needle to Millicent, she plants it in her own flesh, curing her of the scarlet rot. The young woman actually looks strikingly similar to the Scarlet Goddess, from her long red hair to her missing right arm.

If the player gives Millicent the Valkyrie's Prosthesis, she will help them regularly along the path to the Haligtree. At the Haligtree, the formidable sword fighter ends up battling her four sisters, not far from Malenia's final resting place. Indeed, Gowry sent his other four daughters to the tree to kill Millicent. Upon her death, with the needle still planted in her flesh, Millicent will transform into a scarlet flower and offer Malenia a chance at ascending to godhood. The description of the Scarlet Aeonia incantation states: "Each time the scarlet flower blooms, Malenia's rot advances. It has bloomed twice already. With the third bloom, she will become a true goddess." So, Malenia has already bloomed twice, one of those times being during the Battle of Aeonia, allowing the scarlet rot held inside of her to burst forth and bring an end to the endless war. The inscription on a tomb in the swamp confirms: "The Battle of Aeonia. Radahn and Malenia locked in stalemate. Then, the scarlet rot blooms." The other blooming of the scarlet flower is not recorded in the annals of history of the Lands Between; the same is true for many details of Malenia's childhood and youth. The third blooming occurs during her battle with the player, leading to the second stage of the fight with Malenia's other form, the Goddess of Rot.

As for Millicent, at the height of Malenia's power, she is supposed to be reborn as a "scarlet valkyrie," according to Gowry. This plan is supposed to bring about a new Order—another potential ending!—called the Order of Rot, a "cycle of decay and rebirth," again according to the Sage. He believes that Millicent is a "superior bud" compared to her sisters. Millicent also evokes plant imagery in her own dialogue: "I am of Malenia's blood. But in what capacity I know not. I could be sister, daughter, or an offshoot..." An offshoot of Malenia, just waiting to bloom into a scarlet flower, according to her adoptive father.

Millicent does not share this opinion. She returns to the Haligtree, but only to bring Malenia her Unalloyed Gold Needle that she abandoned long ago at the Battle of Aeonia. Millicent explains: "There is something I must return to Malenia. The will that was once her own. The dignity, the sense of self, that allowed her to resist the call of the scarlet rot. The pride she abandoned, to meet Radahn's measure."

At the end of this questline, the player has a choice: they can help Millicent or they can kill her alongside her four sisters sent by Gowry. In the latter case, the bud does, indeed, transform into a scarlet flower, but the young woman does not appear to be reborn as a valkyrie. Millicent is also not the first person to follow or be subjected to this fate: another scarlet flower is found on the way to the arena where you battle Malenia. Next to that flower, you find the Traveler's Clothes, very similar to the garments worn by Millicent. The clothes' description reveals that Millicent may not be the first woman to make this pilgrimage to the Haligtree. Once again, no valkyrie arose from the flower. It seems that the Order of Rot is not destined to take over right away.

When you choose to help Millicent, the quest's conclusion is more satisfying. She pulls the needle out of her own flesh, then gives it to the player before she dies. The player can then bring the needle to its original owner, Malenia, who herself transforms into a scarlet flower after being defeated. As such, the needle was passed down from mother to daughter, before returning to the mother. Millicent offers these last, meaningful words: "Thank you. With your help, I was able to live as my own person, if only in passing." The needle allows the user to overcome the scarlet rot, to avoid its torments and just live one's life. It was a true gift from Miquella to his sister, offered long ago to help her live with her curse.

In time, the relic was unfortunately lost, much like the loving relationship between the twin demigods.

Miquella's curse is very different, as he is condemned to forever remain a child. In the introductory sequence, we see his slender figure and long blond hair inherited from his mother, Marika. He is sleeping in the arms of Mohg. As such, the two aspects of this image of Miquella that really stand out are sleep and androgyny.

There is another mysterious entity in the Lands Between who shares these two particular attributes: Saint Trina. "St. Trina is an enigmatic figure. Some say she is a comely young girl, others are sure he is a boy. The only certainty is that their appearance was as sudden as their disappearance," states the description of the Sword of St. Trina, whose attack inflicts the sleep ailment upon foes.

All of the objects linked to Saint Trina cause sleep, or allow you to craft an object that does so in the case of Fevor's Cookbook. The Fevor in question was an admirer of St. Trina, and there was a time when the saint was beginning to gain more and more followers, particularly thanks to the preaching of her priests. However, Saint Trina suddenly disappeared, just as Miquella's activities suddenly stopped when he was kidnapped by Mohg.

Revelations in the *Shadow of the Erdtree* DLC confirm this intriguing rumor: Saint Trina is indeed a part of Miquella. When he renounced his flesh, abandoning his organs and limbs, the Empyrean also abandoned his love and his fears, in locations very close to what would become the final resting place of Saint Trina. The locations in question are also surrounded by Nectarblood Burgeons shoots that "burgeon forth where the nectar-like blood of abandoned Trina pooled"; they can be compared to the Empyrean-Blood Burgeons which "burgeon forth from where the golden blood of Miquella, the wounded Empyrean, pooled." Not far from the Nectarblood Burgeons, in the depths of the Land of Shadow, we find Saint Trina. We recognize in her the childlike face of Miquella, surrounded by absolutely fascinating purple floral features. We discover Trina, and her eerie resting place, alongside Thiollier, who has long been obsessed with Saint Trina. It must be said that her narcotic powers appear to be particularly captivating, as explained in the description of the Lulling Branch: "In the midst of drowsiness, there is the will to awaken. Feelings that rise from the depths of one's heart."

"Oh, St. Trina... What velvety ambrosia is this? Your poison, and the sweet sleep that follows. Oh, please, let me hear your voice..." Thiollier is under her spell. He drinks in Saint Trina's poison in hopes of hearing her words in his sleep. And he will continue doing so until it kills him. For the player, it's the opposite: they must die and be reborn at least four times to receive, in the deadly, poison-induced sleep, the words of the strange saint. Her words are intended for Miquella, her other half, whose plans to become a god scare Saint Trina. She implores the player to kill her alter ego and thus put an end to his destructive ambitions. According to her, godhood would be like a prison, and killing Miquella would grant him a sort of absolution.

❖ Radagon is Marika

It's interesting to note that the name Saint Trina could be a reference to Christianity's Holy Trinity, the idea that God is divided into three distinct and equal divine entities: the Father, the Son, and the Holy Spirit. However, as we've seen, the major themes of *Elden Ring* tend toward duality rather than trinity, and the divine entity that's central to the Lands Between is none other than Marika and Radagon, two facets of a single god. "Radagon is Marika" is one of the adventure's most important revelations. The simple statement exposes the goddess's surprising dual nature, raising a whole host of new questions. Before we analyze this dichotomy in greater detail, let's take a moment to re-examine the god's two personalities, Marika and Radagon.

Marika

Although she is a shaman, Marika is also a descendant of the Numen. The only information we have about this group is given when the player creates their character at the beginning of the game: they have the option to select a Numen descendant for their character build. The Numen are "supposed descendants of denizens of another world. Long-lived but seldom born." So, they are exceptional beings, and Marika upheld the proud reputation of her people, becoming an Empyrean chosen by the Two Fingers, then the all-powerful goddess of the Lands Between. Marika won many wars with help from a select circle of allies and built an empire thanks to the Greater Will and the Elden Ring. At the height of her domination, she betrayed the Greater Will's Order, as did her Shadow Maliketh, who suppressed Destined Death by binding it within his blade. With this, Marika deceived the Greater Will in order to assert her own vision: a stagnant future without death. She thus became Marika the Eternal.

Radagon

Radagon, meanwhile, is connected to the Giants. His flamboyant red hair is a trait characteristic of this race. "Every giant is red of hair, and Radagon was said to have despised his own red locks. Perhaps that was a curse of their kind," states the description of the Giant's Red Braid. As explained previously, Radagon likely met Marika long ago in the Realm of Shadow, in an age when those lands had not yet been cut off from the rest of the world. Like many other races, the Giants were closely connected to the primordial Crucible, which thrived in that bygone era, particularly in the Land of Shadow. No one knows how, but Radagon and Marika became fused together, allowing Marika to become a goddess. They then had two children, Messmer and Melina, of whom zero records exist in the history of the Lands Between. Similarly, there is no evidence of Radagon's presence during Marika's war against the Giants, on either side of the conflict. His first "official" appearance came during the war against the House of Caria, in which the red-headed warrior led the golden troops of Leyndell, serving his queen valiantly and becoming the capital's champion. He then married Rennala, separating him from Marika for a time. However, when Marika called him back to her side to become her consort and take on the mantle of the Elden Lord, Radagon quickly obeyed. As he abandoned Rennala, he left her an amber egg containing the Great Rune of the Unborn. The forsaken queen became obsessively attached to the gift, losing herself in the darkness of her grief.

The mystery surrounding Radagon and his connection to Marika remains particularly opaque. Certain facts imply that Radagon must have had a life as his own individual: in particular, there's his Giant heritage, but also, later on, his love for Rennala, which was both sincere and out of step with Marika's machinations. Indeed, the fact that he gave Rennala a Great Rune is remarkable, as is the fact that he kept the greatsword that she gave him as a wedding gift. That gift was part of an ancestral tradition of the House of Caria: the queen gives her consort an exceptional greatsword. Ranni actually does the same when she chooses the player at the end of her questline, giving them the Dark Moon Greatsword. So, it seems that Radagon left Liurnia with a certain bitterness, as if he was forced to return to Marika.

Sadly, other clues suggest that Radagon actually manipulated Rennala, probably to weaken her kingdom to the advantage of Leyndell and the Golden Order. First, the Great Rune of the Unborn allows the user to practice a magic of rebirth, a terrible process according to the description of the Juvenile Scholar Robe, a garment worn by young students in Rennala's academy: "Yet their rebirth is not without imperfections, and thus do they repeat the process, eventually becoming utterly dependent upon it. Rebirth is as sleep to them, and with each awakening, memory fades into oblivion."

Given this information, what if Radagon repeatedly used the power of his rune on Rennala? Indeed, the woman who "in her youth [...] was a prominent champion" (Remembrance of the Full Moon Queen) turns out to be "no champion, after all" (Queen's Robe) following Radagon's departure. And we see this for ourselves:

during the battle with Rennala, her mind seems to be elsewhere; she clings to her amber egg while her students assail the player, being constantly reborn thanks to the magical artifact. Just before the second stage of the battle, a new Rennala emerges from the egg. She has been summoned by her daughter Ranni, as if Rennala herself was no longer capable of using her own magic, relying solely on the powers of the amber egg. And indeed, the former champion has lost her shine.

"Lady Rennala was left alone, cradling the amber egg Lord Radagon bequeathed her. Now she devotes herself to it through forbidden rite: the grim art of reincarnation," explains Miriel, the pastor of the Church of Vows, where Radagon and Rennala were married long ago. It's hard to believe that Rennala, the champion who once held her own against the golden army of Leyndell, and also the queen who brought about a rapprochement between the Academy and the Carian royal family, has been left as but a shadow of her former self. Even her kingdom has been gutted, ravaged by the civil war between Caria Manor and the Academy's mages. Should we attribute Rennala's downfall to her grief at Radagon's departure or to her insidious addiction to the amber egg's power of rebirth? Either way, Radagon is at the heart of her disgrace. Even the souvenir of Rennala that he took with him, the greatsword, ends up being transformed: Radagon uses it to forge the Golden Order Greatsword "to proudly symbolize the tenets of the Golden Order."

It's easy to imagine that Radagon "separated" from Marika only to go wage war against the Carian royal family, unfortunately remaining under the goddess's control. It may be that Marika gave him the Great Rune to carry out her plans, as the Elden Ring had not yet been shattered at the time. Once Godfrey had been deprived of Grace and left with the other Tarnished on their pilgrimage, Radagon would have been called back to Marika to again fuse with her. The opportunity was too good for her to miss out on: the champion of Leyndell had become famous across all of the Lands Between, and now Marika could make him her husband. However, certain keen minds like Miriel find these events to be incomprehensible: "The mystery endures, to this day... As to why Lord Radagon would cast Lady Rennala aside... and moreover... why a mere champion would be chosen for the seat of Elden Lord."

Marikadagon

In spite of all the evidence, it's hard to believe that Radagon and Marika really are one and the same person. "Radagon is Marika." An unexpected example of duality. A fascinating one, too. It's the best-kept secret of the Golden Order, one that even the fundamentalists have failed to uncover. Each of the goddess's two personalities represents a fundamental aspect of said Order. Marika embodies causality while Radagon embodies regression. They are closely connected philosophical concepts and are not at all easy to understand. In fact, it's even difficult to describe how each concept connects to each character.

Causality is the idea that behind every effect observed, there must be an action that caused it. On a grand scale, the concept represents an infinite chain of actions (causes) and reactions (consequences) going all the way back from the present to the moment of creation, which you might call the "original cause." What might have caused the fracturing of the One Great, for example, in the universe of *Elden Ring*? Removing a link from this infinitely long and complex chain would mean eliminating every other link that comes after it. Only the last link in the chain of causality can be removed without producing massive repercussions. This process is called "regression." In theory, you could rigorously disassemble the causal chain going all the way back to the original cause. Now, that is not at all the intention of the goddess Marika, but this power to move forward or backward in the creation and modification of all things is a particularly interesting concept.

The description of Marika's Hammer gives a precise example of how causality and regression can come into conflict: it is "the tool with which Queen Marika shattered the Elden Ring and Radagon attempted to repair it." As such, Radagon drew on his power of regression to try to reverse Marika's destructive action. Both characters are imprisoned in the Erdtree, causality and regression clashing with one another in a never-ending duel that plunges the Lands Between into unprecedented stagnation.

When the two fundamental concepts operated in harmony, in balance, Marika made good choices to create and transcend the Golden Order. Her careful decisions used causality and regression in just the right amounts, a system later studied in depth by the fundamentalists of the Golden Order, who developed extensive equations and calculations to understand it. Marika laid down each of her choices, subject to the laws of causality and regression, and this eventually allowed her to realize her own goal of freeing herself from the influence of the Greater Will.

When Radagon split off from Marika to go to war in Liurnia—note, by the way, that he took with him his Great Rune enabling rebirth, a tangible form of regression—it caused a great disruption within the Golden Order. With an important part of the equation cut off, Marika made a bad decision. She deprived her husband Godfrey of Grace and dethroned him from his position as Elden Lord. This came with massive consequences. The greatest warrior the Lands Between had ever known left the capital and abandoned his role as its protector, taking with him a number of his powerful soldiers. In addition to the kingdom's defenses being weakened, the Elden throne was left vacant. Meanwhile, Radagon reproduced a pattern, in a way, with Rennala: they got married and had three children, just like Marika and Godfrey, which we might interpret as a form of regression, or at least of repetition. Through these actions, Radagon also did not make the best decisions, as his three children would later find themselves deeply involved in the schemes of the Lands Between, doing as much as anyone else to overthrow Marika and the Golden Order: Rykard and his Recusants, Radahn fighting Malenia and pushing her to the brink, and Ranni, of course, murdering Godwyn.

Once Marika and Radagon reunited, things calmed down again, but the Golden Order had already been knocked off its axis. And in any case, the two entities remained divided, and undoubtedly less effective than when they were one. The Night of the Black Knives ultimately put an end to their clever blending of causality and regression. Indeed, when you lose a child, all intelligence, all reason, all rational calculations go right out the window. The Golden Order shattered, just like the Elden Ring, plunging the Lands Between into a quagmire of war, leading up to the game's starting point.

Thus concludes our analysis of duality in the game. In this lengthy section, we examined many different subjects, but many others still hide within these fascinating dichotomies that make up the universe of *Elden Ring*. For now, we'll leave behind the theme of duality while staying on the subject of Marika. Indeed, while we've already tried to understand this central character through various lenses, many questions still surround her, particularly regarding her ultimate goal. Why did she do everything she did?

Speculation about Marika's plan

◈ Absolute power

Even though it means stating the obvious, let's just get this out of the way. Marika long strove to obtain the ultimate power. However, once she had it, she still wanted more, more, more. While she was initially persecuted for her heritage, she went on to become an Empyrean, chosen by the Two Fingers to preserve the Elden Ring and bring a new ruler to the Elden throne. She chose to surround herself with the right people to win many wars and reign over a vast realm. After subjugating all of the peoples of the Lands Between, from the hawks of Stormveil to the Fire Giants, she took possession of the Elden Ring and brought prosperity to her kingdom and to the Erdtree.

In Marika's modus operandi for subduing her adversaries, there is a detail that's worth examining. In Leyndell, just before the area where you battle Morgott, a Site of Grace appears called the Queen's Bedchamber. A large bed sits at the center of the room, surrounded by dozens of stone tablets arranged in little piles. The layout is odd, as if this stock of tablets needed to remain within easy reach of Queen Marika.

It actually seems that their function has something to do with subjugation. Indeed, the objects Mohg's Shackle and Margit's Shackle, "made to keep a particular Omen under strictest confinement," are made from these same tablets. They can also be found inside the bodies of certain trolls, held by branches inevitably drawing comparisons to the branches of the Erdtree. These subjugating tablets may originate from very ancient civilizations of the Lands Between. Indeed, statues of old men carrying similar stone tablets can be found in places like Mohgwyn Palace and the ruins of Uld Palace and Uhl Palace. Mohgwyn Palace was built on "the grave of an ancient civilization" (map: Mohgwyn Palace), while the palaces of Uld and Uhl, in spite of their proximity to the Eternal Cities, appear to belong to another era. The monumental architecture and the presence of many Claymen, ancient priests "in service of the ancient dynasty" (Clayman Ashes), speak for themselves. We don't have a lot of evidence of this lost civilization, only a few vestiges remain visible, and the statues might explain the origin of the tablets used by Marika. If her rivals couldn't be convinced, whether by force or by persuasion, to join her, she could always make them change their minds with magic. And these methods were apparently effective given the results the goddess achieved over time. However, they were no replacement for war, for battles and brute, bloody force, the kind that people can see.

Across the Lands Between, battles were held in arenas. Blood flowed for the Erdtree, but also for Marika, so that her divinity would be recognized by all. Some of her echoes transmitted by Melina in her churches clearly evoke this call for violence: "Grow strong in the face of death. Warriors of my lord. Lord Godfrey." Also: "Hark, brave warriors. Hark, my lord Godfrey. We commend your deeds. Guidance has delivered ye through ordeal to the place ye stand. Put the Giants to the sword and confine the flame atop the mount." That particular battle would be decisive for Marika and her followers. In that last quotation, the term "ordeal" stands out, again connecting to the lexical field of religion. From ancient Egypt to the Middle Ages, and even for a time thereafter, the term "ordeal" referred to the idea of submitting oneself to divine judgment through various challenges, each one more awful than the next: walking through fire without being burned, retrieving a sacred object from the bottom of a pool of boiling water, or the most classic example: a fight to the death. The outcome of these ordeals, decided based on the kinds of scars left behind or even just whether or not the person survived, determined if the individual was guilty or innocent. Marika uses the term deliberately, posing the victory of Godfrey and his warriors, who face all sorts of ordeals, as divine judgments pronounced over and over again in their favor. Marika's rise to the position of an all-powerful goddess is nuanced, but also very real, as she ends up wielding the Elden Ring, the most powerful artifact in all of the Lands Between.

However, the power she had acquired remained inextricably tied to the Two Fingers and the Greater Will. Souls continued to be guided to the Erdtree in accordance with the Outer God's plans. Marika remained its vassal and thus she could only use the Elden Ring to compel her people, or even the laws governing the world, to carry out the plan of the higher power. The goddess had aspirations going beyond her position. One of her echoes is suggestive of these desires: "I declare mine intent, to search the depths of the Golden Order. Through understanding of the proper way, our faith, our Grace, is increased. Those blissful early days of blind belief are long past. My comrades, why must ye falter?"

So, Marika took a long time cooking up a plan to free herself from the yoke of the Greater Will. She weighed each and every step from different angles, subjecting them to the equations of causality and regression mentioned previously. The Greater Will was caught off guard when Destined Death was stolen and hidden, leaving the Erdtree to begin its slow decline. The Golden Order replaced the Outer God's Order, and for a very long time, the Lands Between were plunged into unprecedented stagnation. And Marika reigned supreme.

◈ First theory

What follows is pure speculation, but it could be an interesting–if not far-fetched!– explanation for the events that came to shake up Marika's stagnant kingdom. Upon the death of her son, Marika shattered the Elden Ring. With that symbolic action, perhaps she intended to break away, once and for all, from the power granted to her by the Greater Will, which returned to depose Marika and replace her with a new Empyrean. Unfortunately for the Outer God, Ranni also refused to serve the Two Fingers, and Godwyn became collateral damage.

Now, let's imagine that Marika isolated herself within the Erdtree only after plotting for the future. The Tarnished were returning from the Badlands, once again touched by Grace and harboring hopes of ascending to the throne and wielding the Elden Ring, which was left in pieces. The newcomers were fierce warriors, whose vigor and determination Marika could actually take advantage of.

The theory I'd like to examine here arises from this premise: what if Marika was not imprisoned against her will inside the Erdtree? What if, instead, she sealed herself inside in order to amass more power? Indeed, the Tarnished, guided by Grace and driven by their quest for the Elden Ring, explored the Lands Between, took on formidable foes (shard-bearers, for example), and, most importantly, died many, many times. However, instead of encountering Destined Death and returning to the Erdtree to nourish it, as had long been the case, they would be reborn at the nearest Site of Grace or, better yet, next to a statue of Marika. In other words, their souls no longer served the aims of the Greater Will; instead, they went directly to Marika, who could feed on their vital energy bit by bit. This might explain why no Tarnished ever succeeded in dethroning Marika, and even why Grace would eventually end up abandoning each one after a time.

Then, along came the player, or rather, the millions of players brave enough to take on the challenge of *Elden Ring*, a whole heap of new Tarnished to supply Marika with their Grace. It's a very meta theory[8], but let's dig a bit deeper into it. Have you fully taken stock of just how vast and dense the world of *Elden Ring* is? How exhausting it can be to explore the world while keeping up the same intensity for dozens, if not hundreds, of hours? Because of that, many players, convinced that they were entering the homestretch after arriving in Leyndell, then at the foot of the Erdtree, with the incredible battle against Morgott, felt completely dismayed upon discovering that the entrance to Marika's prison was sealed shut. To make matters worse, immediately after that, when the player's maiden Melina–Marika's daughter–tells the player that they must leave the capital, the game's map expands one last time, revealing a whole new area. Moreover, the new area appears to be immense–much more than it actually is. All of this is exacerbated by the fatigue that has set in from the preceding adventure. Many players have reported feeling overwhelmed upon discovering these unexpected challenges. A whole new section of the game begins with climbing a mountain to reach the Mountaintops of the Giants: it's highly symbolic, suggesting a deliberate design choice rather than a simple coincidence. Such a feeling of vertigo is quite rare in video games, and even in other media, but all signs point to it being a conscious decision made by FromSoftware's designers. In a way, we can see that feeling (which is not necessarily a positive one; some might even find it a bit discouraging) as a feat of game design.

So, where does Marika fit into all of this? I'm getting to that. The point of unsettling players is to get them out of their comfort zone. Some even ended up abandoning their game at that point, feeling incapable of continuing for another few dozen hours in order to finish the adventure. We might even say that they lost their Grace, like so many Tarnished before them. In any case, Marika laid out or took advantage of a long odyssey punctuated by obstacles for the Tarnished, with the simple goal of ensuring that they would never reach their destination. Spikes in difficulty, poor

---

8. In its day, *Dark Souls* raised a similarly meta theory about its final boss, who is supposed to be Gwyn, the God of Sunlight and later the Lord of Cinder; however, Gwyn could easily have been replaced by the empty husk of any of the people who had previously sacrificed themselves to renew the cycle of the First Flame. If we push that idea a little further, the empty husk could even belong to one of the players who had chosen, of the two possible endings, the one in which they become the new Lord of Cinder, thus assuming the appearance of Gwyn to deceive future players who would come to do battle and in turn become burnt, empty husks, thus perpetuating the cycle.

character builds, players who simply give up no matter the reason, what's important for the goddess is to discourage even the most determined and to feed off of them until they quit.

When the player reaches the end of the game, and thus destroys Marika inside the Erdtree, it marks the failure of her daring plan. Just before the final battle, Hoarah Loux says: "A crown is warranted with strength!" And after he is defeated, he adds: "Thy strength befits a crown." In her quest for more power, Marika has also embraced the philosophy that might makes right. Before her, there was a whole series of other lords, but she will continue to reign until a more talented upstart challenges her.

Now, you might think that this theory is just a peculiar way of justifying the colossal contents and extreme duration of *Elden Ring*, but there are a few interesting facts to support it. Sir Gideon Ofnir, the All-Knowing, knows more about Marika than anyone else. There's a good chance that he crossed paths with her in the distant past, given that he possesses the Law of Causality, one of the foundational elements of the Golden Order, closely tied to the goddess, as explained previously. And truth be told, Gideon seems to know everyone in the Lands Between. He is nicknamed "the All-Knowing," and yet he is aware that no one can ever know everything. "Knowledge begins with the recognition of one's ignorance. The realization that the search for knowledge is unending. But when Gideon glimpsed into the will of Queen Marika, he shuddered in fear. At the end that should not be." It's a paradoxical concept, "the end that should not be." And it mirrors the description of knowledge, as there is no end to it. Knowledge is infinite. Did Marika envision a reign without end for herself? When the player battles Gideon toward the end of the adventure, the knight's words raise some interesting questions: "I commend your spirit, but alas, none shall take the throne. Queen Marika has high hopes for us. That we continue to struggle. Unto eternity." And as he dies, he adds: "I know... in my bones... a Tarnished cannot become a Lord. Not even you. A man cannot kill a god..." These words, coming from the All-Knowing, are worth examining for a moment. He's a warrior capable of using every type of magic, from Malenia's scarlet rot to the Gloam-Eyed Queen's Black Flame, from the Formless Mother's blood magic to the Academy's glintstone sorcery. He possesses such vast knowledge, and yet his words are so defeatist: this is the starting point that inspired the theory.

During the first visit to Leyndell, Morgott also says some odd things. At the end of the battle against the Omen King, he says: "Tarnished, thou'rt but a fool. The Erdtree wards off all who deign approach. We are... we are all forsaken. None may claim the title of Elden Lord. Thy deeds shall be met with failure, just as I." It doesn't get any more discouraging than that. What's more, Morgott also acts under the guise of Margit the Fell Omen, who, I'll remind you, aims to snuff out the ambitions of those Tarnished who wish to wield the Elden Ring. And indeed, Margit also happens to be the first really difficult boss in the game, and has caused some players to give up after only a few hours of gameplay!

✦ Second theory

Keeping with the idea that Marika was willing to do whatever it took to get out from under the yoke of the Greater Will, and even of the Elden Ring, we can imagine that the goddess might have taken part in the Conspiracy of the Black Knives, and thus in the murder of her own son. This is hard to believe, given that Godwyn must have been the favorite child, or in any case, the only legitimate child of Marika who wasn't afflicted by a curse or connected to her only by marriage.

This theory particularly revolves around the mystery concerning the identities of the women known as the Black Knife Assassins. According to the description of their armor, they were "all women, and rumored to be Numen who had close ties with Marika herself." I brought up this connection in the chapter on the history of the Lands Between, and I suggested that a logical explanation could be that Ranni hired Numen assassins in order to discredit and thus weaken Marika. However, assembling a group of Numen assassins, moreover to conspire against another Numen, would be a real feat given how rare the Numen are in the Lands Between.

As such, it's possible that Marika conspired with Ranni to set the Night of the Black Knives in motion. Ranni was chosen by the Two Fingers to succeed Marika, but the Carian princess had no desire to follow that path. Her fascination with the Dark Moon was stronger than her desire to obtain the ultimate power. It could be that because of Ranni's decision, Marika chose to help her deceive the Two Fingers. She may have told Ranni where to find Maliketh and how to trap him in order to steal a fragment of Destined Death. On the Night of the Black Knives, the Two Fingers lost its greatest asset and Marika lost her firstborn son. However, Marika was given the ideal excuse to destroy the Elden Ring, which she shattered with her hammer. The pieces were shared among the demigods, and all of the kingdoms of the Lands Between were torn apart by war. This gave Marika time to set her new plan into motion. Sacrificing her son made her look like a victim while offering her the opportunity to solidify her own power with a fragmented Elden Ring. And also, what's the point of having an heir apparent when your aim is to hold on to power... for all eternity?

Marika's involvement in the conspiracy might also explain the presence of Black Knife Assassins who arrive to kill Blaidd and Iji at the very end of Ranni's quest. While Blaidd, overcome by a devastating fury, manages to eliminate the Numen, Iji does not survive the attack. This event occurs after Ranni has killed the Two Fingers and decided to overthrow Marika with the player, Ranni's champion, to pave the way for the Age of Stars and the Dark Moon. It may be that Marika did not foresee this turning of the tables and, in an act of desperation, tried to eliminate the people who might try to take her down.

Of course, all of this is just speculation. Marika's true intentions—besides her vengeance against the Hornsent, who she mercilessly slaughters—remain among the greatest mysteries of *Elden Ring*. In truth, while there may be plenty of evidence pointing in one direction, there's an equal body of evidence pointing the opposite way. Might that be her true plan, after all? To throw people off the scent, to cover her tracks, to use the Elden Ring to invent new concepts (like eliminating death or dividing herself in two to reinforce her power) and ultimately to take advantage of thousand-year periods of uncertainty to remain the key goddess of the Lands Between—to become Marika the Eternal.

The people left behind

During her reign, Marika did not treat all people equally. Most humans were accepted because of their souls and their Grace, and thus their utility for the Erdtree. However, any person afflicted by any curse that might cut them off from Grace, especially the Omen curse, was treated quite differently. With any luck, they would be ostracized and excluded from society; those who weren't so lucky would be literally massacred.

For non-humans, their survival would depend on being in Marika's good graces. As we've seen, Those Who Live in Death were hunted and killed. The Beastmen were confined with the rest of their civilization in the floating city of Farum Azula, along with Maliketh. The few remaining Stormhawks were enslaved—we can see chains on their wings—and used to protect the kingdom. The demi-humans were forced into hiding. They concealed themselves within their caves and were finally left alone as the hunters feared their savage and unpredictable nature. Kenneth Haight, a nobleman from the Limgrave region dedicated to bringing about the fall of the tyrant Godrick the Grafted, is the only person to take an interest in the demi-humans. He says that "under the Erdtree, commingling with the demi-humans is made possible." He adds: "Even the vulgar shall not be left behind, under the rule of true Order." Wise words that Marika would never accept. It is interesting to note this idea of "true Order," indicating a desire to change the reigning Golden Order, which discriminates about as much as possible, to move toward a more egalitarian vision of the different peoples of the Lands Between. In other words, Haight's ideas could have led to yet another conclusion of the game!

Finally, with regard to the Misbegotten, they faced a particularly terrible fate.

◈ Hewg and the Misbegotten

The Misbegotten don't really have a consistent appearance from one individual to the next. However, they can be easily recognized by their posture–sort of hunched over–as well as their long arms and the prominent claws on their feet. Other than that, some are winged, while others are not, and some have scales or knots, while others do not. Strangely, those three attributes can be found in the three talismans connected to the primordial Crucible. The Crucible Scale, Feather, and Knot talismans have nearly identical descriptions explaining that certain humans once sported the named attributes; the talismans are described as "a vestige of the Crucible of primordial life. Born partially of devolution, it was considered a signifier of the divine in ancient times, but is now increasingly disdained as an impurity as civilization has advanced." The Misbegotten possess most of these physical peculiarities that are now looked down upon. They also have tails, like one of the Aspects of the Crucible, the incantations used by the Crucible Knights.

The connection between the Misbegotten and the Crucible doesn't stop there. The description of the Winged Misbegotten Ashes states: "The Misbegotten are held to be a punishment for making contact with the Crucible, and from birth they are treated as slaves, or worse." As such, it seems that their ancient connection with the Crucible is the source of their present misfortune. And indeed, Marika lived through that very same era before the Erdtree when the Crucible was powerful and gave rise to numerous lifeforms and primordial gods. The Hornsent–the former persecutors of Marika and her people–were fascinated with the Crucible, a fact that worked against everyone and everything tied to it once the goddess came to dominate the Lands Between.

Certain groups of Misbegotten tried to rise up against their enslavers, like at Castle Morne, on the peninsula in the south of the Lands Between. It's a place that was once controlled by Godrick and his army, but which is now a bloodbath. "The menials have all rebelled," laments Edgar, the castle's warden. He is particularly concerned about the legendary sword of Castle Morne and doesn't want it to fall into the hands of the Misbegotten. The sword in question is the Grafted Blade Greatsword, which you receive after beating the castle's boss, the Leonine Misbegotten, a particularly strong and clever beast.

The Grafted Blade Greatsword is one of *Elden Ring*'s legendary weapons. There are nine such weapons in the game, and three of them are held by Leonine Misbegotten like the one at Castle Morne. So, the Misbegotten apparently prize high-quality, one-of-a-kind, incredibly powerful weapons. It's a detail that leads us to a very interesting theory about the origins of Hewg, the smithing master of the Roundtable Hold.

Hewg is Marika's slave. He has been imprisoned for an eternity and forced to forge the most powerful weapon possible, one capable of slaying a god. It's a task that he never succeeded in accomplishing; that is, until the player finishes his questline and finally brings him the materials he needs. With his ancient-looking scales, his stubby (knot-like) little horns, and particularly his characteristic posture, Hewg ticks most of the boxes to suggest that he is a Misbegotten. Except for that he can express himself perfectly, even if he hates doing so. It's a trait absent in all of the other Misbegotten we encounter. As such, could it be that Hewg was one of the earliest Misbegotten, deriving his extraordinary abilities–in smithing and in speaking, among other things–from the power of the Crucible? As a punishment, Marika decided to make an example of him. Hewg became her slave, and the fate of the Misbegotten was then sealed for the rest of their existence.

The French translation of the term Misbegotten is interesting: *les chimères*. It borrows from mythology: a chimera is a monster with the head of a lion, the body of a goat, and the tail of a dragon. At the same time, the French term erases any suggestion of a link with the peoples of the Lands Between entirely created by humans.

✦ Human creations

From mythology to fiction, from the golem of Jewish folklore to the monster of Victor Frankenstein, the idea of living things created by humans has always been a subject of fascination. The concept implies humans acting as gods and violating the laws of nature, often bringing danger and always producing imperfect results. As it happens, *Elden Ring* is not the first FromSoftware game to present man-made creatures–in particular, I'm thinking of the eerie character that is the doll that resides in the Hunter's Dream in *Bloodborne*.

We have little information about the origins of the artificial beings or how they were made. Still, we encounter them regularly throughout the Lands Between. The quest assigned by the Tarnished warrior Nepheli Loux, whose name obviously makes reference to Hoarah Loux–who may be her relative or just her role model–leads us to encounter a number of different artificial creatures, making it a good jumping-off point for this section.

Your first encounter with Nepheli Loux occurs not far from Godrick's battle arena at Stormveil Castle. She lends a hand to the player in the battle against the Grafted before returning to her adoptive father, Sir Gideon Ofnir, in the Roundtable Hold. The objective of Nepheli's quest is to retake the throne of Stormveil, i.e., to replace Godrick and put an end to his years of cruelty. With Kenneth Haight as a trusty ally, along with the duplicitous Gostoc, Godrick's former slave who has operated behind the scenes, Nepheli becomes the lady (or lord, as the English version doesn't make the gender distinction) of the castle by using the power of storms taken from the giant hawks that once ruled over Stormveil. It is an extremely rare happy ending for the characters of *Elden Ring*. Most of the characters die or lose their minds (or both!) at the end of their storylines. Things are different for Nepheli. She has a difficult time throughout her questline, but if you see it through, she gets a good outcome. On the other hand, Nepheli can die along the way if the player decides to listen to Seluvis, Ranni's preceptor, and give her a strange potion. In that case, you later find her body in Seluvis's secret laboratory, having been turned into a puppet.

In the game, puppets are generally armed and are used to protect sorcerers. They are particularly strong and unpredictable puppet-soldiers—unpredictable because of their four arms (like Ranni) and various erratic, surprising movements. At Caria Manor, Seluvis and his servant Pidia have produced numerous puppets to defend the estate. Unfortunately for Pidia, if Seluvis loses his life, the puppets will exact revenge against his servant, who is totally powerless against them.

Other, much more elaborate puppets can be found in Seluvis's secret lab, located beneath some ruins not far from the towers known as the Three Sisters. Half sorcerer, half artist, the preceptor spends his time creating one-of-a-kind pieces that look exactly like their models. He even goes as far as to kill the models in order to perfect his work, as if his puppets could replace real people. The player can "buy" some of the sorcerer's special puppets, which then act like summoning ashes. After her death from Seluvis's potion, the Nepheli Loux puppet can be purchased to be used as an ally in battle.

A number of obscure figures also appear on the list of puppets, including Finger Maiden Therolina and Dolores the Sleeping Arrow. Dolores is particularly inter-esting as her description tells us: "Dolores once belonged to the Roundtable Hold, where she was both a critic and a friend of Gideon the All-Knowing. It was because of her that he and Seluvis went their separate ways." There is no mention of this character anywhere else in the game! And yet, that description of her puppet offers quite a few revelations. So, Gideon and Seluvis knew each other from the Roundtable Hold, and they had a dispute that had something to do with Dolores. We can easily imagine that Seluvis left the Roundtable Hold, possibly with Dolores, who he trapped and transformed into a puppet to keep her by his side forevermore. Vile. Could there have been a love triangle between Gideon, Seluvis, and Dolores?

Whatever the case may be, Dolores's past presence in the Roundtable Hold and her ability to fire St. Trina's arrows to put her enemies to sleep likely explain Gideon's obsession with Miquella. Every time the All-Knowing talks about Miquella, he shows that he has a real feeling of uneasiness about him. For example, when the player reports that the Empyrean can be found in the palace of Mohg, Lord of Blood, Gideon exclaims: "Ahh, I see! So Miquella was with the Lord of Blood after all! That is some fine intelligence indeed! With it, the final clue has been brought into the light. One of the last few pieces the Roundtable—I need, to put everything together. Well, I wonder what comes next... If he continues his slumber within the cocoon, all will be well. But perhaps it would be safer to destroy it. Miquella is the one thing that remains a mystery to me..." Then, once access to the Haligtree is opened, Sir Gideon says: "With the Haligtree as it is... I suppose Miquella must already be... Ah, my apologies. Lost myself for a moment there. The information you've shared is of great value."

Gideon has long wanted to reach the Haligtree. Ensha, his hostile, mute protector, has been searching for the secret medallion that will activate the Grand Lift of Rold, leading to a secret passageway that marks the beginning of the long path to the Haligtree. Ensha can be recognized by his Royal Remains Armor, made up of bones that belonged to "the soulless king. The lord of the lost and desperate, who was known as Ensha." Now that's quite the mystery! If this ancient king was named Ensha and his bones adorn the armor, who is hiding inside the suit? Is there really someone inside the armor, the pieces of which cover every little part of the body? If so, it seems to be a soulless body that blindly obeys Gideon's orders. Gideon considers himself to be Ensha's "master," and yet he is unable to control him when the player returns to the Hold with half of the Haligtree Secret Medallion and Ensha suddenly attacks the player while Gideon stands by and watches powerlessly, with simply an apologetic attitude. "Ensha got rather ahead of himself, it seems," the All-Knowing comments, aware of how ridiculous this understatement sounds. Indeed, shortly before the attack, Sir Gideon had sent Ensha and a few Omenkillers—easily recognized by their Omensmirk Masks meant to mimic the horned appearance of the Omens—to retrieve the half of the medallion from the Albinauric village. The empty shell of the ancient soulless (at least metaphorically) king took advantage of the outing to terrorize and massacre the residents of the village.

Nepheli Loux was also present in the village at the time. "I witnessed a sight much the same, in my infancy. The oppression of the weak. Murder and pillage unchecked," she tells us. Nepheli is truly shocked by the actions of Ensha and the band of murderous Omenkillers accompanying him, though she is even more disturbed by the fact that the orders came from her adoptive father. "To think he'd order his men to enact such tragedy... Where is the justice he purports, in that? He once told me that if he became Elden Lord, he would never allow the downtrodden to be cheated ever again. Was he simply lying to me?" Nepheli Loux is disappointed and is left reeling. Undoubtedly, this introspection and examination of good and evil helps her collect herself so that she can go on to be the best ruler she can be of

Stormveil. As for Gideon, he regrets nothing. For him, the end justifies the means. He even admits that he took in Nepheli when Grace abandoned her so that he could use her strength and fighting talents for his own purposes. His fascination with Miquella, and probably with his long-lost love Dolores, connected to Saint Trina, takes precedence above all else. If decimating a village of Albinaurics will allow him to achieve his aims, Gideon will do it without a moment's hesitation.

"Albinaurics are lifeforms made by human hands. Thus, many believe them to live impure lives, untouched by the Erdtree's Grace," explains the Albinauric Bloodclot, which is a silvery gray color. A bit like the Mimic Tears of the Eternal Cities–it seems that the color is a direct reference to them–the Albinaurics originate from "ripples" (Ripple Blade). According to the Albinauric Staff, "their innate arcaneness" allows them to spontaneously use sorcery. And, in fact, that "innate arcaneness" influences various stats in the Albinaurics: the object drop rate, holy defense, resistance to Death Blight, and bonuses for status alterations inflicted. As such, the way their stats function is rather arcane, exactly as advertised. The Silver Tear Mask, obtained from the Mimic Tear boss in the Eternal City of Nokron, also significantly increases the arcane stat. It's another similarity that suggests that the Albinaurics were designed with the same objective as the Mimic Tears: to oppose Marika and the Greater Will. Silver is viewed as the opposite of gold, just as the two are symbols of the moon and the sun, respectively. Resistance to holy magic, a strain of sorcery connected to the Golden Order and the Erdtree, is another trait supportive of this idea.

There are at least two generations of Albinaurics, who seem to have no other connection than the method with which they were created.

The second generation is not particularly interesting as it is mainly made up of soldiers, or at least fighters dedicated to watching over and protecting important locations. We encounter many of them throughout the adventure, including around the Academy of Raya Lucaria and Mohgwyn Palace. Their smooth, toad-like heads are unusual, if not absurd. That said, they are agile (the Albinauric Ashes are referred to as "cartwheeling spirits") and are skillful with weapons for hand-to-hand combat. In short, the second generation is only distantly related to the original Albinaurics.

The much-older first generation includes a male model that looks old, sickly, bearded, and bald, with extremely long arms and a hunched-over posture; as well as a female model that looks more like the humans of the Lands Between. While they have legs, none of them can walk normally. To get around, the men drag themselves over the ground while the women ride on giant wolves. Additionally, Commander Gaius, who was sent to assist Messmer in leading the crusade in the Land of Shadow, appears to be an exception. He is neither old nor sickly. Rather, he gives off an air of real power, riding on his faithful battle boar. There is also a female Albinauric not far from the place defended by Gaius. Could she be his companion?

Latenna is another female Albinauric. We meet her in the highlands of Liurnia of the Lakes, accompanied by her impressive wolf, Lobo, who has been killed. Latenna is another person who has been persecuted by Ensha, the "all-hearing brute." She only trusts the player once they show her the right half of the Haligtree Secret Medallion given to them by Albus, the leader of the decimated Albinauric village. As she can no longer get around without her wolf, Latenna accompanies the player in the form of Spirit Ashes, offering her assistance as a peerless archer to help them find the other half of the medallion in order to access the Haligtree. She then appears from time to time on the path to Miquella's sacred tree. The end of Latenna's quest arrives not far from Ordina, Liturgical Town, in the ruins of a building where an Albinauric woman sleeps. The other woman, though much larger, looks exactly like Latenna, right down to the way she's dressed. "Oh young yet towering sister of ours. Let the birthing droplet in. And create life. For us. For all the Albinaurics," says Latenna as she faces her oversized doppelganger. "Our young yet towering sister will give us hope," Latenna then tells the player before thanking them. While we learn from Latenna in another bit of dialogue that the giant Albinauric is named Phillia, her role remains a mystery. We can guess that she represents a new hope for the Albinaurics, or at least for those of the first generation. Perhaps she is supposed to be the mother of a new generation that might be brought about by giving her the "birthing droplet" collected by Latenna in the course of her journey; alternatively, she could be a future spiritual guide who might lead her people to a place where they can finally live in peace, free from persecution. "A chosen land awaits us Albinaurics," says Albus, an obvious reference to the Promised Land in Judaism, also known as the Land of Israel. Moreover, the name Israel shares sounds with the name Elphael, the citadel at the base of the Haligtree, a place of peace and refuge in the far north of the continent.

Miquella and Malenia long ago conceived of the Haligtree to be a haven for the minorities of the Lands Between, those abandoned by the Grace of the Erdtree. The Albinaurics were welcomed there, and Loretta, the former Carian Knight, led a group of them to settle at the giant tree. The description of her Royal Knight Helm recounts: "Loretta, once a royal Carian Knight, went on a journey in search of a haven for Albinaurics, and determined that the Haligtree was their best chance for eventual salvation." Many first-generation Albinaurics lived in Liurnia, which might explain Loretta's inspiration for her initiative. Presently, among the Albinaurics that remain in Liurnia, there's Pidia, the pitiful servant of Seluvis, mentioned previously.

◈ Tragicomedy

Each FromSoftware game has its own batch of zany, absurd, or simply funny characters. These adjectives may be surprising; they seem implausible (absurd even?) given the seriousness and darkness of the universes typically depicted by the Japanese studio. And yet, these characters absolutely do exist. They might grab your attention or put a smile on your face because of their design—like the second-generation Albinaurics mentioned previously—or because of the situations in which they find themselves, or even their dialogue. In *Elden Ring*, given the magnitude of the game and the way it tries to honor the heritage of its predecessors, we of course find a whole slew of funny characters. Unfortunately for them, they almost all suffer a tragic, gruesome fate, which makes the game all the more disturbing and makes the amusement or sympathy of these characters bittersweet.

The Living Jars are a good example, especially as they were created by humans, which also connects them to the subject of the previous section. Indeed, the Living Jars were created "by human flesh and blood," according to the description of the Companion Jar talisman. Said flesh and blood are stored inside the giant jars, which are sealed shut with the seal of the Erdtree, which we can see on top of each Living Jar. They have a funny appearance: they look like big pots with arms and legs of earth and stone sticking off of them. They are perfectly capable of expressing themselves and are very sympathetic characters. Sadly, they are constantly hunted by poachers, as we saw when discussing Diallos, and when they are not being massacred, they are forced to live in isolation from the rest of the world.

To defend themselves, the Living Jars have developed fairly evolved battle talents. Among the Warrior Jars, Iron Fist Alexander is the most emblematic, sort of like Solaire or Siegmeyer from *Dark Souls*. The first time you meet Alexander, he is stuck in a hole. He calls to the player to help him by smacking him until he's knocked loose. It's an extraordinary situation when you're accustomed to FromSoftware's games, in which any little strike against an NPC is usually enough to make them hostile or disappear for the rest of the adventure. But whatever, why not. A young Living Jar in the village describes Alexander: "He used to live here with us, but then he left, to be a champion. I asked to go with him, but he said: 'The path of champions must be trod alone.' So heroic, right? I miss him though. [...] He's big and tough and strong!" Indeed, the Warrior Jar travels around the Lands Between perfecting his fighting skills. In particular, he collects the remains of former warriors inside his jar, which we learn after the Radahn Festival is over. Alexander, who did his best to take part in the big fight, wanders across the battlefield: "The bodies found here are exceedingly fine. Who could expect any less from the very warriors who fought in the Shattering, the greatest of all wars!" After this sequence, Alexander realizes just how powerful the player character is, having managed to defeat even the fiercest of the demigods.

The player and Alexander cross paths a few more times, until the end of Alexander's quest at Farum Azula. Still impressed by the player, Alexander mentions their recent battle against the Fire Giant, who "was practically a god...," according to Alexander. He ends his speech by saying: "I've but one thing to ask of you. Would you kindly undertake my ordeal?" We have previously heard others speak of "ordeals," particularly in words spoken long ago by Marika to her troops. A challenge subject to divine judgment: clearly Alexander takes his quest to become the mightiest of warriors very seriously. However, the outcome of the battle is a foregone conclusion. Alexander dies in an absolutely gruesome explosion of blood and guts, but not before saying: "Victory... was impossible. This vessel... was found lacking..." When he says "this vessel," what he means is that the Warrior Jars pass on their innards from one to the next, in an infinite quest for greater power. The description of Alexander's Innards, which the player collects from the heap of guts left behind after the battle, mentions this tradition: "The jars contain dregs inherited from those who came before. Thus are warriors passed from jar to jar, carrying dreams of greatness." After you give his innards to the young Living Jar in the village, the youth embraces his destiny to become a Warrior Jar and sets out with all of the knowledge and techniques learned by Alexander. And those techniques are truly exceptional, as some of Radahn's remains are included among the innards. Alexander's journey took him far along the path to becoming the greatest warrior, but according to custom, the Warrior Jars must continue finding others stronger than them, making their quest endless.

In spite of his tragic end, Alexander is a sympathetic and endearing character, with his regal intonation and improbable situations—like when he bathes in lava to strengthen his jar. Miriel, the pastor of the Church of Vows, is another of the top silly characters in *Elden Ring*. A giant tortoise wearing a miter on his head? Seriously? His very calm tone and his vast knowledge of Liurnian history make him a soothing and trustworthy character. And while no tragic fate awaits him— other than spending an eternity stuck at his church telling the story of Radagon to every player who stops by—his very presence is surprising. I mean, a tortoise[9] wearing a miter...

Other, even more minor characters add to this other side of the game by being absurd, funny, or even a bit pathetic. I'm thinking of Radahn's tiny horse—named Leonard, according to the game's files—who carries the enormous weight of his

9. A dog.

master on his back. Radahn uses gravity sorcery so as not to crush "his beloved but scrawny steed" (Remembrance of the Starscourge). So goofy!

Among Radahn's inner circle is a man named Jerren. He doesn't seem to have a particularly amusing history: he was once a vagabond and witch hunter, before becoming a guest of the Carian royal family; he then followed General Radahn and organized his festival at Redmane Castle. However, Jerren's character design and manner of dress are totally ridiculous, completely out of step with his role and his surroundings. His colorful tights and puffy pants are reminiscent of the appearance of the eccentric Landsknechts, a band of Renaissance mercenaries who were particularly effective, brutal, and arrogant.

In a totally different register, there's the demi-human seamster Boc, who is on a quest to create the perfect look. We meet him randomly while he's in the form of a bush after having been transformed by a spell; however, he isn't much happier with his true appearance. He finds himself to be so ugly that, if the player gives him a Larval Tear, he will end up going to Rennala to be reborn, costing him his life. Thankfully, there is a possibility of a happier ending for Boc. First, you need to find the Prattling Pate: "You're beautiful"–the Prattling Pates are objects that utter a few words like "Hello," "Thank you," and "Let's get to it." When Boc hears "you're beautiful," it reminds him of his mother. And perhaps it really is her voice that he hears, as the Prattling Pate in question is found near a house in a demi-human village. Boc then concludes his quest with these nostalgic words: "Mum was always the only one who said I was beautiful."

The sorcerer Thops is another character with a tragic fate: he has long searched for a Glintstone Key that would allow him to enter the Academy, which has been sealed shut since the Shattering. As he waits on a bench, his quest having come to a standstill, the player ends up giving him one. Later, we find Thops's body in a room of the Academy. He really should have stayed away from the object of his heart's desire.

Patches is a recurring character in the *Souls* games–he even appears in *Bloodborne*. He is an inveterate traitor and smooth-talker. *Elden Ring* leaves zero doubt as to his duplicity and back-stabbing. The cowardice and dishonesty of this character are palpable, laughable even; as such, it's surprising when, the last time we see him, he reveals that he has deep and sincere feelings. Indeed, when we encounter Patches at Shaded Castle, a fortress in the north of the Lands Between, he is in a particularly bad state and his usual tone has changed. His thoughts are with Tanith, who he met while staying at Volcano Manor with the Recusants, and he exposes his feelings for her. "Makes me sick to see her all bent out of shape," he says, crestfallen. He asks the player to give Tanith the Dancer's Castanets, which he probably stole from her. "Then I can rest easy," he concludes before breathing his last breath. This connection with Tanith is every bit as surprising as the way in which he confides in the player. After getting us accustomed to his trickery and betrayals (concepts relying on the element of surprise), in the end, he really shocks us by sharing his sincere feelings. What a strange sensation!

Big Boggart is an uncouth Tarnished who we find cooking shrimp in the Liurnia region. For a time, we know him only by the epithet Blackguard. He sells boiled prawn and boiled crab, supplies that improve your defenses. The very gourmet descriptions of these items are quite funny, embracing the absurdity of this seafood vendor who we find in the middle of nowhere. Like so many of his fellow tragicomic figures in *Elden Ring*, Big Boggart faces a tragic fate, but also has a sordid past. At one point, he was imprisoned with the Dung Eater, and he actually ends up being killed by him and defiled with a Seedbed Curse.

On the subject of funny yet morbid situations, we also find a few places in the Lands Between that are just unsettling. In particular, I'm thinking of Dominula, the village of windmills, a perfectly minor location that feels like it belongs to another world. In the distance, you see numerous windmills, which evoke the story of Don Quixote and his legendary charge, while riding his steed Rocinante, against a group of windmills he believes to be giants. As the player, riding on Torrent, approaches the Dominula windmills, the ambiance suddenly changes. The epic feel becomes troubling. There are flowers all around, but also strange dancing, laughing women in dirty, even bloodstained, dresses. There's something terrifying about the big smiles frozen on their faces. This macabre ambiguity is highly reminiscent of the film *Midsommar* (Ari Aster, 2019); it may also be a reference to the older film *The Wicker Man* (Robin Hardy, 1973), also belonging to the folk-horror genre. Laughter commingled with tears of terror: how lovely.

We don't talk enough about these characters and situations that are at once dark and comical, largely because of their absurdity. And yet, in each of the titles created by Miyazaki and his team, we find an array of such individuals who clash with the rest of the universe. They maintain the element of surprise that is fundamental to each game. We never know what we're going to find next, nor how we should proceed when faced with a surprise. The contrast is purposeful, cleverly peppered here and there, making it a crucial element in the overall construction of the universe.

Remembrances and projections

The idea of a particularly nebulous timeline is a recurring theme, another foundational element of FromSoftware's universes. As we've seen, it's no easy task to clearly lay out the order of the game's history, and that history is left with many holes; however, I've tried to do so as coherently as possible using the information provided throughout the adventure. Where it becomes even more complicated is when you encounter certain bosses or characters several times, but in different, inconsistent, or even inexplicable situations.

For example, why is there a giant head that looks exactly like the Prince of Death in the depths below Stormveil Castle? The giant head in question bleeds when you hit it, and on it, you find the Prince of Death's Pustule talisman, taken straight from the face of Godwyn himself. It's true that Godwyn is an ancestor of some sort to Godrick, and the presence of his head at the castle could suggest a closer relationship between the two characters; however, the real Prince of Death lies beneath the Erdtree, in the Deeproot Depths. What's more, Godwyn's head appears again deep in some catacombs in the Realm of Shadow. It is the "Prince of Death's cadaver surrogate," if we believe the descriptions of the gear belonging to the Death Knights, who fiercely guard the catacombs. Again, the Realm of Shadow is the place where "all manners of Death wash up"; as such, it may not be such an odd thing for a "surrogate" of the Prince of Death to appear there. The former followers of Godwyn, who initially came to help Messmer, likely became the Death Knights once their crusade was finished.

Another example: how can Loretta defend Caria Manor and also be found at the Haligtree in a much stronger form, using more advanced techniques? One explanation could be that a projection of her remains stuck at Caria Manor, with the abilities and powers she had when the projection was created, destined to forever defend the princess, even though the place seems to have been abandoned for a long time. It's a particularly aggressive memory of a person.

◈ Remembrances from fragmentation

Certain characters in the game, and even certain features, like the Wandering Mausoleums, evoke the important notion of "remembrances." Finger Reader Enia, in the Roundtable Hold, mentions the concept after the player defeats Godrick and collects his Remembrance of the Grafted: "A remembrance of gold has found its way into your possession. Demigods, and even the greater of the champions, are hewn by the Erdtree upon their end, into remembrances. They are... valuable indeed. These remembrances yet house the power of their former masters." When given remembrances, Enia has the power to summon weapons, talismans, sorceries, or incantations closely tied to the corresponding antagonists. It is also possible to replicate the remembrances inside Wandering Mausoleums, which confounds the idea that they're supposed to be one-of-a-kind objects.

So, does this mean that the bosses we battle throughout the game are actually just memories or projections? That would explain how Tarnished like Vyke and Bernahl were once able to get far enough along in the ordeals of the Two Fingers to have real hope of taking the Elden throne. They had already battled the memories of the demigods, like so many millions of players, if we were to extrapolate. Through this lens—which is, admittedly, not very convincing—we can view the quest for the Elden Ring and the exploration of the Lands Between in a whole new way. It's all just memories. It's just a video game, in the arcade game sense, focused purely on gameplay, rather than in the narrative sense, with ambitious stakes. The most concrete way to think of the remembrances of the major bosses is that they are just a way to incorporate a feature of game design allowing the player to duplicate the associated valuable objects and thus claim all of the special gear.

Still, there's all this talk of remembrances and projections, allowing the same character to appear several times, and sometimes in completely contradictory situations. For example, Morgott guards the capital city while Margit the Fell Omen hunts overly-ambitious Tarnished. His twin brother Mohg also appears twice in the adventure in two very different forms. There's the Lord of Blood, of course, but also, in an older incarnation, Mohg the Omen, whom you battle in his original stronghold, below Leyndell where he was long held prisoner. He takes form amid a somewhat inexplicable cloud of black smoke, and his status as a mere Omen naturally makes us think that he is a projection from the past. His presence in the depths of Leyndell suggests that the walls may have absorbed his rage and power over time, and the boss is thus a manifestation of that residual energy.

Radahn is also "duplicated," though this is actually designed to be a plot twist. You must beat him a first time for his soul to be sent to the Land of Shadow, allowing Miquella to resuscitate him using the body of another, who happens to be Mohg. It's a procedure every bit as obscure and esoteric as the previously mentioned projections.

And what are we to make of Igon, the Drake Warrior who once challenged the Ancient Dragon Bayle? Early in the journey through the Realm of Shadow, we find him lying on the ground, terrified, mutilated, missing limbs. However, once at the top of Jagged Peak, he can be summoned in the fight against Bayle the Dread, an incredibly epic battle, and Igon then regains all of his former abilities. He's mobile, powerful, courageous—he becomes an invaluable ally. Two different states, two different physical and mental conditions for two different planes of existence. "My soul yet lies on the mountain," says a quote from him in the description of Igon's Furled Finger, the object allowing you to summon the warrior.

◈ Primal glintstone

Sellen is a glintstone sorceress who uses her powers to project herself into several different locations, notably at the beginning of her questline as she seeks a way to free herself from a tricky situation.

While she was once one of Raya Lucaria Academy's most promising scholars, Sellen was later shunned and considered a "witch," according to the description of the Witch's Glintstone Crown. After receiving this "witch" label, suggesting her magic was viewed with suspicion, she was exiled from the Academy. "It was for attempting to restore the primeval current of glintstone sorcery," she explains. Indeed, she was studying the research of masters Lusat and Azur, the founders of the "primeval current," who also were banished from the Academy long ago. This was explained in the chapter on the history of the Lands Between. Sellen's questline consists of finding the two ancient masters and returning to the Academy to re-establish the primeval current while overthrowing Rennala and the "Carian royal family," as she puts it.

The problem for Sellen is her current situation. She was imprisoned by the Academy beneath some ruins on the Weeping Peninsula, in the south. For a time, the player only interacts with a projection of Sellen in her workshop at the Waypoint Ruins, in the heart of Limgrave—circumstances reminiscent of the encounter with the Dung Eater in the Roundtable Hold. Sellen ends up revealing to the player where her physical form resides and gives them the means to transport her spirit into another body. Quite the plan. After finding her prison, the player plunges their hand inside her body and extracts Sellen's Primal Glintstone. "Seemingly half-alive, blood vessels are visible within. In essence, a primal glintstone is a sorcerer's soul. If transplanted into a compatible new body after their original body dies, the sorcerer will rise again." Her new body resides in Seluvis's secret laboratory. It is a puppet that the Carian preceptor crafted long ago to replace Sellen's original body after her death. Sellen is also somehow indebted to Seluvis, though no one seems to know what that's about; however, the puppet does not really bode well for her. Sellen is eventually revived in the puppet's body. Freed from the constraints of her prison and her projected form, which was restricted to her workshop, Sellen continues her quest for recognition.

◈ Briars of Sin

Another character uses projection to appear in various places and attack nomadic merchants. He is faceless, has a red glow like an Invader, and is surrounded by a light black smoke, similar to the kind we see when Mohg the Omen appears.

He calls himself the "Bell Bearing Hunter," but his armor surrounded with thorns and his battle techniques undeniably suggest that he is actually Elemer of the Briar. The player battles Elemer's true physical form at the top of the Shaded Castle. He wields the legendary weapon known as Marais Executioner's Sword, named after the family to which the castle belongs. "Elemer of the Briar, the Bell Bearing Hunter, snatched the sword from the site of his looming execution, and furnished it with battle skills from his home of Eochaid," states the sword's description.

Eochaid is "a lesser, long-vanished domain," according to the description of the blade Regalia of Eochaid. The names Elemer and Eochaid have deeper meanings: the former means "noble" in Old English, while the latter is the name of a number of kings from Irish myths and legends. This lends a certain cachet to Elemer's character and his mysterious origins. Eochaid was known for its battle techniques, with its fighters' swords whirling around as if dancing. The distant country was also "a land of proudly solitary ascetics," according to the Briar Greatshield's description. Elemer takes austerity very seriously as he has executed and robbed numerous instructors and merchants, hence his nickname "Bell Bearing Hunter" (Bell Bearings being the objects he takes from the merchants' bodies). He was sentenced to death for his actions by the Marais family, who have served as executioners for many generations. Elemer then managed to seize the sword that was to be used to execute him and took control of the Shaded Castle.

It's interesting to note that the image of thorns is used many times in *Elden Ring* and it is a symbol of guilt. We find them, of course, on the Briar Armor, where they are described as "a mark of the guilty," but also on the shields of the soldiers at Stormveil, afflicted by the curse of grafting, and the Shield of the Guilty, which depicts the head of a maiden surrounded by thorns, in remembrance of some unknown sin. Additionally, the Staff of the Guilty boosts the effectiveness of thorn sorceries, like the Briars of Punishment. Absolutely forbidden by the Academy, thorn sorceries are a type of "aberrant sorcery discovered by exiled criminals." The end of their description says: "The guilty, their eyes gouged by thorns, lived in eternal darkness. There, they discovered the blood star." We'll return to this strange "blood star" later, but once again, we find briars or thorns paired with the idea of criminality, or with sin more broadly. Finally, Marika's prison inside the Erdtree is sealed shut by a barrier of briars, likely connected to the Shattering of the Elden Ring and perhaps even the theft of the Rune of Death, which forever changed the plans of the Greater Will. The goddess was found guilty for the ills affecting the Lands Between.

Shadow of the Erdtree offers a different interpretation of the image of thorns. Indeed, they have a deep connection to the Scadutree. In particular, we find them in the Impenetrable Thorns spell, which envelops the caster in "impenetrable thorns grown from the Scadutree"; we also, in particular, find them on the Shadow

Sunflowers scattered all around the Scadutree. The Shadow Sunflowers are equivalent to the Golden Sunflowers that turn to the Erdtree—two flowers held to be sacred in their respective lands. The Shadow Sunflower bears the two main symbols of the Scadutree: shadow and thorns. The Scadutree Avatar—which, by the way, offers one of the best battles in the whole DLC—is a giant Shadow Sunflower whose remembrance tells us: "The Scadutree is the shadow of the Erdtree. Born of dark notions that bear no sense of Order, that twist and bend its stock, rendering it brittle." In this case, thorns are a symbol of protest against the gentleness of the Erdtree, and thus against Marika's influence. Perhaps they even grew in reaction to the goddess's actions? Just as fire was considered a sin in the Lands Between, thorns, in connection with curses and Messmer's secret, could have come to represent guilt over time.

✦ Buds of rebirth

Now that we've talked about thorns, let's stay on the plant theme and talk about buds as a symbol of rebirth. Buds are at the heart of the beliefs of an ancient tribe, undoubtedly closely related to the values of the Crucible: the Ancestral Followers. They now live in the depths of the Lands Between, not far from the Eternal Cities. The description of the Ancestral Spirit's Horn talisman states: "A number of new growths bud from the antler-like horns of the fallen king, each glowing with light. Thus does new life grow from death, and from death, one obtains power." Indeed, the spiritual practices of the Ancestral Followers are centered on the buds that grow from the horns of once-majestic creatures that now live on in spirit form.

The Ancestral Followers belong to a very minor segment of *Elden Ring* lore and they stay away from the Erdtree and all of the drama surrounding it. Still, the interesting thing to look at here is their connection with the Ancestral Spirits. There are two possible battles with the spirit creatures. The lead-up to those battles is the same: light a series of flames on obelisks, then approach the remains of a giant animal, whose dry skeleton suggests that it died long ago. The player is then teleported to a new area—another space-time?—where the animal, an impressive stag, now stands before you, able to move and do battle. Blue buds appear on its antlers and its back, the material manifestation of the beliefs and motivation of the Ancestral Followers. The projections of these animal carcasses into decrepit, but very much alive, creatures raise several questions. While there is no obvious explanation—we can imagine that they are the work of an Outer God or the remains of an ancient god connected to the Crucible, but we have no evidence to support either assumption—the two battles offer all of the drama of an extraordinary boss fight, with enchanting music and lighting. The two bosses are likely an homage to the stag god in the animated film *Princess Mononoke* (Hayao Miyazaki, 1997). The appearance of the Elden Beast, in terms of his size and style, also clearly evokes the immense, ethereal form of the stag god at the end of the film. And let's not forget how the player gallops across the landscape on Torrent, an image reminiscent of the movie's young hero, Ashitaka, riding on his fantastic steed that looks like a cross between a yak and an ibex. A sort of homage from one Miyazaki to another.

◈ *A timeless city*

We've already discussed these two characters who are actually the very same person. Maliketh is tasked with hiding and guarding the Rune of Death; meanwhile, Gurranq searches for deathroot, plants connected to the fragment of the Rune of Death once stolen by Ranni and which give rise to Those Who Live in Death. As such, Maliketh and Gurranq have distinct roles; however, the really odd thing is how they seem to exist in totally different timelines.

For example, even if one of them dies, the other lives on. On the other hand, if the player completes Gurranq's questline and delivers to him all of the requested deathroot, Maliketh's dialogue will change. He will recognize the player, and yet his message will remain essentially the same. Is it just an inconsistency in the game? That would be hard to believe. The floating city of Farum Azula, sometimes called Crumbling Farum Azula, is a world apart from the Lands Between–quite literally, in both space and time. The Ancient Dragon Smithing Stone's description states that it "is said to lie beyond time." Indeed, after the player "completes" the region of Farum Azula by defeating Maliketh and freeing Destined Death, the cinders of the burning Erdtree have already covered most of Leyndell, proof of how time works differently while in the floating city. The Old Lord's Talisman, found in Farum Azula, depicts "the ancient king whose seat lies at the heart of the storm beyond time." The king in question is, of course, the former Elden Lord, the immensely powerful dragon Placidusax. However, his power is gradually declining, much like the slowly crumbling city, the only indication of the strange timeline at play there. Everything else seems to be frozen in time, and Maliketh takes advantage of that to hide out indefinitely within the city to protect Destined Death at all costs.

The separation in time and space from the rest of the Lands Between, and thus from Gurranq, leads to other projections in addition to those discussed previously. However, it's interesting to note that the space-time continuum seems to become distorted whenever you go down into the depths of the earth or when you go high up in the sky. Could this suggest something about the true nature of the Lands Between?

The Lands Between

◈ In the end, what are the Lands Between?

According to the creator

Hidetaka Miyazaki talks about the origin of the name in an interview with *IGN* (June 17, 2021): "The Lands Between is actually a name that was invented by George R. R. Martin himself, when he was coming up with the impetus for this world and writing its history and its deep mythos. So, we wanted to implement that into the game. We hope that as well as taking away the idea of it being the sort of impetus and the starting place for the world, people feel that it's really like an invitation to this mysterious new land. There's a lot of elements of exile and return, and the Lands Between is supposed to invoke this feeling of something that's very mysterious and very ethereal—and we hope that when players play the game, they're going to experience that."

According to myth

So, officially, there is no particular or deeper meaning behind the name. However, the analogy to other similar names is striking. In particular, the name evokes J. R. R. Tolkien's Middle-earth, the setting of his works *The Hobbit* (1937) and *The Lord of the Rings* (1954-1955). It's a fictional world inhabited by imaginary creatures like dragons and trolls, and went on to inspire several generations of fantasy authors, and even creators across all different art forms.

The name Middle-earth is itself a reference to Midgard, literally meaning "middle yard," which is the world of humans in Norse mythology. The lands of Midgard are situated in the exact middle of the nine worlds piled on the great tree Yggdrasil, between the realm of the gods and the underworld, among several others. As for *Elden Ring*'s Lands Between, they follow exactly the same principle. We explore the depths of the world with the Eternal Cities and the "temple in the sky" that is Farum Azula, and the Lands Between are situated right in the middle of those two layers.

According to the game

If we extrapolate out a bit, we can also find explanations more directly linked to the game's universe for the name Lands Between. For example, could it be because the Lands Between are situated between two heavenly vaults? The sky above the surface and the artificial, cracking night sky above the Eternal Cities? As we've seen, the stars are supposed to be direct competitors of the Erdtree, which symbolizes the sun. Whether Ranni on the surface or the Nox belowground, different people have tried to resist the Greater Will and thus isolate their realm between the astral layers.

To this point, we've discussed the Lands Between from a vertical perspective, as that's the way we explore in the game. However, we can also understand the name from a horizontal perspective. Indeed, in the quote above, Miyazaki talks about notions of exile and return, and that's exactly what happened when Godfrey was abandoned by Grace, becoming Hoarah Loux once again, and went into exile with the Tarnished in the Badlands, a faraway region that can only be accessed by ship. The Tarnished later returned to the Lands Between when they were once again touched by the Grace of the Erdtree.

More generally, exile is a recurring theme in the game's universe. Whether criminals or soldiers or knights, the reasons for the exile or banishment of different characters are often shrouded in mystery. Even Roderika the Spirit Tuner belongs to "expatriated royalty," according to the description of the Crimson Hood, which states she likely comes from some faraway kingdom across the sea. The Crimson Hood was "gifted to those who departed on journeys without specific orders, to faraway lands from which they would never return. In other words, the gift of a cloak made it easier for undesirables to be on their way." No one knows anything about Roderika's past, nor what led her to the area of Stormveil Castle, where we first meet her. However, her talents provided in the Roundtable Hold prove to be invaluable for the player in their quest.

Land of Reeds

There are other regions beyond the Lands Between. I've already mentioned the realm of the Numen, as well as Eochaid, the home of Elemer of the Briar, but there's also the Land of Reeds, with obvious Japanese influences. Interestingly, unlike these other regions, we have much more information about the Land of Reeds.

The description of the Land of Reeds Helm tells some of the country's history: "The Land of Reeds has long been locked in a miserable civil war, during which time it has remained alienated from the cultures of its neighbors. Little wonder that the entire nation has succumbed to blood-soaked madness, or so it is said."

The blood and violence of the Land of Reeds are personified by an emblematic individual who has traveled to the Lands Between: Okina. The sharp-minded samurai-sword master once fought Mohg, the Lord of Blood. "When Mohg, the Lord of Blood, first felt Okina's sword, and madness, upon his flesh, he had a proposal, to offer Okina the life of a demon, whose thirst would never go unsated," states the description of the sword, which is known as Rivers of Blood. Okina thus became a Bloody Finger in service to the Lord of Blood, relentlessly hunting other Tarnished alongside his disciples, the Inaba.

The name "Inaba" is a reference to the samurai clan of the same name. They were active in Japan's Sengoku and Edo periods. The information we have about the Land of Reeds generally borrows from Japanese culture and history. For example, the Okina Mask looks similar to the wooden masks used in traditional Japanese theater, and Okina is actually a particular type of play.

It seems that *Sekiro* left its mark on the universe of *Elden Ring*. The *Souls* games also borrowed from Japanese culture, but the references were more vague, mentioning faraway lands to the east. Meanwhile, *Elden Ring* has names taken directly from the era that is the setting of *Sekiro*!

Connections

Some fans have taken these kinds of minor nods to other games and extrapolated to develop complete theories suggesting that *Elden Ring* may be connected to the other universes created by FromSoftware since *Demon's Souls*. Of course, that doesn't make a whole lot of sense, but it's still fun to think about. It's a type of theory often developed around popular sagas. An Easter egg or a subtle reference can be transformed into a deep analysis of the links between universes. We're to believe that Ubisoft's *Far Cry*, *Assassin's Creed*, and even *Watch Dogs* are all interconnected? And the same is true of Fumito Ueda's *Shadow of the Colossus*, *ICO*, and *The Last Guardian*? *Dark Souls* is supposed to be connected to the broken archstone in *Demon's Souls*? These are pure flights of fancy cooked up by fans. However, fantasy can be fascinating, and this idea of a connection beyond the spiritual level between *Elden Ring* and the studio's previous games offers some interesting food for thought.

Among these theories, one makes the link between the universes via the giant trees known as "archtrees" in *Dark Souls*, which are actually seen in the game's introduction. They have no branches or leaves: they're just immense trunks sprouting from the ground and stretching up into the clouds. In the intro, we see dozens, maybe hundreds, of the trees covering the landscape for as far as the eye can see. We later see them again in the subterranean region of Ash Lake. These same trees can be seen in the distance in *Bloodborne*'s Hunter's Dream, but also in the arena of *Elden Ring*'s final boss. In the latter case, they look ethereal and sport the yellowish colors of the Elden Beast. And it's hard not to make the connection between the archtrees and the Erdtree, the Haligtree, the Crucible tree, and all the Minor Erdtrees. What's more, the history of the world of *Dark Souls* included immortal dragons with stone scales, the very same attributes we see in *Elden Ring*'s Ancient Dragons, with their impenetrable granite scales. If we keep stretching the theory, we can draw a link between the Frenzied Flame of the Three Fingers and the First Flame of *Dark Souls*, which brings about the Age of Fire. Finally, the constant theme of the moon in Ranni's questline can be connected to the cosmos from *Bloodborne*, which includes the final boss battle with the fascinating Moon Presence. If we were to draw a straight line from the very beginning of *Dark Souls* to the very end of *Bloodborne*, could we say that the Lands Between are a connector between the two points, which otherwise have no direct correlation? If so, the name Lands Between is well-earned.

Of course, if we start digging down into the details, none of that is particularly coherent, or even serious, but there's something alluring about the idea. Beyond this theory of interconnection between the universes of different games, there's something comforting about finding so many recurring symbols and themes across FromSoftware's productions. Moons, death, giant trees, flames, and moonlight swords—a recurring weapon since *King's Field*—are all elements that show the studio's efforts to create a certain consistency across its games. An Easter egg, an ambiance, a term (*Elden Ring*'s Formless Mother is a reference to *Bloodborne*'s Oedon), a melody, an instrument, a situation (bridges burned by a dragon)—any element can be used to remind us at all times of the creative touch of Miyazaki and his team.

We previously talked about the concept of a palimpsest—when talking about the game's music—a parchment whose writing was purposely erased so that the medium could be reused by another scribe, in a sort of ancient form of recycling. With modern techniques, on certain palimpsests, we can read several layers of text, which blend together and overlap in a chaos of words and ideas. As such, we sort of see this concept of a palimpsest in the games of FromSoftware: their universes, stories, and even their sounds, they are all influenced by a fluid interchange between the studio's various works. *Elden Ring*, the most recent layer of text, is such a sprawling epic that the scribes had to recycle a good number of old rolls of parchment!

What shines through in the game is the impression of discovering a legend rather than a complete modern universe. It's world is full of unknowns and inconsistencies in the history books, depending on who wrote them. The Lands Between sit at the heart of this amalgamation. Given that fact, their name—which remains shrouded in mystery in spite of its connection to Norse mythology—is perfectly apt!

◈ The sky

An unusual characteristic of the Lands Between is that it has two different skies. One above the surface and the other belowground. As has been mentioned already in this chapter, stars are crucially important to the game's universe.

The House of Caria

The ancestors of the sorcerers were the astrologers. These figures from the Eternal Cities read the future in the stars and drew magical power from them. The Carian royal family founded its realm on its belief in the power of the stars; however, other forces intervened to upset that heritage. The description of the Telescope tells us: "During the age of the Erdtree, Carian astrology withered on the vine. The fate once writ in the night skies had been fettered by the Golden Order." To this day, we still find relics of the age of the astrologers, though they are hidden from Marika.

In a locked room in Caria Manor, we find the Sword of Night and Flame, a legendary weapon whose description includes this bit of history: "Astrologers, who preceded the sorcerers, established themselves in mountaintops that nearly touched the sky, and considered the Fire Giants their neighbors." So, here we have evidence of an unexpected connection that might explain how trolls—who, I'll remind you, are supposed to be descendants of the Giants—ended up fighting alongside the Carian Knights against the Leyndell army led by Radagon. What's more, Iji, Ranni's war counselor, is himself a troll. He also wears a Nox Mirrorhelm, created by the Nox of the Eternal Cities, a helmet that "wards off the intervention of the Greater Will and its vassal Fingers."

Another member of Ranni's inner circle wears an item directly connected to the Eternal Cities and the astrologers. Indeed, the Preceptor's Big Hat, worn by Seluvis, has "the movements of the stars drawn on the inside of the brim." The pattern in question is reminiscent of the planispheres created by Andreas Cellarius, a 17th-century mathematician and cartographer who published several remarkable star atlases, such as the *Harmonia Macrocosmica* in 1660. Even the name Seluvis sounds a bit like Cellarius!

And while we're on the topic of references in names, let's take a closer look at the name "Caria." It's actually the name of an ancient region corresponding to the southwest of modern-day Turkey. Caria existed for several centuries and was influenced by different civilizations: the Mesopotamians, the Greeks, the Romans, and the Byzantines. It is said that the Carians worshiped Hecate, a Greek moon goddess. She is even specifically the goddess of the new moon (as opposed to the full moon), which naturally makes us think of the Dark Moon. So, there we can see a direct link to the Moon of Nokstella, the legendary "lost black moon" (Moon of Nokstella talisman) that would later guide Ranni's actions.

Caria derived its name from a hero of Greek mythology, Car. He is an interesting figure for us to look at because he was supposedly the inventor of the *auspicia*. The *auspicia* was a power of divination intended to interpret signs from the gods. It came in many forms, though all of them related to nature. "Augurs" would interpret the flight of birds, while other practitioners of divination would observe the sky and lightning looking for "omens." As such, we can easily see a connection with the Carians in *Elden Ring*, who descended from the astrologers, who also divined the future by observing the night sky.

Finally, a more general parenthesis regarding the ancient region of Caria: around 480 BCE, a famous figure named Herodotus was born. He is considered to be the first historian, as he wrote a text called *The Histories* that chronicled the Greco-Persian Wars and, more broadly, studied the Persian Empire. While offering a mix of historical facts and myth (the prologue to *The Histories* mentions several mythical figures), Herodotus's work served as the very first steps in an exercise of inquiry and writing that has been essential for humanity. In short, if you observe the little fragments of information provided in *Elden Ring*, and the challenge of actually piecing together the game's story, you can understand the difficulty of the historian's work. Ultimately, all of the lore hunters in the game's community are, in a way, following in the footsteps of Herodotus.

Among the Carians in *Elden Ring*, one stands out for his knowledge of Lands Between history. I'm talking about the High Priest Ymir, who once accompanied Rellana to the Land of Shadow. The former glintstone sorcerer ended up establishing himself at the Cathedral of Manus Metyr, built on the site where Metyr, Mother of Fingers, was cut off from the rest of the world. Possibly under the influence of Metyr, or maybe fully aware of what he was doing, Ymir became absolutely obsessed with Fingers. He mastered Finger sorcery, becoming skilled enough to even teach it. He became aware of the Finger Ruins, which he considered to be "hallowed" (Glintstone Nail sorcery). He earned the devotion of two powerful female knights, Jolán and Anna, "Swordhands of Night" (Shield of Night) "born deep underground" (Armor of Night), to protect him. Finally, he decided to become the new Mother of Fingers, as Metyr was unable to fulfill her role. Very strange. While he made it quite far down the road of transformation, he never received any signs from the Greater Will and is eventually defeated by the player. Before this bizarre conclusion to his storyline, Ymir provides us with information on our first few visits to him. Although offering a pessimistic view, his sermon on the "nature of the world," when you ask him about it, is enlightening. He knows all about the forces at play in the Lands Between, involving Marika, the Fingers, Miquella, and the Erdtree. However, we may have reason for skepticism about some of his claims. "Long ago, we began as stardust, born of a great rupture far across the skies. We, too, are children of the Greater Will." What are we to make of this? Is he referring to the One Great and the initial fracturing, as explained by Hyetta? It's possible. It's also possible that he is under the influence of Metyr and the Greater Will. We can have a similar debate about historians and historical truth: no one really knows where we can draw the line between objectivity and bias. Marika herself rewrote history by making Godfrey the "first" Elden Lord. And Ymir is likely trying to write his own history when he makes the wild gamble to become the new Mother of Fingers.

Drawing inspiration from his astrologer ancestors, Ymir is devoted to the distant stars. He even considers the moon, which was viewed by the Carians as being almost divine, to be "merely the closest of the celestial bodies. Nothing more," according to the quote in the description of the High Priest Hat. He studies the life contained in the stars. And according to lore, that life is everywhere!

"The Colour Out of Space"

The astrologers of the Eternal Cities and of the Carian kingdom are not the only people to have a connection to the stars. There is a whole microcosm that revolves around the stars. Between shooting stars and falling meteorites, the Lands Between is the scene of numerous celestial events. As such, the astrologers of old were right to scan the sky in hopes of predicting the future. Every change in the heavens could have great consequences below.

While we don't know hardly anything about the first falling star, carrying Metyr, Mother of Fingers, the fall of the golden star carrying the Elden Beast was one of the first notable—and actually noted—events in the history of the Lands Between. The Greater Will is responsible for sending these falling bodies that would forever change life in the world of *Elden Ring*. Later, Astel, the multicolored "malformed star" (Remembrance of the Naturalborn), fell down on an Eternal City, putting an end to its people's uprising against the Greater Will.

Another star is mentioned in passing in the historical archives of the Lands Between. I'm referring to the previously mentioned "blood star." It appears to criminals and exiles whose eyes have been gouged out by thorns. We also find the words "a blood-stained star is an ill omen" in the description of the Great Stars, a type of weapon called a *morgenstern*, or "morning star" in English, making the real meaning of this phrase ambiguous. In any case, the blood star appears to blinded criminals doomed to an eternity of darkness. This is a constant theme in *Elden Ring*: the blind who see beyond their disability. They are paradoxically able to see the truth in front of them. Adding to this idea, the description of the Prophet Blindfold says: "Why hesitate, if the path leading to the future is clear? Just close your eyes, and walk." We can potentially see in the blood star a connection to the Formless Mother, the Outer God who lives for blood. This theory is supported by the fact that servants of the Formless Mother use roses with incredibly sharp thorns. For example, there's Varré's Bouquet with its steel roses on which "each petal has a sharpened edge, leaving the roses perpetually colored with blood." There's also the Bloodroses, crafting materials that "bloom in festering blood."

We can also consider the blood star from a magical perspective. The glintstones that are the basis for many sorceries come from different sources. The rarest ones come from stars. Sellen tells us, "Glintstone is the amber of the cosmos. [...] It should not be forgotten that glintstone sorcery is the study of the stars and the life therein." Sellen actually considers herself one of the "fallen children of the stars," proof of her fascination with and devotion to the stars. On the other hand, we find red glintstones on Alberich's Pointed Hat, Alberich being a sorcerer who uses thorn sorceries. Moreover, the hat reinforces those very same sorceries, probably thanks to the blood-red glintstones. Also tied to thorn sorceries, the Staff of the Guilty "turns the blood of sacrifices pierced by it into glintstone"—red glintstone, in fact. And interestingly, we see an opposition in the colors of glintstones: the glintstones used by the primeval current are blue (Master Lusat) or Green (Master Azur), colors situated opposite from red on the color wheel.

Onyx and alabaster

There's another kind of magic, represented by a purplish color (thus between the abovementioned blue and red), that's also associated with the stars: gravity sorcery. However, its connection to the stars is very different from that of the Academy's sorceries. Indeed, while the Academy's spells largely rely on drawing power from the stars and their destructive energy when they fall down to earth, gravity sorcery is all about control, both of earth and the stars. For example, Radahn was able to halt the cycle of the constellations thanks to his mastery of gravitational magic. That said, it's not so much the spells themselves that are connected to the stars as it is the masters that teach said spells.

The Alabaster and Onyx Lords are the teachers of gravity sorcery. Starscourge Radahn and Commander Gaius were actually students of an Alabaster Lord in their youth. These lords, with their skin made of stone, whose power has been feared throughout history, are among the great mysteries of *Elden Ring*'s lore. Their opposing colors—onyx being a black stone and alabaster being a white mineral that's also known as "onyx marble"—might make you think that they must be rivals, and yet they seem to share a common goal: to hunt and eliminate "Fallingstar Beasts." These beasts are bosses in the game and are said to have come from meteorites that struck the Lands Between long ago. The arena of the Full-Grown Fallingstar Beast on Mt. Gelmir is actually a crater made by a meteorite. The same is true for the battle arena of the less powerful beast on the Altus Plateau. It's also interesting to note the evolution between the types of Fallingstar Beasts. Their tails seem to grow much longer as the beasts reach adulthood, leaving us to wonder if Astel might be the ultimate evolution of a Fallingstar Beast, given his extremely long tail. There is also a certain resemblance in the impressive mandibles present on both Astel and the Fallingstar Beasts.

The Meteoric Ore Blade is a "katana forged from meteoric ore to dispatch lifeforms born of falling stars." Meteoric ore, of a golden hue this time, is also found in the Onyx Lord's Greatsword, as well as, in tones of blue and white, in the Alabaster Lord's Sword. However, the part of the descriptions of the two weapons characterizing the lords is the same: "A race of ancients with skin of stone who were said to have risen to life when a meteor struck long ago." As such, it seems that they came to the Lands Between to hunt the Fallingstar Beasts, and perhaps even Astel, in that remote era. However, it appears that they failed in their mission.

In response, they then began training followers, like Radahn, to help them in their quest. The Alabaster Lord likely approached Radahn during his time spent in Sellia, Town of Sorcery. In any case, that's what we're told by the Remembrance of the Starscourge. It's a bit odd because the night sorceries practiced in the town are oriented more toward killing and stealth than gravity sorcery. Perhaps it was a coincidence: the ancient lord was wandering through the area looking for a Fallingstar Beast, which turned out to be hiding not far away in the Sellia Crystal Tunnel—becoming a future boss for the player.

A tomb in the Caelid region offers this troubling message: "The Starscourge Conflict. Radahn alone holds Sellia secure. And stands tall, to shatter the stars." What if Radahn used his gravity sorcery on the stars in order to fight back against the Alabaster Lord who had come to Sellia? We actually find the lord locked up in an evergaol not far from Caria Manor, proof that he committed some crime against the House of Caria, and thus possibly against Radahn, the son of Queen Rennala. The Redmane may have used his gravitational magic for protection, for example, to prevent another meteorite from falling and destroying Sellia, just as they had once decimated the Eternal Cities.

The reasons for the actions of the Onyx and Alabaster Lords remain very unclear, just like their origins. Do they, too, come from the stars? Their stone skin could come from meteorites. However, there is zero indication that they have any connection to an Outer God, making them every bit as mysterious as those supreme beings.

✦ The Outer Gods

The call of the Great Old Ones

Fascinating mystery surrounds the Outer Gods, much like the Great Ones from *Bloodborne*. The Great Ones are gods, or at least they are considered to be equivalent to gods, operating on planes of existence different from that of humans. We previously discussed the Moon Presence, which is one of the Great Ones. The name of the group of gods was not chosen randomly: it's a reference to the Great Old Ones from the universe of author H. P. Lovecraft, a group of beings that includes the famous Cthulhu.

Lovecraft's Great Old Ones are terrifying, even unspeakable, extraterrestrials, some of which are worshiped by a handful of followers. Those faithful wait on Earth for their gods to finally awake from their slumber. In Lovecraft's horror mythology, these is also a group of "Outer Gods," the exact same name used in *Elden Ring*. They are cosmic forces that rarely interfere with affairs down on Earth. This is similar to the Outer Gods of *Elden Ring*, who almost never appear in the Lands Between, instead interacting with earthly beings through their vassals, like the Two Fingers or Marika. It's interesting to see how the connection to Lovecraft's works has evolved in the works of FromSoftware: there is always some sort of homage to him. Perhaps their next game will include the Elder Gods from the extended Lovecraft universe, i.e., rivals to the Great Old Ones.

For now, let's take a closer look at *Elden Ring*'s Outer Gods. Because they belong to another plane of existence, we don't really know how many there are, or at least how many there are with a connection to the Lands Between. What's more, certain pieces of information complicate the counting process. Indeed, it's easy to confuse certain gods or god-like beings, i.e., powerful, venerated characters, with the true Outer Gods.

Inner gods

Take for example the "fell god" that "still lurks within the Fire Giants," according to the description of the Flame of the Fell God. It seems that the god in question is just the Fire Giant who the player battles before reaching the Forge of the Giants.

"Once worshiped by the giants, this evil deity is believed to have been slain by Queen Marika," states the description of the One-Eyed Shield. The Fire Giant boss reveals his one eye in the middle of the battle, and his remembrance, obtained after his defeat, allows you to make the incantation Burn, O Flame!, "the power of a fell god." Even Iron Fist Alexander makes a remark about the battle between the player and the Fire Giant: "I doubt there's a single soul who could've handled that giant, other than you. It was practically a god..." In the Realm of Shadow, people talk of "the fell god of fire that haunts the sagas of the Hornsent" (Furnace Visage). This, too, is a reference to the fell god of the Giants; Marika even went as far as to have this fire god's image affixed to the Furnace Golems she sent to carry out her crusade.

The Hornsent, who worship primordial forms of the Crucible, venerate many different gods, such as the divine birds, to get their extraordinary strength and dexterity. Some of those gods were even accessible to mortals, like the tutelary deities, meaning protective gods, present in several forms. The Guardian Deity of Smithery, for example, taking the form of a golem named Taylew, can "imbue weapons with souls" (Smithing Talisman). He is also an expert on the creation of "smithscripts" that make it possible to throw just about any kind of weapon, even big hammers! There is also mention of tutelary deities of the land, hermits who "heighten their spirituality through severe ascetic training," according to the description of the Ascetic's Wrist Guards. Among the tutelary deities, some are really just withered corpses. However, in the palms of their dead hands, Revered Spirit Ash gradually accumulates. That Revered Spirit Ash can be used to boost the power of the person consuming it.

Among the "inner gods," if you will, we of course find Marika and the former partner of Placidusax, a previous Elden Lord, who are considered to be goddesses. The "Serpent God" mentioned in the description of the Serpent-God's Curved Sword is, as we've discussed, connected to Rykard's story. Finally, some believe that Ranni's Dark Moon must be an Outer God. Unfortunately, we have no concrete proof of that, although the Dark Moon's power of attraction is certainly real. After all, it has charmed Ranni, as well as, long ago, the people of the Eternal Cities—and now millions of players.

The five fingers of a hand

Only five Outer Gods are explicitly recognized in the history of the Lands Between. The Greater Will (who we have talked about throughout this book), the Formless Mother, and three others who don't really seem to have a name: the one whose emissary is the Twinbird, the god linked to the Frenzied Flame, and a god tied to the scarlet rot.

While we've talked a lot about the scarlet rot, we haven't yet discussed its associated Outer God. And yet, there is an interesting story about this god, passed down from the distant past. The description of the Blue Dancer Charm tells us: "The dancer in blue represents a fairy, who in legend bestowed a flowing sword upon a blind swordsman. Blade in hand, the swordsman sealed away an ancient god—a god that was Rot itself." We find this talisman on the body of the Guardian Golem boss, a recurring enemy made up of black stone and as tall as ten men, said to have been created by an ancient "civilization now gone to ruin" (Golem Greatbow). As such, the Guardian Golems must have witnessed great changes in the world. One of them apparently picked up the fairy-shaped relic. Incidentally, the fairies still exist in the Realm of Shadow, in the Ancient Ruins of Rauh. They appear to be creatures from the distant past: "sprites thought lost to antiquity," according to the Antiquity Scholar's Cookbook. They are hard to catch, but whoever manages to tame one will benefit from its singular spiritual power. But let's return to our story: that "blind swordsman" who received the "flowing sword" managed to vanquish a god; however, that deity is not named here as one of the Outer Gods. That said, we can make the connection with the map description of the Lake of Rot, an underground region on the Ainsel River where "divine essence of an outer god is sealed away," as well as the description of the Scorpion's Stinger dagger, "fashioned from a great scorpion's tail, glistening with scarlet rot" and "crafted from the relic of a sealed outer god." This mysterious swordsman also appears in the history of Malenia, the Goddess of Rot. Indeed, the description of the Prosthesis-Wearer Heirloom—a reference to Malenia, who has lost limbs as her curse has progressed— mentions "her mentor and his flowing blade," the same words used in the description of the Blue Dancer Charm. In spite of his victory long ago over an Outer God, he continues to travel across the Lands Between to beat back the scarlet rot as it eats away at both people and the landscape. Who knows, maybe we've even crossed paths with him... In any case, this Outer God is a bit different from the others we know, as it is tangible and still present below the Lake of Rot, even though we have no idea in what form.

As for the Formless Mother, she interacts with the earthly realm in a different way than the other Outer Gods. She seems to exist on another plane that can be accessed using the magic of Mohgwyn's Sacred Spear. "As well as serving as a weapon, it is an instrument of communion with an Outer God who bestows power upon accursed blood." This trident can be used in tandem with a unique skill, the Bloodboon Ritual: "Raise the sacred spear and pierce the body of the Formless Mother." The animation for this gruesome attack is just as explicit as its description. A red portal opens up and the player plunges the spear through it, apparently directly into the body of the Formless Mother, releasing a deadly explosion of blood. Mohg, the Lord of Blood, also avails himself of such portals, using the same spear.

The Outer God does not live on the same plane of existence, but she is still immediately accessible, through a portal that looks like a giant wound. "The mother of truth desires a wound," says the spear's description.

It's interesting to note that each Outer God has its own color that characterizes the associated creatures and powers. Blood red for the Formless Mother, golden yellow for the Greater Will, a purplish red for the god of scarlet rot, black for the god of the Twinbird, and an orangish yellow for the Frenzied Flame.

The color of the Frenzied Flame is really not all that different from the gold of the Greater Will, though it is much more vibrant, symbolizing the constant similarity and rivalry between the two Outer Gods and their mouthpieces, both "Fingers." We find these similarities between the two in many details, like the Warming Stone and Frenzyflame Stone, whose designs are nearly identical: they are stones surrounded by a yellow halo—though each halo sports the yellow of its corresponding Outer God! The two stones also seem to have very similar effects and descriptions—you need to read carefully to learn that the Three Fingers' stone comes with a risk of madness. "Take care not to mistake this for its gentler cousin," warns the description of the Frenzyflame Stone.

Something that the game's story doesn't really get into is the fact that there's a whole group of people who long ago embraced the will of the Three Fingers and the Frenzied Flame. They are the nomadic merchants, including Kalé, an odd character who welcomes the player to the Lands Between by offering them a few supplies and a crafting kit to make their first weapon improvements. He and his fellow merchants, or perhaps their ancestors, belonged to a race of merchants who formed the Great Caravan—in French, the word *kalé* is actually another name for the Roma (the people known by the derogatory term "Gypsy"). The description of the Nomadic Merchant's Chapeau tells the story of their tragic fate: "These merchants once thrived as the Great Caravan, but after being accused of heretical beliefs, their entire clan was rounded up and buried alive far underground. Then, they chanted a curse of despair, and summoned the Flame of Frenzy." If you go down far into the depths of Leyndell, a few levels before the room of the Three Fingers, you'll find hundreds of nomadic merchants lying all about. However, instead of wearing their merchant outfits, they're left wearing nothing but loose rags. Deprived of their merchant identity, they simply became nomads, "member[s] of a tribe that was entombed in the earth so as to bury the maddening disease that followed them" (Nomad Ashes). Some of them still play their strange stringed instrument. Most of them are immobile, but those who continue to wander about will summon the Frenzied Flame with little warning, the fire pouring from their cursed eyes.

I've generally avoided mentioning in this book any of the game's deleted content (some of which remains present among the game's files) out of respect for the studio's creative choices—if they decided to delete or set aside certain elements, they did so for a good reason. Still, data miners have found among the game's files an entire questline centered on Kalé and the Frenzied Flame. The idea was that the player would cross paths with the merchant throughout their journey to the capital city and leading all the way to the door of the Three Fingers. In the course of the questline, Kalé would discover within himself a deep hatred for the Order of the Greater Will and would end up giving himself over to the Three Fingers and the Frenzied Flame, returning to the roots of his nomadic people. Once again, it's a tragic fate, but on a backdrop of folklore not often seen elsewhere in the game. All of this was supported by a talented voice actor, Nabil Elouahabi, whose emotions grew more and more intense as the questline progressed.

Shadow of the Erdtree also adds to our understanding of the Frenzied Flame. Indeed, it includes an entire subregion tied to the Outer God's ravages: the Abyssal Woods. The paths through the woods are plagued by the Aging Untouchables, with their giant heads filled with yellow, rotting eyes. It's best to stay out of their sight, otherwise you might find yourself afflicted with a dose of madness strong enough to kill you. That said, death is almost a release, given the anguish the creatures inspire. Even Torrent, the spectral steed, is afraid of these woods and cannot be summoned while in the area. Within the Abyssal Woods, we find the sanctum of the Sage Midra. It's a forbidden place for the Hornsent, who are wary of the Frenzied Flame and the chaos and madness it leaves in its wake. Midra's Manse is really just a hellscape of ruins. While we can see in an old painting how the mansion used to look, a majestic structure in a meadow filled with colorful little flowers, the build-ing's present-day appearance is almost unrecognizable: a black, forbidding castle; ten individuals are lined up in front of the entrance, on their knees, with some sort of golden needle planted in the tops of each of their heads. While it's easy to assume that these must be Miquella's golden needles "crafted to ward away the meddling of Outer Gods," they are actually meant to serve as a warning. The needles are Greatswords of Damnation, plunged into the bodies of people who were once touched by the Frenzied Flame. A spiral of barbs surrounds the shaft of the needle: when the needle is plunged into the head, and then body, of the victim, the spiral gradually opens up, inflicting unimaginable suffering. These charming tools are used by the Hornsent inquisitors, who hunt all those they consider "heretics." Jori, the Elder Inquisitor, is found at the entrance to the Abyssal Woods, while some of his underlings occupy Midra's Manse.

Midra is the local patriarch and the area's boss. He also has a Greatsword of Damnation planted in his skull. However, being somewhat stronger than his comrades, he lives on. When he decides to remove the torturous spiral that has long pierced his body, the greatsword rips off his head, which is replaced by a ball of Frenzied Flame. He thus becomes the Lord of the Frenzied Flame. How did all of this transpire? The sordid history of Midra's Manse is shrouded in mystery.

However, it seems that a woman named Nanaya knows something about it. "In a distant land, in an age long past, was born a man who failed to become the Lord of Frenzied Flame. All that remains of him is cradled gently by Nanaya," we learn from the description of Nanaya's Torch. The timeline and geography are still very vague, but still: we know that the Lord of the Frenzied Flame is a title that some hope to perpetuate and that certain people have failed to secure. A bit like the title of Elden Lord. Nanaya, probably under the control of the Three Fingers, is searching for a Lord of the Frenzied Flame. She has already failed before and fled to start over, then failed again with Midra, as he dies—but not without putting up a fight!—at the hands of the player. It's interesting to note that the player can obtain the title of the Lord of the Frenzied Flame if they follow the path of the Three Fingers. Becoming a lord is always a test of one's strength and will.

And resistance is another such test.

Resistance

Just to remind you, once you have been touched by the Three Fingers, the only way to sever the connection with the Frenzied Flame and have any hope of a conclusion other than the Age of Chaos is to use Miquella's Needle. As we know, Miquella also gave Malenia an Unalloyed Gold Needle to help her channel the scarlet rot, connected to another Outer God. "Unalloyed gold," closely tied to Miquella and different from other materials in the Lands Between, can thus be used to resist the Outer Gods. Malenia's full set of armor is made from unalloyed gold. We can also find the material used in the shields of certain Haligtree soldiers, as well as in some of their armor. It is not unusual to see an unalloyed gold crown atop the helmets of knights devoted to Miquella.

Although the Outer Gods, and even their emissaries, possess great power and are constantly trying to subjugate the peoples of the Lands Between in order to accomplish their plans, there is always someone standing up to them to counter or weaken their influence: Miquella and his Unalloyed Gold Needles, but also the ancient, anonymous swordsman who triumphed over the scarlet rot, Marika and her plan to use the Golden Order to throw off the Greater Will, and even Melina, who stands up to the Frenzied Flame if the player follows the path of the Lord of Chaos. It's a natural equilibrium that is more or less maintained in the universe of *Elden Ring*. Each wave of action may come with a millennium of inertia, but it is eventually countered by an opposite event. The game's world appears to be stagnant, but in fact, it is constantly moving and adapting to the choices of various individuals, from the most powerful to the most opportunistic.

One of the turning points in the player's story comes when Finger Reader Enia, the ancient mouthpiece of the Two Fingers, tells you: "The realm, and all life, in ruins. Impossible events transpire, beyond the ken of the Fingers. Who is to say that the cardinal sin must be cardinal forever? Go on. Finish the job. Take the course you deem most worthy." These are surprising words, especially given Enia's position, but they are filled with reassuring wisdom. Indeed, if the balance of the world is threatened, then the rules simply need to be changed.

CHAPTER 5
THE MANY MEANINGS
OF ELDEN RING

While we have examined *Elden Ring*'s lore from many different angles throughout this book, given the density of the game's universe, it is sadly impossible to cover absolutely everything. It would be hard for me to go into every detail without nauseating my readers, and just like for FromSoftware's previous games, players will continue to find symbols and other elements hiding in the backgrounds for years to come. For now, let's zoom out and take stock of the creative works that inspired *Elden Ring*, as well as the game's major themes.

Inspirations and references

◈ A few reminders

Just like in FromSoftware's previous games, particularly those directed by Miyazaki, we find in *Elden Ring* a number of clear references to works of pop culture. We've previously discussed the allusions to the folk-horror films *Midsommar* and *The Wicker Man* (in the village of Dominula), and there is even a nod to a famous song from Disney's *Frozen* (Blaidd's Armor). There are also references to TV and literature, like the Grafted Blade Greatsword, which is really a whole bunch of swords fused together, much like the structure of the Iron Throne in *Game of Thrones*. According to the weapon's description, it is "the storied sword of Castle Morne." And as it happens, Morne is the name of a castle off the coast of Westeros, one of the continents in the world of *A Song of Ice and Fire*. G. R. R. Martin's Morne was also the home of a legendary knight named Galladon, who was said to have a magic sword... And that reminds me of another reference, this time to the world of video games: *Blasphemous* (The Game Kitchen, 2019). That game makes various references to the *Souls* games; in exchange, we find in *Elden Ring* a nod to *Blasphemous*: the

Blasphemous Blade is reminiscent of the weapon wielded by the eponymous game's unsettling protagonist, with the obvious reference in the sword's name, but also its appearance, with the "remains of the countless heroes [Rykard] has devoured writh[ing] upon the surface of this blade" in the form of a thorny briar wrapped around it, just like the thorns on the sword in the game cooked up by The Game Kitchen. Everything comes full circle!

Besides these few references to various modern pop-culture media, it is above all the artistic medium of painting that is the lifeblood of *Elden Ring*. Each of the game's panoramas is an ode to the Romantic painters of the 19th century, with the explicit goal of showing the sublime side of nature. I've previously mentioned the references to works by Caspar David Friedrich and Théodore Gudin, whose fascinating, rugged Brittany landscapes bear a striking resemblance to the cliffs of the Lands Between. I would also be remiss if I didn't mention John Martin's *Pandemonium* (1841), brought to life by the village adjoining Volcano Manor. The colors, the lighting, and the ambiance of both the painting and the game's environment are, indeed, very similar. This vision of hell, made sublime by John Martin, previously provided inspiration for the *Souls* games: here I'm thinking in particular of Lost Izalith from the first *Dark Souls* and the Iron Keep from the second volume. The engravings and universe of Gustave Doré are also reflected in the game's unsettling landscapes and characters, as well as a few curiosities, like the bodies piled pell-mell among the roots of the Erdtree, deep in the catacombs, creating an image that's a near-exact replica of Doré's scene of refugees from the biblical great flood clinging to one another (1866). We also see inspiration from Doré's studies of light, particularly the way that the sun's rays—intense and indirect—shine through a cloudy sky, images seen regularly during our exploration of the Lands Between.

Belonging to a totally different artistic style, a more recent one this time, the oppressive and yet dreamlike ambiance of the paintings of Polish artist Zdzisław Beksiński is often felt throughout the game: in Caelid, with its red, misshapen landscapes and the gigantic beings that seem to have fused into the ground, or the fascination with crucifixion and crosses in general, as well as the colossal, almost surreal-looking buildings that rise up in the middle of nowhere, like the Academy of Raya Lucaria. And how about the giant skeletons found in the Eternal Cities? We see a similar idea in several of Beksiński's paintings! Finally, again borrowing from more recent art, *Elden Ring* takes a lot of inspiration from the illustrators of fantasy literature: there's Frank Frazetta, with his washed-out colors—tarnished, you might say!—seen constantly across the Lands Between, Ciruelo Cabral and his love for depicting dragons, as well as Alan Lee and John Howe, illustrators famous for their work on *The Lord of the Rings*, having created an incredible vision of Middle-earth and its inhabitants.

✦ Miyazaki's admitted inspirations

As is true for so many creators within the realm of fantasy, Tolkien's *The Lord of the Rings* is one of the key inspirations for Miyazaki's work. The game's English translator, Ryan Morris, introduced in the first part of this book, described Miyazaki's history with the fantasy epic in a wide-ranging interview with *Rock Paper Shotgun* (February 22, 2022): "He used to struggle through English fantasy books like *Lord of the Rings* in his youth. He is really into Western fantasy. And that's how he ends up making something like *Demon's Souls*. It's his own take, but it's heavily inspired by Western fantasy." So, growing up, Miyazaki discovered both the fantasy genre and the English language together, with this segment of Western culture forever shaping his sensibilities and influencing his games to varying degrees.

In *Elden Ring*, we find many facets of *The Lord of the Rings*. There are elements borrowed directly, like the name of the Lands Between, which could easily be synonymous with Middle-earth, or the obvious Elden Ring, which, like the One Ring from Tolkien's universe, grants immense power to its owner. "One Ring to rule them all," as the famous phrase from the book goes. However, in an interview with *Edge* magazine, Miyazaki denies the existence of a tacit link between the two rings, underscoring the fact that Sauron's ring is, above all, a material object, while the Elden Ring possesses an abstract nature and connects to metaphysical concepts. That said, it's hard to ignore the similar themes and symbolism between the two objects, both being the highly-coveted ultimate source of power! And there are other themes shared by both works. Notably, there's the way that desiring or obtaining power corrupts a person, or, more broadly, the notion of hubris, the immense pride of humans (or, in this case, the demigod children of Marika) who always want more, more, more. Finally, the captivating imagery of Peter Jackson's film adaptation of *The Lord of the Rings* is also reflected in *Elden Ring*. *The Fellowship of the Ring* (2001), the first movie in the trilogy, begins with the story of the forging of the Rings of Power. It's a series of shots that collectively form one of the greatest prologues in the genre, immediately establishing the atmosphere and context, i.e., the distribution of the Rings to their elf, dwarf, and human recipients, then the war against Sauron. Although the story is different, the introduction to *Elden Ring* functions in exactly the same way. The first two shots show Marika and then Radagon, who both appear to be trying to forge an artifact—except that Radagon is actually trying to reforge the Elden Ring destroyed by Marika. From there, the intro presents the demigods bearing shards of the Elden Ring, and then war in the Lands Between.

More on the dark side of the fantasy genre, Miyazaki tells *Edge* magazine (issue 367, February 2022) that he was very much inspired by the works of

Michael Moorcock, especially his novels featuring the Eternal Champions, with Elric of Melniboné, the titular character of the Elric saga (1961-1989), being the most famous of the bunch. In Moorcock's stories, an Eternal Champion is a sort of guardian whose job is to create balance between the opposing cosmic forces of Law and Chaos. If this sounds familiar, it's because one of the main "cosmic" confrontations in *Elden Ring* is between Order (the Greater Will) and Chaos (the Three Fingers). If we follow that same line of reasoning, the equivalent of the Eternal Champion would be none other than the Elden Lord! We also find other similarities between the two universes: a dying, stagnant kingdom, characters who are at once both powerful and weak, charismatic and pathetic—odd paradoxes delivered by sober, bare-bones, suggestive storytelling that is at times poetic in the case of Moorcock's stories. It is an interesting approach, and one that has been tried and tested in Miyazaki's narrative design since *Demon's Souls*.

Finally, again in conversation with *Edge*, Miyazaki mentions the tabletop role-playing game *RuneQuest* among his strongest inspirations for *Elden Ring*. George R. R. Martin is also a fan of *RuneQuest*, and on his blog, in August 2021, he gave a moving tribute to the game's late creator, Steve Perrin. It's important to understand that along with *Dungeons & Dragons*, and to a lesser extent *Chivalry & Sorcery*, *RuneQuest* was one of the first tabletop role-playing games to become a hit in the 1970s. Each game works on different systems and presents a different universe, although all of them can more or less be considered medieval fantasy. Glorantha, the world of *RuneQuest*, is home to a series of gods and their respective runes. The runes represent things like the elements, such as Fire and Earth, but also broader notions, like Truth and Death. In *Elden Ring*, these notions are also embodied by runes, brought together in the Order represented by the Elden Ring; there's also the infamous Rune of Death, stolen and concealed by Maliketh, which transformed the natural laws of the Lands Between for ages and ages. Some devoted players of *RuneQuest* on Reddit have compared the traits of Glorantha with the world of *Elden Ring*, finding interesting similarities, like Ranni stealing the Rune of Death from Maliketh, which connects to the story of Humakt, Glorantha's God of Death.

Miyazaki likes to inject his passion for role-playing games into his own games: in their design, recreating in video game format the things he has loved about tabletop RPGs; and in their worlds, which are always constructed to feel like universal, eternal mythologies, which the player discovers within the context of a scenario or campaign that barely scratches the surface, allowing the imagination to fill in the holes.

◈ An homage to Berserk

Although Miyazaki has been broadly influenced by Western fantasy literature, with the references mentioned previously, and also the *Choose Your Own Adventure* books, which he often mentions in interviews, he still carries in his heart all of the Japanese works that shaped his youth. That includes the manga *Berserk* by Kentaro Miura, which was first published in 1989 and which Miyazaki read as a teenager. Miyazaki immersed himself in the new dark-fantasy–truly the darkest!–universe inhabited by sinister, merciless characters, deeply shaping his sensibilities.

As with *RuneQuest*, Miyazaki is constantly injecting *Berserk* into his games. *Demon's Souls* with its fire lizards and iron maidens, for example. *Dark Souls* more directly borrowed the skeleton wheels and muscular snake men, but also made clear references via its characters: the onion-looking Siegmeyer of Catarina evokes Bazuso, and the blacksmith Andre of Astora evokes Godo. *Dark Souls III* even features a glowing red eclipse in its final part, recalling one of the most powerful moments from *Berserk*. More generally, Miyazaki's appreciation of Miura's main character, Guts, shines through in all of his games, whether taking inspiration from his gear, like his massive sword or his armor, or from some of his most memorable stances. The cover art for the *Prepare to Die* edition of the first *Dark Souls* comes to mind: it shows the knight Artorias crouching down just like Guts in one of the manga's most popular cover images. Both *Berserk* and Miyazaki's works share certain key themes, particularly having to do with fate and eternal cycles that must be broken, but also the insatiable thirst for power and the desire to become superhuman, in the philosophical sense of the term, in order to improve one's status and rival the gods. They are solemn themes rooted in dark fantasy, from which FromSoftware's games, particularly *Bloodborne*, draw without hesitation.

The development of *Elden Ring* offered a new opportunity for Miyazaki's teams to declare their love for the work and universe of Kentaro Miura. From the time of the first trailer in 2019, fans made the connection between Malenia's Winged Helm, with its broad visor, and the helmet of the ruthless Lady Farnese de Vandimion. In the same trailer, a seconds-long shot shows Radahn, alone on a battlefield tinged with red tones, evoking an image, almost point for point and color for color, from the anime series based on *Berserk*. It really set the tone, announcing to future players that *Elden Ring* would have its own batch of *Berserk* influences. And indeed, the game once again features many references. For example, the Prisoner Iron Mask, available for one of the starting character classes and thus heavily featured in advertising for the game at the time of its release, resembles the mask worn by Griffith before the previously mentioned eclipse. Moreover, in *Shadow of the Erdtree*, Miquella, with his androgynous charm and beauty, appears to directly reference Griffith. From there, it's hard not to mention the first meeting with Blaidd, perched atop some ruins and crouching in the previously mentioned posture adopted by Guts. The silhouette, the sword, the armor: everything about the image points to the main character of *Berserk*. We also find echoes in the themes and major inspirations of both works. The notion of causality, for example, discussed previously in this book, resonates throughout *Berserk*. Alchemy and gnosticism are also important to both universes, which we will discuss in a bit.

Going beyond the act of referencing the manga and demonstrating an affinity, the homage to Berserk could not have been easy for Miyazaki with *Elden Ring*. Indeed, the manga's creator, Kentaro Miura, died suddenly in May 2021 at the age of 54. He left behind an incomplete work and tens of millions of inconsolable fans, devastated by the loss of such a great artist. In the Lands Between, on several occasions, we come across groups of swords planted in the ground. Large swords, standing straight up like gravestones. In the middle of each group, there's always an even bigger sword on which we can read an epitaph, often having to do with a battle that happened nearby. While all of this fits perfectly into the lore and art direction of *Elden Ring*, some have seen the sword markers as a vibrant final tribute to the creator of *Berserk*. A subtle and touching commemoration.

One of the strengths of *Berserk*, and of many other Japanese works, by the way, is its ability to blend together all sorts of heterogeneous ideas, symbols, and cultures to create a universe that is at once unique and familiar. The image of a giant tree, for example, is found in both *Berserk* and *Elden Ring*, and is largely borrowed from Yggdrasil in Norse mythology, but used differently in each of the works. This form of syncretism, this way of combining dissimilar elements by transfiguring them with a new aesthetic and sensibility, is a real hallmark of FromSoftware's games, and *Elden Ring* is no exception, which explains the game's abundance of themes.

Elden Ring, or the transfiguration of the self

◈ The universality of themes

Taking on the subject of analyzing the themes present in *Elden Ring* can seem like a monumental and complicated task, given the number, variety, and universality of the references, subjects, and symbols. Indeed, you've probably seen already in this book, there is an impressive array of themes to be explored... to the point that you may feel like the game touches on everything under the sun! Reddit forums, Twitter feeds, and YouTube comments are teeming with analyses, each one more interesting than the next. It's enough to think that you could just take any idea and search for evidence–particularly among the universal elements–in the game and always come up with a cogent argument. Fans have gotten the same impression with FromSoftware's previous titles, in which we can identify a whole range of major themes, many of which make a reappearance in *Elden Ring*: greed, for example, but also stagnation, death, curses, a cycle to be broken, chaos as an alternative, fathomless darkness, etc.

Could we say then that *Elden Ring* was designed to be a theme-generating engine? The studio's previous experiments, combined with the opening up of the game's world into a particularly wide and varied playground, support the idea. Still, we can also, particularly, see the game as a myth generator. Indeed, each player produces their own myth. Their journey is (more or less) unique—at the very least, it's the player who decides which areas they want to explore, which bosses they want to battle, and which Great Runes they wish to collect to progress to the end of the game. The player also gets to choose their own conclusion depending on certain choices and discoveries, thus crafting a singular myth at every turn. And mythology goes hand in hand with major underlying themes. Each player, as they make their way through the adventure, will form their own essential ideas about the game; they will identify themes with which they personally connect, depending on their sensibilities, their culture, and their background. Isn't that what myths are all about?

Neil Gaiman, the best-selling British author, explains in the introduction to his book *Norse Mythology* (2017) how he tried to effectively stitch together the scattered and incomplete information available on Scandinavian mythology in order to tell—in his own version—its most famous tales. "History and religion and myth combine, and we wonder and we imagine and we guess, like detectives reconstructing the details of a long-forgotten crime," he says. "I've tried my best to retell these myths and stories as accurately as I can, and as interestingly as I can. Sometimes details in the stories contradict each other. But I hope that they paint a picture of a world and a time." With similar proportions, the discovery of the myths of *Elden Ring* shares this same spirit, in a way. The experience of the Lands Between is divided between inquiry, fascination, and a handful of personal interpretations.

Many of the recurring themes and motifs have already been discussed in this wide-ranging chapter on the game's universe, often in the context of analyzing certain characters and situations that form the glue that holds the story together. However, we can go deeper into our deciphering of the adventure: if we delve into its syncretism, *Elden Ring* gradually reveals a thematic backbone that structures its messages and ambitions.

◈ Architectural syncretism: macrocosm and microcosm

The blending of architectural styles in the game is striking. As far back as *Demon's Souls*, and even more obviously in the first *Dark Souls*, the studio drew inspiration from various movements and eras of architecture, combining them to construct the forms and features of their universe. *Elden Ring* continues that tradition while applying it on a massive scale, across dozens of gargantuan monuments, hundreds of secondary structures, and thousands (and thousands) of broken paving stones, warped and rotting wooden planks, and corroded pieces of metal. Blending of architectural elements, blending of materials, blending of styles, all largely inspired by European historical monuments. The decaying structures of the Lands Between, and also of its depths and its airspace, in the case of Farum Azula, borrow from thousands of years of architecture, from ancient Greece (Mohgwyn Palace is almost a replica of the Parthenon) to the Victorian era of the 19th century, which we see, for example, in the facades of Volcano Manor.

Exploration of the Lands Between takes us on an organic journey to visit all of these monuments with their different styles and functions. Austere medieval fortified castles, built to robustly defend everything within their walls, can be found alongside Roman arenas and buildings whose domes are reminiscent of the gentler Renaissance era. And what about the tower of the Hornsent, Enir-Ilim, with its spiraling architecture? It's a place that resonates physically and symbolically with the Tower of Babel, as the Hornsent hope to meet their gods, even worshiping the Gate of Divinity at the top of the tower. Additionally, no matter the history of the place, everything seems to be on the verge of ruin; and yet, every corner of the world is inhabited by creatures, often hostile toward strangers, and each one lives it own life, whether alone or in a community.

Thus, we explore a magic academy, extravagant manors, fortified castles, wooden hovels, incredibly expansive catacombs and tombs, massive cities, etc. It's a fascinating and varied corpus of architecture, and one that makes sense within this fictional universe! As one of the finishing touches on this masterpiece, our visit to Farum Azula toward the end of the game presents us with an exceptional monument, badly damaged and half in ruins from being caught in a storm. Pieces of the temple's structures whirl around in the tempest like leaves, adding to the architectural charm of the place. The walls move, the décor and architecture seem to do an elegant, chaotic dance.

Going beyond looking at each of the buildings individually, the overall architecture of the regions of the Lands Between represents a massive and riveting body of artistic work. Even the natural areas, which are thus symbolically free of all human intervention, were designed by FromSoftware's architects—which can seem like a bit of a paradox! An unknown, intense, hostile world just waiting to be discovered, singular spaces just waiting to be explored, offering a combination of emotions than can only be delivered in video game format.

All of this said, what is the purpose of such diversity and syncretism in the architecture? What is the reason for the fabulous and varied aesthetic? Is it to flesh out the lore using environmental storytelling, using the symbolism of architecture and the meaning that such symbolism can bring to forms and materials? Is it about the excitement of spotting one of the structures in the distance, knowing that you will soon be exploring it, like a child yearning for adventure, for something extraordinary? Of course, *Elden Ring* essentially does all of that. As architecture is an art form in its own right, it has a way of conveying emotions. Unlike the lines and colors of a painting, or the carefully chosen words of a literary work, architecture is seen and observed from both the inside and the outside. You must physically move in and around a piece of architecture to appreciate its details, and it's also in that act of walking around that we construct meaning, in the relationship between the macrocosm and the microcosm. The appreciation—and emotion, too—evolves depending on the time of day, the weather, and the viewpoint, offering infinite possibilities! *Elden Ring*, like many other video games, embraces those possibilities, offering a faithful virtual recreation of this spatial art. While we lose the sensation of touch—and of smell, too—thus lessening the authenticity of the architectural art form, the results are still quite captivating. Thankfully, the construction of buildings in the virtual world is not as long or difficult as it is in the real world, but it still requires a remarkable upstream design phase. Each monument has its place in the game's environment, and also in its themes—vertical lines can accentuate the idea of seeking divine status, just as colors and lighting can convey a connection to an emotion or abstract idea. None of this is without meaning: the player's place within the game's environments expresses various key concepts. Standing at the heart of these phantasmagorical visions, filled with deeper meaning, the Erdtree singlehandedly synthesizes the multiple meanings of *Elden Ring* and the way in which the game draws from ancient myths and religions.

◆ Mythological syncretism: polytheism and the new quest for the Holy Grail

The first *Dark Souls* was partially founded on a very free interpretation of Greek mythology, with Gwyn being the divine father figure who uses lightning, just like Zeus, and Anor Londo being the city of the gods, in parallel to Mt. Olympus. *Dark Souls II*, meanwhile, drew elements from *Cath Maighe Tuireadh*, a legendary saga of the Irish, and of Celtic people more broadly. Before that, *Demon's Souls* blended together various elements of Norse mythology to flesh out its dark and dreamlike universe.

As we've already seen many times, *Elden Ring* also borrows from ancient Scandinavian tales: the Erdtree mirrors Yggdrasil, the Lands Between are analogous to Midgard, the Giants are like the powerful *jötnar*, connected to both fire and ice. By the by, the ancestor of all *jötnar* was a being named Ymir—a name that we also find in the game—and upon his death, his head was used to create the earth, his hair for the forests, and his teeth for the rocks and mountains. Doesn't that remind you—to a more limited extent, of course—of the Caelid region, with its mounds formed by giants? In Radahn's red-tinged region, we can make out the shapes of enormous heads in some of the cliffs. It's a mysterious and fascinating environment that gives the impression that the land of Caelid was formed upon the remains of strange and massive creatures, ones much larger than the beings that the game calls Giants. We also find similar forms in the cliffs at the Mountaintops of the Giants, bordering ancient battlefields filled with the bodies of Giants, which are indeed much smaller.

Among the notable figures from Norse mythology, the three Norns, Urd, Verdandi, and Skuld, represent the past, present, and future, respectively. The name "Urd" sounds a lot like Uld and Uhl, two ruined palaces of the Lands Between. The two palaces don't offer much of an explanation about their history, and they seem to be disconnected from the world's present. They are simply vestiges of a time long ago, of an ancient and mysterious dynasty belonging to the distant past, as if governed by the mythological Urd.

The reference to the valkyries of Norse mythology, the warrior goddesses who are messengers of Odin, is a more obvious one. The term is even used explicitly in the name of the Valkyrie's Prosthesis, a prosthetic arm used by Millicent that is exactly identical to the one used by Malenia. Even if we just look at the character design of the Goddess of Rot, evoking paintings inspired by Richard Wagner's *The Ride of the Valkyries*, with her winged helmet, her long red hair, her cape flapping in the wind behind her, and her elaborate armor, some even see a deeper connection with descriptions from medieval texts. The Twitter user @albertdevanves, for example, draws the link between Malenia and the true bloodthirstiness of the valkyries on the battlefield, particularly with the red color of the scarlet rot, evoking a trail of blood-soaked ground left in the wake of the valkyries. Relinuss also adds: "Indeed, Malenia inspires a certain terror in her enemies and in players. Like the valkyries, there is a contrast between her 'shiny' armor, her long, feminine hair, and the ruthless fury she unleashes."

One final Norse reference we'll discuss, even though I'm sure we could find many other elements that inspired the game's developers and designers: the Ancestor Spirit, the enigmatic, deer-like boss, can be compared to Eikthyrnir, a fantastic creature whose antlers were believed to be the source of the world's rivers. We battle the two forms of the Ancestor Spirit in the depths of the Lands Between, where the Siofra and Ainsel Rivers flow endlessly. There's even this historical note, imbued with myths and legends, on the map of the Ainsel River: "The vast region is said to be the grave of civilizations that flourished before the Erdtree."

With the studio always embracing this syncretism, amid this amalgam of references to Norse mythology, we also find a heavy dose of influence from the Arthurian legends. As far back as *Demon's Souls*, Hidetaka Miyazaki has often mentioned the movie *Excalibur* (John Boorman, 1981) as one of his inspirations. The film presents a rich and thrilling story based on the myth of King Arthur. While there had always been occasional Arthurian references in Miyazaki's games, they are much clearer and more numerous in *Elden Ring*. For example, the Lands Between, and particularly the Limgrave region, with its green plains and countless sheer cliffs, constantly evokes Arthur's kingdom on the British Isles and in Armorica. In an interview for the game's official guide, Miyazaki mentions Scotland—the superb and picturesque Isle of Skye!—and Wales among his influences for the design of the landscapes.

Then, there's *Elden Ring*'s Roundtable Hold, another iconic location inspired by the Arthurian legends. Even though the vast table appears to be in a state of abandon when the player arrives—an impression reinforced by the scattered empty chairs and the old swords planted in its center—the idea of a past filled with intense discussions among the Tarnished continues to resonate in the place. The parallel to King Arthur and his knights is undebatable. However, the metaphor behind the round table—everyone sitting around it is treated as an equal—is largely distorted in *Elden Ring*: Sir Gideon, the "leader" of the Hold, initially considers the player to be nothing more than a novice, a nobody destined to fail like all the others. There's also the blacksmith Hewg, who has been chained up for ages and ages, putting the Roundtable Hold at odds with the virtues of equality found in the Arthurian legends. The moral code that knights are supposed to abide by has no value in the Roundtable Hold: it is perfectly acceptable there to judge anyone and everyone, and even to kill your neighbor—Ensha suddenly attacks the player in the course of the adventure, and Fia betrays and kills D. It's a pessimistic vision of the concept of the round table, whose values appear to have been mutilated over time. In other words, the round table is a farce! Moreover, the Roundtable Hold is actually just supposed to be the recreation of an abandoned place in Leyndell; it serves the purposes of the Erdtree, far from the virtues of Arthur's Knights of the Round Table. Miyazaki discusses it, again in the game's official guide: "The Roundtable Hold is a place far away from the world, although it is modeled on the Fortified Manor in Leyndell, and its power comes from the Erdtree. That's why, when the Erdtree burns, [the Hold] burns too."

The great quest of the Knights of the Round Table from the Arthurian legend was to seek the Holy Grail, a magical artifact believed to confer immortality or abundance—no one really knows which. But ultimately, its true function doesn't really matter. The point of the search for the elusive Grail was really to build the character of the men brave enough to go on the holy mission. Instead of finding the prized Grail, they would find the spark of a new era, the opportunity and the strength to abandon old traditions and beliefs. This is a central point of the Arthurian myth: the abandonment of the magical world of the Celts, with its wizards, fairies, and druids with bewitching powers, to enter a more "modern" world, represented in the Middle Ages by the growth of Christianity–which is indeed symbolized by the Grail, as it is sometimes interpreted as being the cup in which Christ's blood was collected. *Elden Ring* makes a direct parallel in its messaging. The Elden Ring, or becoming the Elden Lord, is, quite simply, the Holy Grail. The person seeking the throne will have to undertake a quest, both physical and spiritual, to become powerful, influential, and intelligent enough to change the current stagnant state of the world and to usher in a new era. And that's exactly what the player does when they choose their preferred ending.

◈ Religious syncretism: Christianity and gnosticism

In addition to ancient myths, *Elden Ring* blends ideas from various religious movements and thus expands on this interpretation through the lens of the metaphysical quest for the Holy Grail. Indeed, the Grace that guides the people of the Lands Between to the Erdtree connects to a very important idea in Christianity. In the most basic terms, grace is divine salvation given to humans in order to save them from damnation. And grace even extends beyond believers down on Earth, as the archangel Lucifer, for his pride and rebellion against God, was stripped of grace and cast out of Heaven. Thus, losing one's grace does not bode well for one's future. In *Elden Ring*, many different people see their Grace abandon them, becoming Tarnished. If we were to consider the Greater Will to be analogous to the Christian God, we could imagine it taking away their Grace to punish or condemn them. After losing their Grace, a number of Tarnished went into exile on a pilgrimage, another significant term anchored in religious practices.

Along the same lines, the Erdtree and its surrounding country, the Lands Between, could be compared to the Tree of Life and Paradise. The Tarnished, having fallen from Grace, thus had to leave the Lands Between, just as Adam and Eve were forced out of the Garden of Eden (Elden?). Much later, as the Tarnished saw their Grace restored, a sort of desperate epiphany granted by the missionaries of the Two Fingers, and thus by the Greater Will, they returned to conquer Paradise. However, the Greater Will did not foresee that one of those Tarnished would commit the cardinal sin–another term borrowed from Christianity–by burning the Erdtree, destroying the Tree of Life and bringing an end to the world as we know it.

While we can draw parallels between the Greater Will and God, we can also see in Marika inspiration from the figure of Christ, both an ordinary mortal and God's chosen representative on Earth. This description also fits Marika quite well.

And then there's all the iconography surrounding her, immediately evoking Christ's crucifixion—we see it in her many statues at every holy site. In the introduction to the final battle, we find her once again in that same position, as if crucified on one of the runes of the Elden Ring, a blade planted in her side, just as Christ's side was pierced by the Holy Lance. In addition, the illustration of Marika seen in the game's intro is reminiscent of the Salvador Dalí painting *Christ of Saint John of the Cross*, because of the top-down perspective and the use of both chiaroscuro and warm colors.

In addition to this abundant iconography, Marika's embodiment of Jesus Christ is also emblematic of some of the game's key ideas. I previously mentioned how the quest for the Holy Grail represented a changing of eras, but Marika's ascension to godhood could be viewed as a syncretic reference to the symbolic dividing line between the Old Testament and the New Testament, together forming the age-old, divine epic that is the Bible. Among many other themes, the Old Testament describes the coming of a Messiah who will save humanity, while the New Testament is dedicated to that savior, Jesus, via his words and acts. While it's not an exact comparison, of course, we can make the connection between Marika's ascension and aura, and those of Jesus in the New Testament.

In both cases, the Church plays a key role in spreading the good word and presents the people with an important paradigm shift. The Greater Will is the god that connects the two "testaments," but its presence changes somewhat after Marika becomes the center of attention. Whether willingly or by force, all eyes are now glued to her, the Messiah in the flesh. Similarly, Jesus, the son of God, is the heart of the New Testament: he is sometimes considered to be the incarnation of the *Logos*, the Word of God. In Catholic theology, the doctrine of consubstantiality states that the parts of the Holy Trinity possess the same nature, and thus the Son (Jesus) and the Father are one and the same. In *Elden Ring*, Marika becomes the object of all worship. Her existence brings with it a new era: she erases the history of the former Elden Lords, as Godfrey is declared the "first Elden Lord." Similarly, Christianity erased older polytheistic beliefs, considered to be "pagan," while actually appropriating certain aspects from them. I'll give one of the most famous examples, Christ's birthday: it was set as December 25 to coincide with and replace the date of a celebration tied to the Roman god Sol Invictus—though it's worth noting that December 25 was also the feast day of the Persian god Mithra, whose religion, according to some historians, competed with early Christianity. This all adds to the parallel with the quest for the Holy Grail, marking the passage from the magical world of the Celts to the hegemony of Christian monotheism.

In addition to those already mentioned, there are more Christian theological terms to be found in *Elden Ring*, notably in *Shadow of the Erdtree*, in which seduction leads to betrayal, and then to original sin. All of that under the influence of a mysterious serpent. There seems to be an obvious parallel to the temptation of Adam and Eve, who were convinced by the serpent to taste the forbidden fruit of the (Erd) Tree of Knowledge. Their doing so caused the fall of humanity; after that, God announced that a Messiah would come to save them. For its part, the DLC explicitly invokes the theme of crusade, with Messmer leading a holy war in honor of his mother, Marika, an idea that connects to dark and bloody periods in the history of the Catholic Church...

True to form, again using syncretism, *Elden Ring* borrows from religions other than Christianity. Indeed, we can also find gnostic inspirations in the game. Although gnosticism was derived from early Christianity, it was deprecated, and even labeled as heretical once Christian dogma was solidified. Gnosticism is more esoteric, with concepts that are somewhat different from its original model. The (very) basic idea behind the movement is that there is a material world created by an evil god (sometimes identified as the vengeful Christian God of the Old Testament, hence the persecution of the gnostics) where humans live, and a spiritual world, governed by a higher god. However, that supreme god maintains a connection with humanity, via personal spiritual knowledge. The quest for knowledge, particularly of oneself, is at the heart of gnostic beliefs: it is what's known as gnosis (from the Greek γνῶσις, *gnōsis*, meaning "knowledge"), which was believed to bring salvation of the soul. This duality of the physical body and intangible soul resonates with one of the major themes of *Elden Ring*, discussed in detail earlier in this book. In fact, could it be because of this gnostic dualism that the game so frequently offers ideas having to do with the body, both in its crudest material form and in its absence? Between Malenia's rotting body, which she literally strips bare, the grotesque, bloated body of the Prince of Death, the fractured body of Marika/Radagon, the puppet body of Ranni, the suit of armor that serves as a receptacle for D, the player's body branded by the Three Fingers, the body inhabited by Radahn after the resuscitation of Mohg's corpse, not to mention all of the bodies and faces hidden by armor, masking the true physical nature of the people we encounter, the entire adventure of *Elden Ring* pushes us to contemplate the concept of dualism.

There were several different currents of gnosticism in the first few centuries AD, and they were influenced to different degrees by the myths and theologies of the time and of the regions where each of the religious thinkers lived. It's all very fascinating to learn about and explore, but not all of it is relevant to *Elden Ring*! Valentinus, who lived in the 2nd century, was Egyptian and then Roman (and then heretical). He was the founder of one of the largest gnostic movements. His explanation of the origin of the gods offers some ideas relevant to us—which is why I will briefly summarize his teachings here.

The Pleroma is the spiritual world, where primordial forms of existence reside—the supreme god, Propator, and his female counterpart, Ennœa. In the beginning, they produced many aeons, metaphors for abstract concepts like truth, love, hope, and understanding. The aeons were created in pairs, always with one masculine and one feminine. The youngest of them was Sophia, wisdom. She wished to know Propator, which led to a schism: she was evicted from the Pleroma. The fall of Sophia split her into two: a higher being who remained intangible, and a fallen, lower being. From that lower being was born the Demiurge, the evil god of the material world mentioned above. Humans were thus considered to be the children of Sophia, their bodies being held back by matter and destined to remain in the inferior world, but their spirits remaining connected to the higher, celestial form of Sophia. As such, knowledge of the divine, representing knowledge of the self, was believed to be key to the elevation of the soul: Sophia was believed to have put in each human being the *pneuma*, the divine "breath," a spark from the Pleroma, in order to allow their ascension.

Those are the basic concepts of Valentianism that are relevant to us here. We can draw analogies between certain characters in *Elden Ring* and this gnostic mythology, starting with the One Great and Propator. Indeed, certain currents of gnosticism call this superior being the One. In that case, the connection is all the more explicit! If we compare the Outer Gods to the aeons, the Greater Will and its two "fallen" entities cast down to the Lands Between (Metyr and the Elden Beast) could represent the fall of Sophia; and finally, we could draw a line between the Empyrean achieving godhood and the Demiurge.

However, this direct parallel may appear to fall short in terms of what we might glean by viewing the game through the lens of gnosticism. As Marika's role is central to the story of *Elden Ring*, perhaps the keys to understanding the many mysteries surrounding her might be found in this religious movement? Indeed, we can see that the principle of male-female duality among the aeons is found in a literal form in Marika and Radagon. The fall of Sophia is the key event in the gnostic theogony described above. Sophia hoped to know that which cannot be known: the One, the absolute. Her desire led to the creation of the inferior material world; human beings thus come from below and must raise themselves up and shed their material nature in order to reconnect with their divine forebears. This original sin by the female aeon of course echoes the Book of Genesis, in which Eve is enticed by the serpent and causes the fall of humanity. If we make a parallel between Marika and Sophia, we can discern a number of insights. Marika is not the cause of the creation of the material world–although her usage of gold helped her redefine the contours of the Lands Between! Still, she is responsible for a cardinal sin, not the result of forbidden curiosity, but rather of a desire for emancipation: by breaking the Elden Ring, she brought disorder to the world and precipitated its fall. She cast a veil over the Lands Between–literally in the case of the Realm of Shadow–by refusing the influence of the Greater Will. The Outer God thus found itself powerless and deprived of information, much like how, in a sort of subtle inversion, the gnostic Demiurge is ignorant of the existence of the higher world, the Pleroma. The Tarnished must regain their lost Grace, their *pneuma*, to build the foundations of a new era, to reconceptualize the world. Just as the gnostics were guided by the word of Christ to obtain knowledge, the Tarnished collects, all throughout their journey, the words of Marika, as reported by her daughter, Melina.

In addition to drawing the parallels between myths and names, we can see gnosis as a key part of the universes and experiences of FromSoftware's games, i.e., the idea of transcending the limits of the lower world, and even approaching the divine. "The current imperfection of the Golden Order, or instability of ideology, can be blamed upon the fickleness of the gods no better than men," states the description of the Mending Rune of Perfect Order, which we find on Goldmask's body at the end of the game. As we've seen previously, the entire quest surrounding this strange character is about demonstrating that the gods are not as all-powerful and trustworthy as one might think, while humans can learn and improve their knowledge, to the point of achieving a sort of clairvoyance close to that of the gods. The hierarchy between the gods and humans becomes blurred, and that's precisely what happens at the end of *Elden Ring*–and in many other Japanese RPGs!–when the player battles Marika/Radagon, the deity that has reigned for an eternity. By the by, I'll remind you that Marika has not always had her divine status–she, too, was once a common mortal, a Numen (a word that actually sounds quite close to "human"). Finally, after first battling the god, the player faces off against the Elden Beast, an emissary of the Greater Will, the highest power that we know of in the game's universe. When you win this final battle, the words "God Slain" appear on the screen. And there is certainly a bit of gnosticism in that final message!

If we zoom out even a bit further, it is the knowledge collected throughout the adventure that brings the player to that point (finishing the game), which also means choosing an ending, i.e., choosing a successor to the reigning goddess. Knowledge of the self, of others, of the divine, of the stakes of the Lands Between– these are the gnosis of *Elden Ring*. However, this process of transfiguration also resembles the principles of a famous occult science: alchemy.

◈ The Magnum Opus: alchemical transmutation

For centuries, or even millennia, alchemists worked on the transmutation of metals. They were particularly focused on what they called the Magnum Opus, meaning the creation of the Philosopher's Stone, a fantastic substance that would be able to change ordinary metals of no value into precious metals, like gold or silver. The alchemists believed this "purification" would "cure" the metals and eliminate their impurities in order to elevate their nature. We find this same transformation metaphorically in the story of *Elden Ring*, with a Tarnished—a term that takes on extra meaning in this context—trying to become the sovereign of the Golden Order, or else the consort of Ranni, the moon goddess, symbolizing silver for obvious reasons.

There is also meaning to be found in the importance given to metals in *Elden Ring*'s lore. For example, the ancient Crucible Knights—"crucible" being another term frequently associated with alchemy—wear armor of a reddish-gold color that looks dull in comparison to the shining gear of the Golden Order's knights. Over time, the Golden Order and the Erdtree came to replace the primordial Crucible and its prehistoric tree. This evolution also symbolically represents the transformation of the alchemical process. It's an idea that resonates with a parallel previously discussed in this book, that of the Arthurian legend and the search for the Holy Grail. The Philosopher's Stone was also frequently associated with the Grail, and alchemists claimed that the stone possessed other virtues, like the power to confer immortality. If the Philosopher's Stone could "cure" metals, why wouldn't it also cure humans of the illness of aging?

Just as we can interpret the quest for the Holy Grail as a symbol of changing times, we can also view alchemy on a more metaphorical level. Indeed, beyond the idea of metals being elevated by a curative substance, transmutation can also be spiritual.

In the 4th century, Zosimos of Panopolis tackled that very concept, studying the dissociation of the *soma* from the *pneuma* (that term again!), the body from volatile matter, i.e., the spirit. No matter the substance, and often working with metals, the idea was that, using distillation, one could separate the spirit from its body, its matter. And what if the substance were a human being? Would it be possible to liberate the soul from the physical body by alchemical processes? Of course, this question touches on a philosophical, even metaphysical, approach reminiscent, as you may have noted, of gnosticism, as discussed previously. Indeed, Zosimos was influenced by gnostic doctrines. Zosimos studied this idea of separating the spirit from matter, but also the reverse, reunifying the spirit with its substance, by means of what he called "divine water," which was really just mercury. So, the idea was to separate the spirit from impure metals to alloy them with mercury and create precious metals, like gold? And to do the same for the human spirit and thus achieve divine status? An interesting point here is that the top of the Elden Ring, with its arc pointed up toward the sky and linked to a number of circles below it, is reminiscent of the alchemical symbol for mercury, as if mercury were the binding agent in the ring, pointing toward the heavens, toward the divine. In this case, it's easy to make the parallel between the Elden Ring and the Philosopher's Stone: the Elden Ring brings the peoples of the Lands Between into a golden age and transforms the Empyreans into gods.

Moreover, we see numerous similarities between the form of the Elden Ring and the visual symbols of alchemy. Notably, the interlocking circles are reminiscent of certain incredible images from the *Amphitheater of Eternal Wisdom*, a work created by the German alchemist Heinrich Khunrath in the 16th century. The same can be said for *The Rosary of the Philosophers* by Arnaldus de Villa Nova (13th century) or the scrolls of George Ripley (15th century). The Philosopher's Stone, the Magnum Opus, has its place in all of these illustrations, which are overflowing with details and symbols. Alchemy was studied and communicated through symbolism. I mentioned the symbol for mercury previously, but an arc of a circle can also be used to represent the moon, and a circle itself can represent the sun. Gold and silver, as we've seen, form a central motif in the story of *Elden Ring*. Ultimately, the study of and search for meaning are ideas present in both the–almost mythological–images from alchemical treatises and *Elden Ring*. Each symbol connects to an idea, a concept; as such, can we say that assembling and understanding the cryptic puzzle is sort of like obtaining the Philosopher's Stone? The Holy Grail, gnosis, the Philosopher's Stone: the parallels are almost endless. Perhaps I digress, and undoubtedly I've gotten carried away, but the game most definitely features a number of universal symbols, and the emotions and sense of discovery are very real.

Finally, to delve further into these few parallels between alchemy and *Elden Ring*, in the early 20th century, the famous psychiatrist Carl Gustav Jung, a dissident disciple of Sigmund Freud and the founder of analytical psychology, also relied on alchemical principles–among other ideas, including gnostic beliefs!–to lay out his theory of individuation. To summarize the idea in the most basic terms, because it would be overkill to go into the details, individuation is based on the notion that a person is an individual, a being that is completely different from all the other beings around them.

Marika, at one time, was just a shaman, but she transformed herself into a goddess via certain principles connecting analytical psychology to alchemy. This is probably a good time to note that there are supposed to be three stages in the creation of the Philosopher's Stone, and Jung borrowed those stages for his theory of individuation. And each stage is associated with a color: *nigredo* (black), *albedo* (white), and *rubedo* (red). We could fill an entire book with analysis of the alchemical and psychological symbolism tied to these three colors, but the story of Marika explores it in singular fashion. Indeed, she succeeded in escaping her demons and freeing herself from the clutches of death that likely awaited her, given the way the Hornsent massacred her people. And that all happened in a place that would become the Realm of Shadow, where death converges. This dimension of her story can be linked to *nigredo*. The *albedo* would be her ascension to godhood, to a state of purity. Lastly, *rubedo*, which represents the alchemical union of opposites, such as man and woman, while also being the final phase where the "self" becomes complete, very directly echoes the union of Radagon and Marika within one person. This gives extra meaning to Radagon's red hair. Thus, the phrase in the story trailer for *Shadow of the Erdtree*, "an affair from which gold arose," offers another level of meaning, an alchemical one this time. With Marika's individuation complete, like a Philosopher's Stone, she will transform Order into the Golden Order—achieving the Magnum Opus.

In a more measured fashion, the principle of individuation also applies to the player's anonymous Tarnished avatar. "A Tarnished of no renown," as the game's introduction indicates, who in the end will become the central individual of the Lands Between, a lord. Whether that will be the Elden Lord, the Lord of the Frenzied Flame, the Lord of the Golden Order, or the Lord of the Duskborn, the title will be determined by the player's choices. This transmutation of the Tarnished into a lord—in other words, going from an anonymous nobody to a renowned individual—is thus the result of an incredible alchemical process!

◈ Ambition, free will, or fate?

Becoming a lord—and thus symbolically completing your transmutation!—marks the end of the game's main questline. That end comes after a crucial decision, which is itself preceded by countless decisions weighed by the player throughout the adventure. While the idea of choice is innately linked to the idea of free will, many elements of the game seem to be based on the idea of an inevitable fate. These two concepts exist side by side, constantly clashing with one another, giving a singular tone to the Lands Between and its many stories, first and foremost the player's story.

By taking the Elden throne, the player will determine the kingdom's future. After spending dozens or even hundreds of hours choosing a path to follow, the areas to explore, the demigods to defeat, and the different builds to develop, including weapons and styles of magic, the adventure ends with one final decision. And yet, each of the six possible endings is tied to a particular character or entity. Indeed, the player is ultimately asked to defend their causes more than the player's own ego. To protect Those Who Live in Death, to spread a curse, to restore the primordial order, or to follow Ranni in bringing about the rise of the Dark Moon: it's hard to talk about free will when you are ultimately just a receptacle for someone else's ideology. Incidentally, Godfrey was also once the Elden Lord, but in reality, he was nothing more than a puppet and was stripped of his title as soon as signs of decline appeared. Ultimately, only the conclusion tied to the Three Fingers—and to a lesser extent the ending tied to the "classic" progression alongside Melina, resulting in the Age of Fracture—represents a special case, in which chaos spreads all across the Lands Between. The result is a sort of freedom guided by violence and destruction, nevertheless thanks to a power granted by another Outer God. Furthermore, if you have the misfortune to be won over by Miquella's Age of Compassion in *Shadow of the Erdtree*, you will have to allow yourself to be killed in the battle against Radahn. But doing so doesn't even result in a true death; instead, it just leads to a game-over that forces you to start the battle over again. Clearly, according to the game's designers, the Age of Compassion is not to be counted among the game's canonical endings, further complicating this distorted vision of free will. As such, it seems that Miquella was destined—by his creators—to never impose his will!

Marika's fate was also sealed, long ago, by the Greater Will. However, one of the major themes of *Elden Ring* is the idea of "breaking the cycle." It's a notion that represents a sort of realization of one's need for freedom, always coming from one presumed to be weaker in the hierarchy. In an interview on the Xbox official site (June 9, 2019), Hidetaka Miyazaki says of an unnamed character featured in concept art that he represents a theme: "That theme is the will, or ambition, of mankind."

Marika wished to free herself from the control of the Greater Will, just as Ranni refused her fate as an Empyrean, with all the consequences that ensued. From there, the Golden Lineage of Marika and Godfrey, with Godwyn representing perfection and most likely the future of the Golden Order, became tarnished. The cursed Omens Morgott and Mohg broke their chains, both literally and figuratively, and emerged from their underground prison to rise to the positions of protector of Leyndell and Lord of Blood, respectively. As for Godwyn, against his will, he became the Prince of Death, thus obliterating his golden destiny that had been laid out for him since birth. The same is true for the twins of Marika and Radagon, who represent a new lineage of Empyreans who are ultra-powerful, and yet cursed from the moment they entered the world. Malenia and Miquella also tried to break the cycle in their own way, using the Haligtree; however, the Shattering dashed their plans.

In *Elden Ring*, we often find ourselves navigating the space between free will and inescapable fate. It's a dichotomy that we find in the two major aspects of the Golden Order, the concepts of causality and regression, represented by Marika and Radagon, respectively. Fate and causality appear to be closely linked, notably in philosophical schools like stoicism, according to which the universe is governed by unwavering determinism. In opposition to causality, Radagon's regression is able to unravel the chain of causes and consequences in order to refine the branching possibilities and directions followed at each decision point. Could that be a form of free will, emerging from inextricable fatalism? In any case, that seems to be a key message in *Elden Ring*, one conveyed by most of the characters—and there are a lot of them!—and by the player's many adventures and gradual development of understanding, with the player's unique story constantly revolving around this fascinating subject.

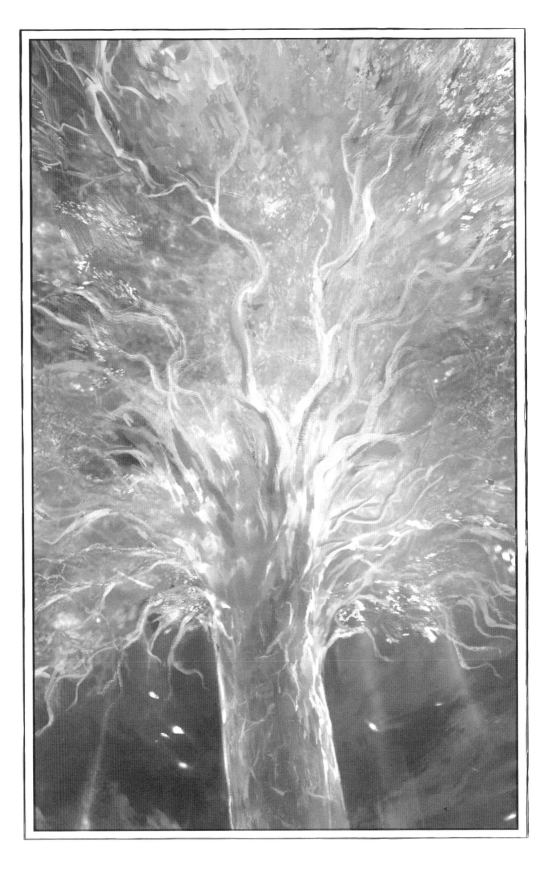

THE MONUMENTAL
ELDEN RING

FROMSOFTWARE'S MAGNUM OPUS

CONCLUSION
THE NEW MYTH(S)

LDEN RING is a monumental creation whose depth of gameplay and themes becomes apparent, not just over hours and hours of play, but even beyond the virtual format, as the game has driven long and fascinating discussions, whether between two sessions of play, or over several months, or even years after reaching the conclusion. The *Souls* games—and their other descendants made by the studio—stoked their own lively community engagement in their time, but in the case of *Elden Ring*, the ambition and magnitude have been multiplied. And *Elden Ring* has numerous awards it has received over the years to prove it. It conquered the video game market while inspiring people in a much wider audience. Indeed, the game's creator, Hidetaka Miyazaki, was included on the *Time* 100 list in 2023, a prestigious annual selection by *Time* magazine of the 100 most influential people in the world. Only one other video game figure had previously appeared on the list: Shigeru Miyamoto, the famous creator of *Mario* and *Zelda*, in 2007.

Elden Ring is an extraordinary "world-building" work, much like, in literature, Stephen King's *The Dark Tower* series (volumes published between 1982 and 2004) or Alain Damasio's *La Horde du Contrevent* (2004). These two examples of world-building books immerse the reader in other worlds, ones governed by unique and surprising rules unknown to the audience at first. The process of discovery is both dense and intense, driven by a style that can be changing and complex, or by a singular narrative structure connected to the very universe in which the stories are rooted. The audience can get lost in these fictional universes when they are laid out and used with great artistry. In other cases, the audience might not fully understand at first, with all sorts of different information coming at them fast. Moreover, the concepts of the fictional universe can be blended with particularly powerful mythological and philosophical themes, and audience members often find themselves thinking back on key moments years later. People will re-read certain chapters, they'll discuss the book with other fans, and they gradually come to appreciate the richness of these world-building works, which never reveal everything all at once. *Elden Ring* belongs to this category of creations.

Beyond the richness of its themes and its singular concepts—"Radagon is Marika" will always remain one of the highlights—FromSoftware's flagship title is also an incredible myth-building tool. It's an aspect specific to the video game medium, enhanced in this case by the many themes, symbols, and situations encountered by players, each one having their own sensibilities and culture. As such, each personal perception of *Elden Ring*'s world is exciting to discover! In this context, the feeling of accomplishment that Hidetaka Miyazaki holds so dear goes beyond merely triumphing over a difficult obstacle: it's also about learning to decode the game's universe itself. Our perception, our fears, our moral and philosophical conceptions are all put to the test. Like all myths, *Elden Ring* can provide us with food for thought and help us elevate our consciousness to a higher plane. The title of Elden Lord is really just a metaphor; it's up to us to build a new meaning for it out of the ashes of the past.

THE MONUMENTAL

ELDEN RING

FromSoftware's Magnum Opus

BIBLIOGRAPHY

Online Articles

ANONYMOUS. "Director Miyazaki Discusses Elden Ring: Shadow of the Erdtree – New Weapons, Approach to Difficulty, GRRM's Involvement, and More." *Frontline Gaming Japan*, March 17, 2024. Available at: <https://www.frontlinejp. net/2024/03/17/ director-miyazaki-discusses-elden-ring-shadow-of-the-erdtree-new-weapons-approach-to-difficulty-grrms-involvement/>

ANONYMOUS. "Elden Ring Release Interview with Director Miyazaki (Part 1/2) – Discussing Lore and Field Design." *Frontline Gaming Japan*, March 5, 2022. Available at: <https://www.frontlinejp.net/2022/03/05/ elden-ring-release-interview-with-director-miyazaki-part-1/>

ANONYMOUS. "Elden Ring Release Interview with Director Miyazaki (Part 2/2) – Discussing Design Philosophy." *Frontline Gaming Japan*, March 8, 2022. Available at: <https://www.frontlinejp.net/2022/03/08/discussing-design-philosophy-elden-ring-release-interview-with-director-miyazaki-part-2-2/>

ASHCRAFT, Brian. "Miyazaki Gives Clear Answers On The Future Of Dark Souls, Armored Core." *Kotaku*, September 21, 2016. Available at: <https://kotaku.com/ miyazaki-gives-clear-answers-on-the-future-of-dark-soul-1786887531>

BIRO, Alexis. "Insights from the Localization of Elden Ring." *Terra Localizations*, April 6, 2022. Available at: <https://www.terralocalizations.com/ja/2022/04/06/ elden-ring-localization-insights/>

BUNTING, Geoffrey. "How much does From Software crunch?" *Games Industry*, November 29, 2022. Available at: <https://www.gamesindustry.biz/ how-much-does-from-software-crunch>

DEALESSANDRI, Marie. "Bandai Namco: 'Elden Ring is just the beginning.'" *Games Industry*, October 3, 2022. Available at: <https://www.gamesindustry.biz/ bandai-namco-elden-ring-is-just-the-beginning>

DRUCKMANN, Neil. "The 100 Most Influential People of 2023." *Time*, April 13, 2023. Available at: <https://time.com/collection/100-most-influential-people-2023/6269962/hidetaka-miyazaki/>

EVANS-THIRLWELL, Edwin. "The jolly co-operation of localising Dark Souls." *Rock Paper Shotgun*, February 22, 2022. Available at: <https://www.rockpapershotgun.com/the-jolly-cooperation-of-localising-dark-souls>

KAIN, Erik. "FromSoftware's 'Elden Ring' Marketing Is Pure Genius." *Forbes*, December 13, 2020. Available at: <https://www.forbes.com/sites/erikkain/2020/12/13/fromsoftwares-elden-ring-marketing-is-pure-genius/>

KRABBE, Esra. "Elden Ring is an Evolution of Dark Souls Says Creator – E3 2019." *IGN*, June 21, 2019. Available at: <https://www.ign.com/articles/2019/06/21/elden-ring-is-an-evolution-of-dark-souls-says-creator-a-e3-2019>

LUMB, David. "Elden Ring Creator Hidetaka Miyazaki Talks Shadow of the Erdtree, New Weapons and More." *CNET*, June 17, 2024. Available at: <https://www.cnet.com/tech/gaming/elden-ring-creator-hidetaka-miyazaki-talks-shadow-of-the-erdtree-new-weapons-and-more/>

MIDDLER, Jordan. "Hidetaka Miyazaki says Elden Ring's release was 'not a very pleasant time." *Video Games Chronicle*, March 9, 2022. Available at: <https://www.videogameschronicle.com/news/hidetaka-miyazaki-says-elden-rings-release-was-not-a-very-pleasant-time/>

NIGHTINGALE, Ed. "Elden Ring Shadow of the Erdtree is FromSoftware's 'largest expansion' ever." *Eurogamer*, February 21, 2024. Available at: <https://www.eurogamer.net/elden-ring-shadow-of-the-erdtree-is-fromsoftwares-largest-expansion-ever>

PARKIN, Simon. "Hidetaka Miyazaki Sees Death as a Feature, Not a Bug." *The New Yorker*, February 25, 2022. Available at: <https://www.newyorker.com/culture/persons-of-interest/hidetaka-miyazaki-sees-death-as-a-feature-not-a-bug>

PRESCOTT, Shaun. "'It's a tier above': How a giant, cryptic RPG like Elden Ring gets translated." *PC Gamer*, March 10, 2022. Available at: <https://www.pcgamer.com/its-a-tier-above-how-a-giant-cryptic-rpg-like-elden-ring-gets-translated/>

SAITOH, Tsukasa. "Elden Ring composer Tsukasa Saito on creating the game's score and his favorite track." *PlayStation Blog*, September 9, 2022. Available at: <https://blog.playstation.com/2022/09/09/elden-ring-composer-tsukasa-saito-on-creating-the-games-score-and-his-favorite-track/>

SALTZMAN, Mitchell. "Elden Ring Director Answers All of Our Shadow of the Erdtree DLC Questions | IGN Fan Fest 2024." *IGN*, February 21, 2024. Available at: <https://www.ign.com/articles/hidetaka-miyazaki-elden-ring-shadow-of-the-erdtree-interview>

SALTZMAN, Mitchell. "Elden Ring: The Big Hidetaka Miyazaki Interview – Summer of Gaming." *IGN*, June 17, 2021. Available at: <https://www.ign.com/articles/elden-ring-miyazaki-hidetaka-full-interview-summer-of-gaming>

TURI, Tim. "An interview with FromSoftware's Hidetaka Miyazaki." *PlayStation Blog*, January 28, 2022. Available at: <https://blog.playstation.com/2022/01/28/an-interview-with-fromsoftwares-hidetaka-miyazki/>

TUTTLE, Will. "E3 2019: Hidetaka Miyazaki and George R. R. Martin Present: Elden Ring." *Xbox Wire*, June 9, 2019. Available at: <https://news.xbox.com/en-us/2019/06/09/hidetaka-miyazaki-and-george-rr-martin-present-elden-ring/>

Miscellaneous

@albertdevanves. X (Twitter), October 22, 2022. Available at: <https://x.com/albertdevanves/status/1583800102728388610>

@TsuboiKlein. X (Twitter), July 6, 2022. Available at: <https://x.com/TsuboiKlein/status/1544772979988520960>

CONSPICOR. "Elden Ring – Chinese Interview Translation." Reddit, May 2, 2024. Available at: <https://www.reddit.com/r/Eldenring/comments/1ci9slp/elden_ring_chinese_interview_translation/>

theangryfurlong. "Full translation of the Famitsu interview with Miyazaki for Shadow of the Erdtree." Reddit, February 22, 2024. Available at: <https://www.reddit.com/r/Eldenring/comments/1awzsrq/full_translation_of_the_famitsu_interview_with/>

theangryfurlong. "Miyazaki Famitsu interview translation [Part 1]." Reddit, June 15, 2021. Available at: <https://www.reddit.com/r/Eldenring/comments/o0680a/miyazaki_famitsu_interview_translation_part_1/>

Books

ANONYMOUS. *Elden Ring – Books of Knowledge, Volume 1: The Lands Between*. Future Press. 2023. 512 pages.

ANONYMOUS. *Elden Ring – Books of Knowledge, Volume 2: Shards of the Shattering*. Future Press. 2023. 528 pages.

CHEVALIER, Jean and GHEERBRANT, Alain. *Dictionnaire des symboles : Mythes, rêves, coutumes, gestes, formes, figures, couleurs, nombres*. Robert Laffont, 1997. 1,100 pages.

GAIMAN, Neil. *Norse Mythology* W. W. Norton & Company. 2017. 288 pages.

JUNG, Carl Gustav. *Psychologie et Alchimie*. Buchet Chastel. 2014 (edition). 720 pages.

Videos

BANDAI NAMCO ENTERTAINMENT AMERICA. "ELDEN RING – OST Behind the Scenes with the Budapest Film Orchestra." YouTube, September 9, 2022. Available at: <https://www.youtube.com/watch?v=S4ZQ-CrnT_k>

BANDAI NAMCO EUROPE. "ELDEN RING Shadow of the Erdtree – OST Behind the Scenes performance." YouTube, July 10, 2024. Available at: <https://www.youtube.com/watch?v=zIKUzL1cLpA>

BANDAI NAMCO EUROPE. "ELDEN RING Shadow of the Erdtree | Story Trailer." YouTube, May 21, 2024. Available at: <https://www.youtube.com/watch?v=6uT8wGtB3yQ>

BANDAI NAMCO EUROPE. "ELDEN RING – Story Trailer." YouTube, December 9, 2021. Available at: <https://www.youtube.com/watch?v=K_03kFqWfqs>

Websites

Fextralife (Wiki): https://eldenring.wiki.fextralife.com/

FromSoftware (official website): https://www.fromsoftware.jp/ww/

Moby Games (*Elden Ring* credits): https://www.mobygames.com/game/174989/elden-ring/

Moby Games (*Elden Ring Shadow of the Erdtree* credits) : https://www.mobygames.com/game/226510/elden-ring-shadow-of-the-erdtree/

VGMdb (information on original soundtracks): https://vgmdb.net/

Magazines

Edge. February 2022. No. 367.

Famitsu. March 10, 2022. No. 1742.

Famitsu. March 28, 2024 No. 1841.

AUTHOR'S ACKNOWLEDGMENTS

I would like to thank Third Éditions, especially Damien for all your help throughout the writing of this book. You provided me with support, ideas, fascinating texts (particularly on music)– you have a heck of a job as an editor of such varied subjects!

And thank you to FromSoftware, of course, for the great adventures you have offered us, past, present, and future. We'll see you at the next destination.

Also available from Third Éditions

✹ RPG COLLECTION

Berserk. With Darkness Ink
BioShock. From Rapture to Columbia
Dark Souls. Beyond the Grave - Volume 1
Dark Souls. Beyond the Grave - Volume 2
Decoding The Last of Us. The Remnants of Humanity
Devolver: Behind the Scenes. Business and Punk Attitude
Fallout. A Tale of Mutation
JoJo's Bizarre Adventure. Manga's Refined Oddball
Metal Gear Solid. Hideo Kojima's Magnum Opus
Resident Evil. Of Zombies and Men - Volume 1
Sekiro. The Second Life of Souls
The Heart of Dead Cells
The Impact of Akira. A Manga [R]evolution
The Legend of Dragon Quest
The Legend of Final Fantasy VI
The Legend of Final Fantasy VII
The Legend of Final Fantasy VIII
The Legend of Final Fantasy IX
The Legend of Final Fantasy X
The Legend of Kingdom Hearts - Volume 1: Creation
The Mysteries of Monkey Island. Pirates Ahoy!
The Rise of the Witcher. A New RPG King
The Saga Uncharted. Chronicles of an Explorer
The Strange Works of Taro Yoko. From Drakengard to NieR: Automata
The Works of Fumito Ueda. A Different Perspective on Video Games
The Works of Hayao Miyazaki. The Japanese Animation Master
Zelda. The History of a Legendary Saga - Volume 1
Zelda. The History of a Legendary Saga - Volume 2: Breath of the Wild

Legal submission: November 2025
Printed in Turkey by TypoLibris

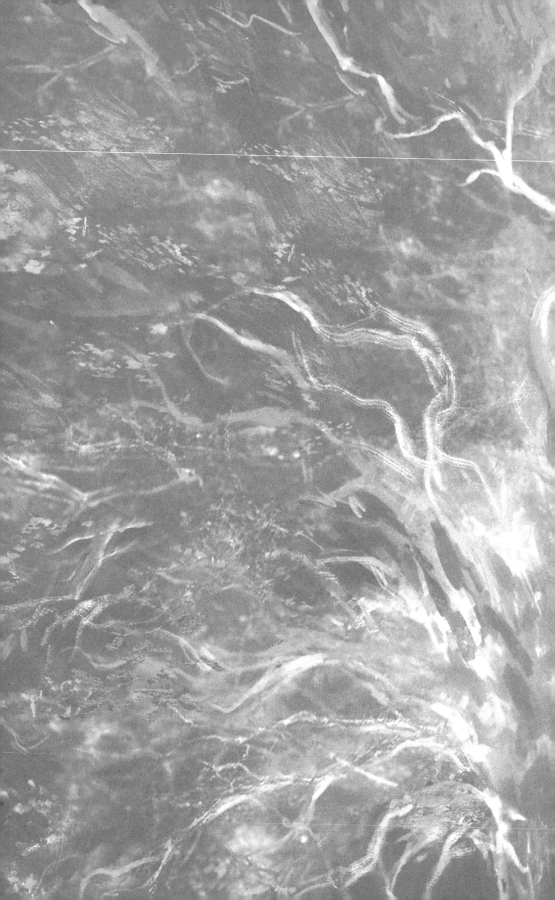